The
Jerome Holtzman
Baseball Reader

◆

JEROME HOLTZMAN

TRIUMPH
B O O K S
CHICAGO

Library of Congress Cataloging-in-Publication Data

Holtzman, Jerome.
    The Jerome Holtzman baseball reader / Jerome Holtzman.
      p. cm.
    Includes index.
    ISBN 1-57243-493-7 (hc.)
     1. Baseball—United States—Anecdotes. I. Title.

GV873 .H58 2003
796.357—dc21

2002044368

This book is available in quantity at special discounts for your group or organization. For further information, contact:

Triumph Books
601 South LaSalle Street
Suite 500
Chicago, Illinois 60605
(312) 939-3330
Fax (312) 663-3557

Printed in the United States of America
ISBN 1-57243-493-7
Interior design by Sue Knopf

CONTENTS

Foreword by Ira Berkow.................................... v
Calvin Griffith... 1
Brian Kingman 4
Ambidextrous 7
Leon Cadore.. 11
Bob Feller.. 15
Ron Necciai.. 19
Jerry Manuel... 23
Lady Umpires 27
Fathers and Sons 31
Edward Gaedel 34
No-Hitters Lost with Two Outs in Ninth 38
At Last, Aparicio's Headed for Hall..................... 44
Lights *Were* OK'd for Wrigley Field.................... 47
A Word for '69: Unforgettable 50
Stan the Man: A Living Monument...................... 53
A Crowded Field of Rose Admirers...................... 56
Maris Heard Only the Boos 59
Brosnan Pitches Write Stuff 63
Hank Greenberg Mixed Religion with Greatness 67
A Splendid Pitch on Art of Hitting 71
Hugh Alexander, a Good Scout, Always Remembers
    the Ones That Got Away 75
Campanis Guilty Only of Not Being Slick Enough
    to Escape Koppel's Trap........................... 78
Scouting Amateur Free Agents Could Be
    the Toughest Job of All in Baseball................. 81
A Bright Future Seen for Maddux....................... 87
Babe Ruth's Called Shot.............................. 90
Ryan Past Prime, Still a Cut Above 97
Durocher Warms Up in the Bull-Session Pen 101
Santo's Numbers Hall of Fame Size 105
Spring Training a Lousy Yardstick...................... 108
"Shoeless" Was Hardly Blameless 111

President Holds a White House Conference
    on a Critical Matter: Baseball 117
A Midsummer Classic: Where It All Began 120
Buckner Survives That Infamous E-3. 124
Bill Veeck: An Uncommon Man Merits the Fanfare 127
DiMaggio Still a True Yankee Blue Blood 130
Father of the Hall Loved His Baby 133
Tinkering with Cub Double-Play Legend 137
It's Been a Long, Deliberate Journey
    for the Ump His Colleagues Call "God" 140
Marge Schott and Freedom of Offensive Speech 144
Lasorda's Godson Could Well Become a Godsend 148
Cardinals' Smith Works His Wizardry to Ward Off Age 151
Briefing on Nixon: Fan of White Sox, Appling, Baseball 154
Billy Sunday Was a Heavy Hitter—When He Preached. 157
Cubs' "Mr. Wrigley" Made a Difference, but Not Noise. 160
Worst Deal Ever? Principals Deny It—and They Should Know . . . 163
In '45, a Warm Body Could Get a Man in the Major Leagues. . . . 166
Nice Try, Mike, but You Belong in Basketball 169
Gehrig's Legacy Far Surpasses 2,130-Game Streak 172
Sosa Destined to Enter Game's Elite Territory. 175
At 65, Being Mr. Cub Still Fits Banks Perfectly 178
Andre Dawson: The Mantle of His Time. 181
Courageous Flood Staked Career on Free Agency 184
How Wendell Smith Helped Robinson's Cause 186
Stealing Signs: Grand Larceny a Part of the Game 189
Interleague Play Validates Veeck's 75-Year-Old Vision 192
He Had Many Loves: People, Baseball, Chicago—and Life. 195
For Baseball's Real First Black, Fame Wasn't Even Fleeting. 198
This Was Brickhouse: He Knew Everybody and They Knew Him . . . 201
A Great Companion. 204
Baseball's Hitters in Waiting. 210
Introduction to *My Greatest Day in Baseball* 219
Index 225

They Had Ice Cream Every Friday

JERRY HOLTZMAN—JEROME HOLTZMAN to the readers of his baseball column in the *Chicago Tribune*—grew up like many of us, in a house with kids. Unlike the homes of many of us, the house contained 300 kids, about 150 boys and 150 girls. It was on the west side of Chicago, and was called the Marks Nation Jewish Orphan Home.

Jerry went to live there when he was 10 years old, along with his younger brother and sister, after his father died in 1936. His mother, left a widow in those dark Depression days, was unable to properly look after her children.

The mind builds its own castles and its own dungeons, and an orphanage during the Depression conjures up the life of Oliver Twist, complete with gruel and water and stinging raps on the ear. Surprisingly, Holtzman did not feel that way. "I thought it was terrific," he has been known to say. "The building was about a half-block square, and there was a ball field beside it, and we had ice cream every Friday night. My wife, Marilyn, says there has to be something wrong with someone who liked an orphanage."

There was pain, certainly, in separation from his family home, but Jerry Holtzman learned somewhere that you try to make the best of a situation, and you do not look back in anger or sorrow or bitterness.

So Jerry Holtzman, stocky with a shock of wavy gray hair, eyebrows furry as caterpillars, wearing suspenders and smoking a cigar not quite as long as his arm, has made his way to become one of the brightest, most respected men in his profession. So good, in fact, that in 1989, in Cooperstown, New York, he was awarded the J. G. Taylor Spink Award, which honors a baseball writer "for meritorious contributions to baseball writing," by the Baseball Hall of Fame.

Once Holtzman walked over to a ballplayer with a surly reputation and introduced himself. "I'm not talkin' to the press today," said the ballplayer.

"No problem," said Holtzman, lighting his cigar. "Maybe I'll catch you next year. Or the year after that."

Some time ago Holtzman discovered something he hoped he could use to augment his sportswriter's salary. He bought the rights to 10 of the finest sports books, bound them handsomely, and reissued them in a set. "I took a bath on it," Holtzman recalled. Nonetheless, behind a batting cage in Shea Stadium one evening, he was introduced to Nelson Doubleday, who then owned Doubleday & Company. "It's nice to meet a fellow publisher," Holtzman said.

In his remarks at the induction ceremony in Cooperstown, as ballplayers Jim Palmer and Joe Morgan sat nearby waiting to receive their induction plaques, Holtzman thanked first his wife for her support, and then his family, including his three daughters and his son. One of his children wasn't there, however.

"We lost Catherine Ellen six months ago, to cancer, three days before her 37th birthday," said Holtzman. "A day or two before she died, she said to me, 'I'm sorry I won't be with you in Cooperstown, Dad.' She was a much loved person and an avid baseball fan. I taught her how to keep score when she was a freshman in high school, and she learned to keep an almost perfect scorecard."

He spoke with a still heavy heart, and yet Jerry Holtzman wished to share the memories of this much-loved person and something that she loved with those in the modest-sized but packed Cooperstown Central

High School auditorium (the ceremonies had been moved indoors because of the pelting rain).

That is like Holtzman himself, a man who hums when he types, who shares with his readers his love of baseball and of sportswriting. Holtzman said he grew up not with dreams of becoming a baseball player, as many youngsters did, but of becoming a baseball writer. He worked on his high school paper and, he said, discovered he had "a modest flair for writing." He joined the *Chicago Times* in 1943 as a copy boy immediately after "graduating" at 17 from the orphanage. "They gave me a suit and $10," he said.

He spent two years in the marines, returned to the newspaper in 1946, covered high school sports for 11 years, and then in 1957 became a local baseball writer for the *Chicago Sun-Times*. He moved to the *Tribune* in 1981 as its national baseball columnist.

In 1974 Holtzman recorded and edited the sportswriting classic *No Cheering in the Pressbox*, a warm and provocative collection of interviews with veteran sportswriters.

"I remember Jimmy Cannon telling me, 'A sportswriter is entombed in a prolonged boyhood,' because we're always writing about youth, the athletes," said Holtzman. "But I also remember Shirley Povich saying that when he was young, all the players were heroes; but it seemed he matured overnight, and stopped writing about the roar of the crowd. I know what he meant."

Another writer who is also enshrined at Cooperstown discussed the coming honor with Holtzman. "It'll change your life," the man said.

This concerned Holtzman. "I don't want my life to change," he said. "I like it the way it is."

—Ira Berkow

Calvin Griffith

NOVEMBER 12, 1999

AN OLD BASEBALL SOLDIER DIED LAST MONTH. He was properly eulogized by the Minneapolis/St. Paul media, his home base, but his obit was buried nationally, crowded out by the World Series. His deeds were seldom acknowledged and he took his lumps, almost always without complaint.

This is what the late Bill Veeck said about him: "It's not just that he marches to his own drum. I don't even think he hears anyone else's. He doesn't identify with the fans—never has. He doesn't do things because they're good PR or politically smart. It's a strange thing to say, with that big, fat belly of his, but in a perverse way I find him gallant."

I agree, except he did identify with the fans. He was continually concerned about the gate and fielded the best possible baseball teams within the limits of his financial capabilities.

He was Calvin Griffith, who died at the age of 87, a baseball lifer, a majority owner who was his own general manager and operated the old Washington Senators and later the Minneapolis Twins. He had been a minor league catcher and manager and was the epitome of the common man.

Never a slick talker, he was the exact opposite and provided a bundleful of laughs because of his inability to come up with the appropriate word.

And although he sometimes butchered the King's English, it was easy to understand what he was saying.

Late in his career after he was honored at home plate and greeted with cheers, he said, "The fans were really great. I've been hung in apathy before so I didn't know what to expect."

Calvin's malaprops, in addition to some of his more captivating (and truthful) bizarre meanderings were much enjoyed and delivered with such frequency that they were assembled in a 30-page pamphlet titled *Quotations from Chairman Calvin—The Collected Wit and Wisdom of the Former Minnesota Twins' President and Chairman of the Board,* published in 1984 by Brick Alley Press of Stillwater, Minnesota.

Some samples: "I can't tell you exactly what I intend to do, but I can tell you one thing: it won't be anything rational."

On his knee surgery: "They took out the cartridge."

When accused of having the lowest payroll in baseball: "If I do, it shows I'm not a horse's ass."

On Jim Eisenreich, then the Twins' rookie center fielder: "He's doomed to be an All-Star."

On the possibility of re-signing some of his high-priced free agents: "We ain't America's farm team. I think we're smarter than hell to get rid of some of those guys."

On his fellow owners: "They're all egotists. They've got so much money but nobody knew who they were before baseball. Who the hell ever heard of Ted Turner or Ray Kroc or George Steinbrenner?"

On how he hopes to be remembered: "As someone who did his best to give the people something they can be proud of. The ovations I have received at various places lately, like out at the airport the other night, have been most appreciative. It makes you know you're not too bad a guy overall."

Calvin Griffith was always a good guy. Because of his frumpy appearance, his lumpy speech, and general disdain for the changing times, most of his fellow moguls regarded him as a so-called dinosaur, a leftover from the previous age and beyond.

He was all of that. Born in Montreal, in near poverty, he was adopted when he was 11 years old by his uncle, Clark Griffith, a star pitcher at the turn of the century, then the majority owner of the Washington Senators.

Uncle Clark, who as a youth had watered Jesse James' horses, was a stern parent; he watched Calvin closely, and made him earn his way up the baseball ladder. Calvin was the batboy for the 1924 Walter Johnson Senators. He attended George Washington University for three years and left because, "They don't teach baseball there."

The elder Griffith made him make the minor league rounds. He was a catcher and later the manager and general manager of the Chattanooga Lookouts of the Southern Association. His first major league assignment was in the concessions department.

Calvin became the majority owner when Uncle Clark died in 1955. The bleak financial circumstances forced the team to move to Minneapolis/St. Paul in 1961; they were renamed the Minnesota Twins.

Despite his reluctance to pay huge salaries and his reputation as base-ball's most penurious owner, Calvin, with the help of his few scouts, rebuilt the club with judicious signings and trades. The Twins won the American League pennant in 1965 and divisional titles in 1969 and 1970.

My favorite Calvin Griffith story was the night he brought his Chattanooga club to Kissimmee, Florida, for an exhibition game with the Houston Astros.

"Do you know what the gate receipts were for that game?" Calvin asked Minneapolis columnist Pat Reusse. "Twenty-five cents. That's what it cost to get into the game, 25 cents, and we had only one fellow who paid to get in. I walked over to him and gave him his quarter back."

Brian Kingman

JANUARY 7, 2000

PITCHER BRIAN KINGMAN, who had a brief and disappointing big-league career, has his priorities straight. Today, 20 years later, he is part owner of a Los Angeles financial services company and no longer embarrassed because he was a 20-game loser.

"At the time I took it real hard," he admitted last week. "There is no question it shortened my career. But my feelings have changed 360 degrees. What if I had lost 18 or 19? Nobody would have talked about it. I would have been a nonentity."

Instead, Kingman, who was 8–20 with the 1980 Oakland A's, is a footnote in baseball history: the last 20-game loser in the 20th century.

Sometime this year he plans to reward himself with a "Pud Galvin Memorial Trophy." Galvin is Kingman's hero. He lost 20 or more games in each of his first 10 seasons, from 1879 to 1888. But he also averaged 30 wins in those 10 seasons, and twice won 46 games. He retired with 361 victories, sixth on the all-time list, and in 1969 was elected to the Hall of Fame.

"It's really just an excuse to have a trophy with my name on it," Kingman explained. "Maybe I could give one to the next guy who loses 20, but he might hit me over the head with it."

In the two decades since, a half dozen pitchers have come close to matching Kingman's dubious achievement. But all were stuck at 19.

It happened to Jose DeLeon twice, with Pittsburgh in 1985 and again five years later when he was with the White Sox. The others were Scott Erickson, Minnesota, 1993; Kirk McCaskill, California Angels, 1991; Tim Leary, Yankees, 1990; Mike Moore, Seattle, 1987; and Matt Young, Seattle, 1985.

Last year's major league leader, with 18, was the Cubs' Steve Trachsel. In mid August, when Trachsel was 4–14, Kingman told Chicago baseball writer Dave van Dyck that he was rooting for Trachsel. "Tell him to keep going out and doing his best," Kingman advised. "He's making me very, very nervous."

Curious, Kingman has plowed through the record books and discovered there is no great stigma in a 20-loss season.

Eighteen Hall of Fame pitchers lost 20, some more than once. The legendary Cy Young was a three-time 20-game loser. So was Vic Willis. Walter Johnson, Steve Carlton, and Phil Niekro did it twice. Denny McLain, baseball's last 30-game winner, 31–6 in 1968, was 10–22 three years later. White Sox knuckleballer Wilbur Wood lost 20 in 1973 but also led the league in victories with 24.

"It's just something that happens," Kingman said. "If you tried to lose 20, I don't think you could do it. Anyway, the manager probably would take you out of the rotation."

Unless, of course, the pitcher has been consistently effective, which Kingman was. In five of his losses, Oakland was shut out. During the 30 games he started, the A's averaged 2.9 runs per game, almost two runs fewer than their season average.

"Losing 20 of 30 starts is no fun," Kingman said. But there were moments of satisfaction. On Friday the 13th (in June) he went the distance in a 4–3 win over the Yankees' Ron Guidry, who at the time had the highest winning percentage of any active pitcher.

Kingman was the hardest thrower in Oakland's 1980 rotation and was 7–11 in early August, certainly no indication he would lose 20. But he lost nine consecutive decisions in the next six weeks. His only regret is that it occurred in his first full season. Most of the other big losers were established pitchers.

"It marks you when you break in like that," he said.

Kingman had been brought up at midseason the year before and won eight games. He recalled that Tom Weir of *USA Today*, then with the *Oakland Tribune*, predicted that if he maintained that pace for a full season he was likely to win 20 the next year.

Ambidextrous

MARCH 3, 2000

AN MLB WEBSITE CLIENT, Bill Ruhl of Miami, Florida, has asked if "there has ever been a pitcher who pitched with both arms? Kind of a switch-pitcher."

Greg Harris of the Montreal Expos, a natural right-hander, is the only pitcher in modern baseball history (since 1900) to throw with both hands in a major league game. It was on September 28, 1995, against Cincinnati in the final week of the season when the Expos were 24½ games out of the lead in the National League East.

The ambidextrous Harris worked a scoreless ninth inning in a 9–7 loss. Using a special reversible six-finger glove, which had two thumbs, Harris faced four batters, two right-handed and two left-handed. He allowed one runner, on a walk.

The play-by-play follows: pitching right-handed, Harris retired the lefty-hitting Reggie Sanders who swung at the first pitch and grounded to short. The next two batters were Hal Morris and Ed Taubensee, both right-handed hitters. Throwing with his left hand, Harris walked Morris on four pitches. Taubensee carried Harris to a full count and hit a nubber in front of the plate. Harris switched back to his right hand for the righty-hitting Bret Boone who grounded to the mound for the third out.

It was the next-to-last big-league appearance for Harris, who was with six clubs and had a 15-year career beginning in 1981. Used mostly in middle relief, he retired with a 74–90 lifetime record, 54 saves, and a 3.67 earned-run average. He appeared in 703 games, 605 out of the bullpen.

Talking about it last week in a telephone interview from his home in Newport Coast, California, where he operates a weekend pitching camp, Harris said he strengthened his left arm when he was a teenager. "I did a lot of woodworking," he explained. "I sawed and hammered with my left hand."

But it wasn't until he was in his sixth big-league season, in 1986 with Texas, after he got his left-handed fastball into the mid-80s, that he became confident that he could throw both ways against major league competition. But there were two strikes against him: (1) the belief that he would be making a mockery of the game, and (2) there was no need for him to throw left-handed because he was consistently effective right-handed.

Bobby Valentine, then the Texas manager, told Harris he would allow him to parade his wizardry in the final series of the 1986 season. The plan was scrapped because the Rangers were in first place and fighting for the division title. Harris was traded to Philadelphia where the management was indifferent to his desire.

His next move was to Boston prior to the 1990 season. The Boston writers, eager for a good story, pleaded each year for the next five years with the Red Sox brass to give him a chance in a spring-training exhibition game. General manager Dan Duquette refused to oblige. "We pay Greg to pitch right-handed," Duquette insisted.

American League president Dr. Bobby Brown, a one-time Yankee infielder who batted .349 in 17 World Series games, was aware a two-way pitcher would have a rare advantage and would neutralize and diminish the effectiveness of every batter. Unwilling to weaken his kinship with the offense, Dr. Brown prepared for the possibility by issuing a directive to his umpires:

a) The pitcher must indicate which hand he intends to use.

b) The pitcher may change arms on the next hitter but must indicate the arm to be used.

c) There will be no warm-up pitches between the change of arms.

d) If an arm is injured, the pitcher may change arms; the umpire must be notified of the injury. The injured arm cannot be used again in that game.

Harris' opportunity came in his last season, in 1995 when he was in his second term with Montreal. To be certain he would be ready, manager Felipe Alou alerted Harris in late August, a month before the event: "Felipe said he wanted to see for himself how I would do and that it would be good for the game."

According to the on-the-spot reports, Harris was baseball's first ambidextrous pitcher since Elton "Ice Box" Chamberlain in 1888. Chamberlain was with Louisville in the American Association, then a major league. He gave up a ninth-inning home run and lost 9–8.

It has since been established that Tony Mullane, with Baltimore in the N.L. against the Cubs, was Harris' immediate predecessor. Mullane, in 1893, worked the ninth inning and gave up three runs in a 10–2 loss. He also threw with both hands in 1882 when he was with Louisville. In 1884, Larry Corcoran, in a game when the Cubs were running out of pitchers, worked four middle innings, the record for longevity.

There were probably as many as a half dozen ambidextrous pitchers in the 20th century who threw on the sidelines but never in a game. Among them were Cal McLish, a 15-year veteran who was with six clubs; Ed Head of the old Brooklyn Dodgers; Dave "Boo" Ferris of the Red Sox; Tug McGraw, Mets; and Jeff Schwarz, who had a brief stay with the White Sox.

The ambidextrous Paul Richards, who later had a distinguished managerial career with the White Sox and the Orioles, claimed that when he was in high school, in Waxahachie, Texas, he was featured in *Ripley's Believe It Or Not!* after winning a doubleheader by pitching right-handed to the right-handed batters and left-handed to the left-handed batters.

When he was in the minors, with Muskogee in the Western Association, Richards was confronted with the ultimate dilemma: the switch-pitcher versus the switch-hitter.

Summoned in ninth-inning relief, Richards was ready to pitch right-handed Charlie Wilson, a switch-hitter. Wilson countered by crossing the plate and stepping into the left-handed batters' box. The amusement continued for several minutes as Wilson jumped from one side to the other.

Exasperated, Richards threw his glove on the mound and faced Wilson with both feet square on the rubber.

"I put my hands behind my back," Richards recalled, "and shouted 'I'll wait until you choose your poison.' "

Leon Cadore

APRIL 15, 2000

IN TODAY'S GAME OF BULLPEN SPECIALISTS, a manager often tells his starting pitcher "Give us six or seven good innings and we'll take it from there."

The complete game is a dinosaur. In 1995 the Colorado Rockies had only one completion. Last season and the season before the Milwaukee Brewers had two. The biggest rarity is the game when both starting pitchers go the distance—12 last season, in an aggregate schedule of 4,586 games, 10 times fewer than grand slam home runs.

This is brought to mind because May 1 is the 80th anniversary of baseball's longest game, a 26-inning marathon between Brooklyn and Boston. It was called because of darkness with the score tied 1–1.

What made that game especially memorable is that the starting pitchers, Leon Cadore of the Dodgers and Joe Oeschger of the Braves, pitched the entire 26 innings. One more inning and they would have worked the equivalent of three games.

It was in 1920, in the midst of the labor movement. *The New York Times* responded with an editorial titled "Overtime Without Pay." The editorialist, unimpressed by the endurance record, commented: "Pitchers in these times are fragile creatures, most of whom think that nine innings in a day is about enough and that two appearances in the same week are as much as can be expected from the hardiest." He recalled that Charlie "Old Hoss" Radbourne, who won 60 games in 1884, pitched and won nearly every day for as much as two weeks in a stretch.

It was the first day of daylight saving time in Boston. The game was played at Braves Field in a dreary mist before a crowd of 2,000. The time of the game was three hours and 50 minutes, approximately an hour and 15 minutes for each nine innings. There were 171 at-bats, nine walks, and six sacrifices, a total of 186 batters faced. Walter Holke, the Braves' first baseman, had 42 putouts.

Cadore and Oeschger met a week later.

"How do you feel?" Cadore asked.

"I've been waiting to see how you feel." Oeschger replied. "We've ruined ourselves."

The popular opinion was they had thrown their arms out, that neither would recover from their heroic duel. It was an erroneous assumption. The next year Oeschger was 20–14, his only 20-victory season. The following season, Cadore, essentially a .500 pitcher, was 13–14, two wins less than his career high.

Cadore was given a 1–0 lead in the fifth. Catcher Ernie Krueger walked, took second on a fielder's choice, and scored on Ivy Olson's single to left. The Braves tied the score in the sixth. Wally Cruise tripled to the foot of the center-field scoreboard. Holke lined to left for what seemed to be a hit but Zack Wheat made a shoestring catch and almost doubled Cruise off third. Tony Boeckel brought Cruise home with a single to center.

Neither team scored again. The Dodgers had their biggest scare in the ninth when the Red Sox filled the bases with one out. Charley Pick then grounded into a side-retiring double play.

The Dodgers also loaded the bases with one out in the seventeenth. Their final threat, Harold Elliott, next up, tapped back the mound and into a force at the plate, Oeschger to catcher Hank Gowdy who fired to first baseman Holke in an attempt for a double play. When Holke fumbled the throw, Ed Konetchy tried to score from second but was out, Holke to Gowdy who made a diving tag for the third out.

Instead of weakening, Cadore and Oeschger grew stronger as the game progressed. Neither allowed a hit in the last six innings. The National League record for longevity was broken in the twenty-third inning, the American League mark in the twenty-fifth.

The reporter covering for *The New York Times* wrote: "After the twenty-sixth inning, umpire [Barry] McCormick yawned twice and observed that it was nearly bedtime. He didn't seem particularly thrilled by what was going on. To him and his brother arbiter [Eugene] Hart, it was merely an infernally long day's work. McCormick held out his hand in the gloaming and thereupon called the game to the satisfaction of himself and Mr. Hart and to the chagrin of everybody else concerned."

In response to my query, part of a letter received from Cadore, dated February 10, 1956, follows: "Some of the ballplayers, particularly Ivy Olson, begged the umps to let it go one more inning but they overruled him and called it. Maybe it was just as well. Just what would have happened if they had lights in those days, is hard to tell.

"What most people don't recollect is that about seven days before that game Oeschger and I tangled down here in Brooklyn, the game went 11 innings, and I was the lucky one in that, beating them 1–0.

"You ask, do I think the long game had any effect on my arm, etc? I couldn't raise my right arm for a couple of days after the big one, and as far as sleeping for a couple of days, well, that is for the birds. Sure, I was tired and did a little sleeping, which reminds me that Wilbert Robinson, our manager, asked if I was getting tired in the twentieth inning.

"I remember saying, 'Sure, but I can go one more,' figuring something just had to happen one way or the other, but that was the way it went through the twenty-sixth. True, maybe a couple more innings could have been played. But as you can see, what a crime it would have been to have a loss marked up against either pitcher.

"Let me state right here the way they rate pitchers today is little short of criminal. Here was a game that neither pitcher got much credit for as far as averages are concerned. I contend that any pitcher, win or lose, who pitches nine innings of shutout ball should be given credit for a winning performance."

Cadore died in 1958, Joe Oeschger in 1986. Both were born in Chicago, 16 months apart.

Bob Feller

MAY 15, 2000

BOB FELLER, GREAT AMERICAN. That's how I often have described the Strikeout King of the mid 20th century, two generations removed. "Rapid Robert," as he was known then, had a 98 to 101 mile-an-hour fastball, the antecedent of Nolan Ryan of more recent vintage and Randy Johnson and Pedro Martinez of current times.

He was the first major league ballplayer to enlist in the armed forces after the bombing of Pearl Harbor and joined the navy on December 10, 1941, three days after the attack. He earned five campaign ribbons and was decorated with eight battle stars serving on the battleship USS *Alabama*, which prowled both the Atlantic and the Pacific theatres during World War II.

Appropriately, he will be the grand marshal for baseball's annual Memorial Day parade and festivities at Cooperstown during the weekend of May 27–29. Can there be a better way to honor the 292,131 gallant American servicemen who fell in World War II than to march behind Chief Petty Officer Feller? I don't think so.

Feller didn't have to enlist but put aside his draft deferment. He was the sole support of his family—his father, who was dying of cancer, his mother, and a younger sister. He was sworn in a month after his 23rd birthday at precisely the time he was approaching the peak of his career.

He was a teenage phenom. In 1936, at the age of 17, in his first American League start, he struck out 15 St. Louis Browns to tie Dizzy Dean's single-game big-league record. He broke the record in 1938 against the Detroit Tigers with 18 Ks. And two years later, on April 16, 1940, against the White Sox, he pitched the only Opening Day no-hitter. In the three seasons prior to his enlistment he won 76 games: 24 wins in 1939, 27 in 1940, and 25 in 1941.

He heard about Pearl Harbor when he was crossing the Mississippi River, en route to Chicago from his Van Meter, Iowa, farm to negotiate his 1942 contract with Cy Slapnicka, then the general manager of the Cleveland Indians. "I was never a big hero," Feller recalled last week in a telephone interview from his home in Gates Mills, Ohio. "It was just time for me to help in any way I could."

Six months later, his training completed, he was assigned to the newly commissioned *Alabama,* one of four battleships of the swift South Dakota class. Normally it carried a crew of 2,300. It was 700 feet long and had a main deck large enough to accommodate a hard-throwing pitcher. When fully loaded, the ship weighed 45,000 tons.

His first 11 months aboard the *Alabama* were spent in the European theatre, mostly in the North Sea, convoying British and Russian troop and supply ships against a German U-boat armada. From the bitter Arctic, the *Alabama* made a nonstop 6,600-mile voyage through the Panama Canal to the simmering heat in the New Hebrides in the South Pacific, a staging area halfway between Hawaii and the Philippines.

Assigned to the Third Fleet, the *Alabama* was in constant action and, in order, was involved in the battles of the Gilbert and Marshall Islands, in the Marianis, in Peleliu, in New Guinea, then back to the Marianis, this time in the battle for Truk. It was also engaged in the capture and occupation of Guam, the epic struggle for Saipan, and in the landings in the Western Caroline Islands, and supported the invasion of Okinawa. After the surrender documents were signed, the *Alabama* led the fleet into Tokyo Bay.

Feller was in charge of a 40-millimeter antiaircraft mount, usually manned by 10 gunners and capable of firing 160 rounds a minute. The day he remembers most was in June 1944 when the army, eventually rescued by the marine corps (General "Howlin' Mad" Smith, commanding), was securing the Saipan beaches. The Third Fleet shot down 474 Japanese planes in one day. It is still known in the navy, a half century later, as the "Great Turkey Shoot." There was no way of keeping score. Every ship in the fleet was firing simultaneously.

"Which ships took credit for the 'splashes' [when an enemy aircraft plunged into the water] was not important," Feller said. "What mattered was the damage to the fleet. We were not hit but some of the bombs came close."

Remarkably, the *Alabama* never lost a man in an enemy action, then or later. It was known as the "Lucky A."

"Hell, we weren't lucky, we were good," insisted Captain John Brown of Keller, Texas, who was among Feller's shipmates.

Feller was aboard the *Alabama* for 34 months before returning to a hero's welcome. He was discharged on August 22, 1945. After an absence of almost four years, he reported to the Indians. Five weeks remained on the schedule. He made nine starts and finished with a 5–3 record and a 2.50 earned-run average but the big strikeout pitch was missing in action: a comparatively modest 59 Ks in 72 innings. Many baseball insiders immediately predicted, at best, he would be a .500 pitcher thereafter.

The doomsayers were wrong. He won 26 games the following season, including his second no-hitter, on April 30 against the Yankees, in his first New York appearance, and led the majors with a one-season record 368 strikeouts. He struck out every regular American League position player with one exception. Only Barney McCosky of Detroit escaped. This record stood for 20 years. If not for Feller's short 1945 season, he would have led the league in strikeouts eight years in a row and in victories five times, also in succession.

This was the stone age of baseball technology. There were no radar guns to measure velocity. So Feller agreed to several pregame stunts. His fastball beat a motorcyclist who was given a running start. A *Life* magazine photographic crew clocked him at 100 miles an hour. Lew Fonseca, a former American League batting champion and then the director of baseball's motion picture bureau, caught him at 99 and 101.

The comical Lefty Gomez, a pitcher with the Yankees, contributed to the Feller legend:

> Along about the eighth inning I got up for the third or fourth time. Hadn't hit the ball yet. Feller winds up and lets it go. I never saw it. It just went "bzzz," and into the catcher's mitt. The umpire hollered, "Strike 1."
>
> I dug in and waited for the next pitch. "Strike 2," Then he winds up again. It was just a blur of white and that noise, "bzzz." The umpire screamed in my ear, "Strike 3." I don't think the umpire saw it, either. So I turned and beefed, "Hey, Mac, didn't that one sound low?"

Feller retired after the 1956 season with a 266–162 record. He had three no-hitters, 12 one-hitters, and 10 or more Ks in 45 games. A baseball analyst subsequently determined that if he hadn't been in the navy he would have won an additional 107 games. Feller has no regrets.

"Every time I went out to pitch I thought about how lucky I was to serve my country and come back with all my limbs," Feller said. "I did what I thought I should. You'll never hear me cry about it."

Ron Necciai

JUNE 15, 2000

RON NECCIAI WASN'T AT HIS HOME in Monogahela, Pennsylvania, when
the telephone rang. He was helping his brother-in-law put in a kitchen
at nearby North Huntington. His wife, Martha, answered the phone.
When he returned she told him she wasn't sure if she could pronounce
or spell the caller's name, but he left his number and said he had played
first base at Bristol.

"Sure, I know who he is," Necciai replied, and he called Phil Filiatrault
in Vancouver.

"I hadn't heard from him in 50 years," Necciai explained. "He had
read the morning paper and said, 'Ron, I don't want anyone to surpass
your record or even equal it.'"

And that was the first Necciai (pronounced Netch-Eye) knew that Brett
Gray, a 23-year-old right-hander with the London, Connecticut,
Werewolves in the independent Frontier League had struck out 25 batters.

Gray's performance triggered the memory not only of Filiatrault, but
also those of many senior fans who remember that Necciai, a slender 6'5"
right-hander, struck out 27 batters, also in a nine-inning game, on May
13, 1952. Necciai was a Pittsburgh farmhand with the Bristol, Virginia
club in the Class D Appalachian League.

19

Necciai has the box score framed. No hits, no runs, 31 batters faced in a 7–0 rout over the Welch, West Virginia, Miners. Four batters reached base: on a walk, an error, another hit by a pitch, and the fourth and last when he swung and missed a third strike that would have been the final out. But the ball hit the crease in front of the plate and bounced past catcher Harry Dunlop. It was scored as a passed ball. The next batter struck out.

After the game Dunlop told Necciai, "You know, you struck out 27 batters."

And I said, "They've been playing this game for 100 years. Someone must have done it before."

No one had done it before or since.

"I was 18 and he was 19," recalled Dunlop, a veteran big leaguer and now a coach with the Cincinnati Reds. "In about the sixth inning the fans began chanting numbers. '16! 17! 18!'—I didn't know what it was all about. I came into the dugout and I asked, 'What are all the numbers about?'

"They told me he was striking out everybody. And I thought I better start bearing down."

The natural assumption, when reading about a 27-strikeout performance, is that it was 27 up, 27 down, with the catcher making all the putouts. But two of the putouts were made by first baseman Filiatrault, on a fourth- or fifth-inning line drive that bounced in front of him, and a midgame, swinging, dropped third strike that required a throw.

Prior to the ninth inning, according to Filiatrault, the primary concern was protecting Necciai's no-hitter.

"We knew Ron was having strikeouts galore but essentially we were thinking of the no-hitter," Filiatrault recalled. "As the game progressed, it became more pressure-filled. We just didn't want to make an error or let a line drive go past us without maximum effort.

"We didn't realize there was a possibility of 27 strikeouts until the ninth inning. The batter hit a high foul ball between first base and home plate, about 12 feet foul. Harry was underneath faster than I was. As he was looking up, getting ready to make the catch, I yelled 'Drop it! Drop it!'

and then the crowd chimed in. It didn't mean anything. We were way ahead. Harry let it fall.

"Ron struck him out on the next pitch."

Then came the crucial moment.

"He was an overhand pitcher," Dunlop said. "He had a great curveball, an old-fashioned drop. A lot of them dropped in the dirt. He wasn't easy to handle. There were two outs and he had two strikes on the batter. That's when the ball hit the plate. The batter swung and missed but the ball bounced away and he reached first base."

Necciai struck out the next batter and the game was over, his fourth strikeout in the inning. If the game hadn't been prolonged, Necciai would have finished with 26 strikeouts.

Necciai's unprecedented achievement was put to verse:

> Ron fanned the side at will that night,
> His Bristol Twins put Welch to rout.
> A flawless romp? Well, not quite.
> One Miner batter grounded out.
>
> A shutout, though not neat at all,
> Welch men on base with every glitch;
> One walk, one error, one passed ball,
> A Miner struck by Ronnie's pitch.
>
> Yet goofs did not the runners leaven;
> Strikeouts erased them tit for tat,
> As Bristol's ace whiffed 27.
> Ye pitchers hence—try topping that.

"There were no radar guns in those days, but his fastball was in the middle and upper 90s," Dunlop said. "I thought he was going to be a great major league pitcher."

In his next start with Bristol, before an overflow crowd of 5,235, Rocket Ron celebrated "Ron Necciai night" with a two-hit, 24-strikeout win over Kingsport, Tennessee. The Pirates then promoted him to their Burlington, North Carolina, club in the Class B Carolina League. He struck out 14 in his Burlington debut. Pittsburgh was the next stop.

It was the great American Horatio Alger story. But it was aborted. Once in Pittsburgh, Necciai injured his arm. He was 1–6 in nine starts with the Pirates and never pitched in another big-league game.

But he hasn't been forgotten. A monument with a huge plaque was erected in his honor at the Bristol ballpark last August, and in January he was invited, for the first time, to the Pirates Fantasy Camp commemorating their 1960 World Championship.

"It was wonderful," Necciai said. "I was there with all the Pirate stars— Dick Groat, Vernon Law, [Bill] Mazeroski, Elroy Face, and Bob Friend. I had a great time."

Jerry Manuel

MARCH 3, 2001

CASEY STENGEL, WHO MANAGED THE YANKEES to 10 pennants in a 12-year sequence, from 1949 to 1960, often said he "couldn't have done it without the players."

It's a well-worn quote and the general assumption, then and now, was that Stengel was being modest. But it wasn't modesty. It was honesty. How else could it be explained that in his previous nine seasons, when he was managing the Brooklyn and Boston clubs, his teams never finished in the first division?

Today, almost a half century later, Jerry Manuel of the White Sox has the same approach. Last season Manuel guided the Sox to their first divisional title since 1983, and is aware that the manager gets too much credit when his team wins.

"The worst part of this job," Manuel insists, "is that the manager gets too much exposure."

He was genuinely embarrassed last season by the flood of national stories that described him as a dugout wizard.

"It was the players who were entitled to all of the press," Manuel said. "They were the ones who did the job. The players and the organization. I didn't hit a ball or run a base. I was just the guy who tried to keep everything in order."

Manuel, who is starting his fourth season at the helm, was a landslide winner in the balloting for the American League Manager of the Year. Dusty Baker of the San Francisco Giants was selected, for the third time, as the National League Manager of the Year. Like Manuel, Baker is also from Sacramento, California.

Manuel is grateful of course for the honor but knows that sometimes the Manager of the Year is dismissed in the very next season. Some of these victims, in recent years, have been Davey Johnson, Gene Lamont, and Jack McKeon. Heroes one season, goats the next.

Manuel says he is a novice and still learning the trade. "I've learned a lot each year. When I stop learning it will be time for me to be doing something else."

The first season he learned the necessity of patience. "I had a young club and wanted everything to work right away. The second season we were trying to put together a pitching staff. It was a big chore. And again I had to be patient. It takes time for everything to fall in place.

"If they [the Sox front office] had listened to me, we probably wouldn't have been where we wanted to be. I like to win—the sooner the better. But it was worth waiting for. And no doubt I became a better manager."

Manuel doesn't subscribe to the long-held theory that the Sox will now have a more difficult time to contend because the other clubs will make a greater effort against them.

"That's a lot of baloney. Every time you're playing a major league club, they're trying to win. It doesn't make any difference where you are in the standings."

Manuel is often asked how many victories a manager is responsible for.

"I tell them I can't answer that because I don't know. What I do know is a manager must communicate and develop a good relationship with all of his players. Everybody in uniform is important. From the best player to the 25th man. And when you have good communications, a player will always give you a full effort."

He was told that when the Sox won in 1983, it was Jerry Dybzinski, a utility infielder, the 25th man, who provided the initial spark. Dybzinski was in the starting lineup every day for two weeks in May and turned the club around.

"I can believe that," Manuel said. "No doubt about it. The 24th or 25th man can be just as important as your big hitter."

Manuel knows this from his personal experience. A weak-hitting second baseman, he appeared in only 96 big-league games, 60 with Detroit and 36 with Montreal. Combined, he batted .150.

"I wasn't the 25th man," Manuel said. "I was the 26th man, always waiting to come up from Triple A. I would hope I would appreciate them anyway, but obviously I have some experience in being that man."

Manuel broke into professional baseball in 1972 and spent 10 years in the bushes, most of them in upper minors. He was also a minor league coach and manager and put in time as a major league field coordinator.

Is he another example of a failed player who became an outstanding big-league manager?

"I hate stereotypes," Manuel observed. "An argument could be made that we don't make the best managers. I've had to work hard. The only way to get things accomplished is to work hard at it."

He says he learned the most from Felipe Alou and Jim Leyland. He put in six years as Alou's third-base coach with Montreal and another season with the Florida Marlins under Leyland. He also played for Leyland when they were in the Detroit organization, in Triple A.

"I played for a lot of managers. Dick Williams was very smart. Ralph Houk had a reputation as a tough-guy manager. I liked him. He was very honest.

"They all had something to offer. Especially Felipe Alou. He was an innovator, not necessarily in redefining the game but in thinking ahead. He seemed to always know what the opposition was going to do—not just the other managers, what they were thinking, but what the opposing players were trying to do. He just has that knack."

Manuel also has the knack and though he is a comparatively new manager at the big-league level, he is an expert at handling and inspiring the troops.

He was an all-around sports star at Cordoba High School in Sacramento and received more than 150 football scholarships but instead signed with Detroit when the Tigers plucked him out of the 1972 free-agent draft.

Dusty Baker, five years older, graduated from nearby Del Campo High School. They played basketball together in the off-season.

"It never occurred to me that either of us would become a big-league manager," Baker said. "That we would be Manager of the Year in the same season is hard to believe."

Lady Umpires

A HEARTY HELLO AND GOOD FORTUNE to the new lady umpire! She is Ria Cortesio from Rock Island, Illinois, a graduate of Rice University and the Jim Evans Umpire Academy, a five-week course that has a slim survival rate.

"They tell 90 percent of the students to go home and have a nice life," Cortesio said.

She hasn't gone home and is working in the Class A Midwest League, her third season in the minors. And, yes, she's having a nice life, and doing just fine according to league president George Spelius.

"She's going in the right direction," Spelius reported. "Otherwise, she or any of our other umpires wouldn't still be here. They're all young and learning."

The right direction is the road to the major leagues. Whether she'll make it to the top nobody knows. What is known is that she's the fifth female umpire to work in organized baseball. None of her antecedents graduated to the big time, including Pam Postema, who had the longest and most distinguished career—13 years—including seven seasons in Triple A, four as a crew chief.

In her 1992 book, *You've Got to Have B*lls to Make It in This League*, coauthored by Gene Wojciechowski, Postema revealed she "got plenty of

27

weird proposals." She said Carmelo Martinez, who had a brief stretch with the Cubs, spent half his time in the batter's box trying to sweet-talk her.

" 'I love you, honey,' he'd say.

"I'd ignore him.

" 'My amor,' he'd try again.

"He'd asked me to marry him. I would laugh and tell him, 'Not until you get to the big leagues and make a million dollars.' "

So far Miss Cortesio, 24, 5'10" and a slim 145 pounds, with light brown hair, has not had any marriage proposals. But she has been asked out.

"A couple of stupid players have tried for a date," she conceded. "I chewed them out and humiliated them in front of their teammates. You get the whole dugout laughing at them and they won't do it again."

And what if another umpire wanted to go dancing?

"I'd shoot them down as well."

Cortesio is all business and seems determined to reach the top. Unlike Postema, who practiced lowering the pitch of her voice, bound her chest for a more masculine appearance, and tucked her ponytail inside her cap, Cortesio doesn't conceal her femininity.

"I'm not trying to look like a man," she insisted. "You don't have to be a man to umpire.

"I'm just out there doing the same thing that my partner is. We're just like all the other crews. My gender doesn't matter. Ball! Strike! Safe! Out! Fair! Or foul! It doesn't change whether the umpire is male or female. It never comes up in my mind.

"And the players have their own agendas. They're trying to get to the big leagues just like we are. They care more about 'What's this guy going to throw me on a 1–2 pitch?' They hate me just like they hate every umpire."

But this time around there is a huge difference. Cortesio has an advantage. Her colleagues are generally sympathetic and in her corner. They may not all be rooting for her but they are not publicly hostile, as was the case with her predecessors.

The pay in Class A is minimal, approximately $2,000 a month, plus expenses, for a four-month season. But there is a pot of gold at the end of the rainbow. Major league rookies open at $75,000 a year, with annual increases of $5,000. After 10 years it's $120,000, after 20 years it's $170,000.

Good plate-work is absolutely essential. "You try for consistency," Cortesio explained. Whereas big-league umpires have the plate every fourth game, she is working in a two-person system. It is beneficial. She and her partner, Scott McClellan, call balls and strikes in every other game.

Bernice Gera, 5'2", 130 pounds, a housewife out of upstate New York, was the trailblazer. Following a six-year court battle for women's rights, she worked her first and only game on June 24, 1972, in the opener of a doubleheader between Geneva and Auburn in the New York/Penn League.

She worked the bases and reversed a call after she had ruled an Auburn player safe at second base. Nolan Campbell, the Auburn manager, rushed out in protest. Gera admitted she had made a mistake. Nonetheless, she gave him the thumb. Her partner did not intercede.

"Why are you throwing me out?" shouted Campbell. "You're the one who made the mistake."

After the game she told Joseph McDonough, the Geneva general manager, "I've just resigned from baseball. I'm sorry, Joe."

And she walked to a car and was driven off by friends. Witnesses said she had tears in her eyes.

Christine Wren, out of Seattle, was number two and the first woman to work the plate. One night there was a frying pan at home plate. She was repeatedly taunted with sexist comments such as "Go home and do the laundry!" Players asked, "Why does a nice-looking broad like you want to be an umpire?" All accompanied with a stream of obscene language.

When a reporter asked if she was fronting for women's lib, Wren said, "I don't believe in it. I believe in people lib. And given this opportunity, I'm going to prove I'm not a token woman umpire because I'm not going to quit. They'll have to fire me first."

She quit in 1979 after four seasons in Class A.

Theresa Cox, a Southern belle out of Alabama, also gave it a whirl. She worked two years in the Arizona Rookie League and was released in

1990, one year after Pam Postema departed. Postema holds the record for longevity, from 1977 to 1989.

At the time, the general belief was that Postema was ready. According to published reports, the late Bart Giamatti, when he was commissioner, was "grooming" her for a major league assignment. She worked major league spring-training exhibition games in 1989. But Giamatti suffered a fatal heart attack and she never got the call.

"I've read Pam's book," Cortesio said. "I hope someday I'll get to meet her."

Cortesio became interested in umpiring when she was 17 and attending games in the Midwest League. "I met some of the umpires and that's when I realized they were just normal people. Everybody has a tendency to think of umpires as dirty, fat, grouchy old men. It's a terrible misconception."

Umpires, at every level, must be aggressive. They are constantly challenged. Jerry Dale, a former National League umpire, wrote his master's thesis on the changing umpire personality. The higher they advance the more their aggressive behavior escalates. Otherwise, Dale concluded, they aren't likely to survive.

Although Cortesio claims she has heard no sexist comments, she has felt an underpinning of resentment by several of the older managers. "That's their problem, not mine," she said.

Whatever, it may be well to remember the limerick by Ogden Nash:

> There was once an umpire whose vision
> Was cause for abuse and derision.
> He remarked in surprise,
> "Why pick on my eyes?
> It's my heart that makes the decision."

Fathers and Sons

JUNE 15, 2001

STEVE TROUT WAS ONLY NINE YEARS OLD but the memory is still vivid. He was playing catch with one of his older brothers at a family picnic when suddenly his father, Paul "Dizzy" Trout, began shouting to his mother: "Pearl! Pearl! C'mon over here and see your son throw the ball! We finally got our pitcher!"

A former major league pitcher, the late Dizzy Trout fathered ten children, seven of them boys. "We knew one of us would be a professional ballplayer," Steve recalled with amusement. "I was the dumb one with a strong arm. I knew it would be me."

The Trouts won 258 games, Dizzy 170, Steve 88, for many years the most victories for a father and son, since surpassed by Mel Sr., and Todd Stottlemyre, with 302 going into this season.

According to Larry Tamman, an expert on the subject, there have been 153 fathers who played in the majors and have enjoyed the thrill of seeing their sons do the same—from the Adamses, Bobby and Dick, to the Wrights, Clyde and Jaret, both pitchers. Jaret is now among the stars on the Cleveland staff.

This list also includes such well-known players as Barry and Bobby Bonds; the Griffeys, Ken Sr. and Ken Jr.; the Alomars, Sandy Sr. and sons

31

Roberto and Sandy Jr.; Fred and Jason Kendall; Bob Boone and his sons Bret and Aaron; Maury and Bump Wills; and George Sisler and his sons Dick and David.

Also, Randy and Todd Hundley; Felipe and Moises Alou; Hal and Brian McRae; Jose and Danny Tartabull; Bob and Joel Skinner; Bob and Terry Kennedy; Tito and Terry Francona; Vern and Vance Law; Yogi and Dale Berra; Chuck and Bruce Tanner; and Thornton and Don Lee, the only father-son duo to strike out Ted Williams.

There is an even more exclusive group: the three-generation families—father, son, and grandson. There are only three such royal baseball house-holds—the Boones, the Bells, and lately the Hairstons. Considering the odds, it doesn't seem likely a fourth generation will appear.

The Boone family, through action of June 12, 2001, leads in major league games, 5,104, combined. The Bells are next with 4,790, the Hairstons a distant third, 1,003.

Some lineage is required: Ray "Ike" Boone, a 13-year big-league short-stop who retired after the 1960 season, begat Bob Boone, a distinguished catcher, second to Carlton Fisk (by one game) in total games caught. Bob begat Bret and Aaron, both third-generation players. They are still active, Bret with Seattle, Aaron with Cincinnati.

Gus Bell, a reliable outfielder, a .281 career hitter in 15 big-league seasons, sired Buddy Bell, a five-time All-Star third baseman, a strong hitter who was also brilliant in the field. Buddy fathered David, a hard-hitting infielder with the Seattle Mariners who is beginning to leave footprints.

The Hairstons, until now, have been comparatively obscure. Grandpa Sam was a husky reserve catcher who appeared in only four games, all with the 1951 White Sox. Sam had two sons who made it to the majors. The first, John, a catcher, played three games with the 1969 Cubs. Sam's second son, Jerry, persevered, and had a 14-year career, all in Chicago, as a utility infielder, pinch-hitter, and designated hitter.

Jerry's son, Jerry Jr., a second baseman, is in his fourth season with the Baltimore Orioles, and is emerging as one of the American League's leading hitters. Good fortune to Jerry Jr. His father and grandpa were among my good friends.

The Griffeys, Ken Sr. and Ken Jr., Seattle teammates, are the only father and son to play in the same regular-season game. In their first game together, against Kansas City on August 31, 1990, they opened with back-to-back, first-inning singles that helped the Mariners to a 5–2 victory.

"I was so nervous, it was like being a rookie again," said the 40-year-old Griffey, who described it as his biggest thrill in baseball. The senior Griffey, who had an outstanding 18-year big-league career—148 home runs and 832 RBIs, won a free dinner from his 20-year-old son, betting on who would get the first hit.

Young Griffey said, "It seemed like a father/son game, like we were out in the backyard playing catch."

A royal pedigree can also present personal difficulties. Bob Kennedy, then the Cubs' general manager, almost acquired his son, Terry, in the 1977 summer draft. "Our scouts tell us he's the best catching prospect in the country," Kennedy said. But he decided it would be a disadvantage if Terry was in the same organization with his father. There would be too much pressure. Terry signed with the Cardinals.

And what if the son doesn't live up to expectations? This happens more often than not. Al Campanis, the former front office boss of the Los Angeles Dodgers, was confronted with this weighty problem. He traded his son Jim, a weak-hitting catcher, to Kansas City.

Several field managers—including Felipe Alou, Hal McRae, and Yogi Berra—managed their sons.

McRae told his son, Brian, "Never be late and stay out of the hotel bar."

"I think it's great," Yogi said after the Yankees had acquired his son in a trade. "It'll be good to get a chance to see him play."

Edward Gaedel

JULY 15, 2001

"BASEBALL IS A FUNNY GAME," said Joe Garagiola. And it was never more amusing than 50 years ago almost to the day, August 19, 1951, when Barnum Bill Veeck, then the owner of the St. Louis Browns, used a midget pinch-hitter in the first inning of the second game of a doubleheader against the Detroit Tigers,

It's properly noted in the baseball encyclopedias: Gaedel, Edward Carl, born in Chicago, 1925—height 3'7", weight 65 pounds, no official at-bats, no hits, no runs, no batting average—and one walk. And, of course, a story goes with it.

It was Veeck's best-known stunt. Wearing uniform ⅛, Gaedel popped out of a papier-mâché cake, walked to the plate, and was announced as a pinch-batter for leadoff man Frank Saucier. Gaedel drew a four-pitch walk from Bob Cain. Jim Delsing ran for him.

The assumption was that only Veeck's wife Mary Frances, field manager Zack Taylor, and a few club officials were in on the gag. Not true. Bob Broeg, St. Louis' Hall of Fame baseball writer, had been tipped off.

"We had been out drinking the night before," Broeg recalled. "About midnight, Veeck looked at his watch and said, 'I guess you're in with your last edition.' And Veeck told me, 'I'm going to use a midget tomorrow.'"

"I'm glad you're telling me," Broeg replied. "We don't have many photographers working on Sunday."

At the ballpark the next day, Broeg sought out Jack January, a *Post-Dispatch* photographer. January told Broeg he was just shooting the first game.

"No, no," Broeg told him. "You've got to stay for the second game."

In those days photographers were allowed on the field. January kept creeping closer and was within 10 to 12 feet of the plate when he took the picture of catcher Bob Swift on his knees with Gaedel at bat. It is among baseball's classic photographs and was printed the next morning in newspapers throughout the country. Without it, the amusement would have been muted.

January had plenty of time because plate umpire Ed Hurley, after one look at Gaedel, started toward the Browns' bench and shouted to Zack Taylor, "Hey, what's going on here?"

Veeck, in his autobiography *Veeck—as in Wreck* told the rest of the story:

> Zack came out with a sheaf of papers. He showed Hurley Gaedel's contract. He showed him the telegram to [the American League headquarters in Chicago] duly promulgated with a time stamp. He even showed him a copy of our active list to prove we had room to add another player.
>
> The place went wild. I will never forget the look of utter disbelief that came over Cain's face when he finally realized this was for real. Bob Swift rose to the occasion like a real trouper. I could not have improved one whit upon his performance.
>
> Bob, bless his heart, did just what I was hoping he would do. He went to the mound to discuss the intricacies of pitching to a midget. To complete the sheer incongruity of the scene—and make the picture of the event more memorable—he got down on his knees to offer his pitcher a target.
>
> I had called Marty Caine, a booking agent, and asked him to find me a midget who was somewhat athletic. Marty found Gaedel in Chicago and sent him to St. Louis. He was a nice little guy, in his mid twenties. He had sad little eyes and a squeaky voice that sounded as if it were on the wrong speed of a record player.

"Eddie," I said, "how would you like to be a big-league ballplayer?"

When he heard what I wanted him to do, he was a little dubious. I had to give him a sales pitch. I said, "Eddie, you'll be the only midget in the history of the game. You'll be appearing before thousands of people. Your name will go into the record books for all time. You'll be famous, Eddie. You'll be immortal."

Eddie had more than a little ham in him. The more I talked, the braver he became. By the time I was finished, he was ready to charge through a machine-gun nest to get to the plate.

I asked him how much he knew about baseball. "Well," he said, "I know you're supposed to hit the ball with the bat. And then you run somewhere."

Obviously, he was schooled in the fundamentals. "I'll show you what I want you to do." I picked up a little bat and crouched over as far as I could, my front elbow resting on my front knee. The rules of the game say that the strike zone is between the batter's armpits and the top of his knees "when he assumes his natural stance." Since he would bat only once in his life, whatever stance he took was, by definition, his natural stance.

When Eddie went into that crouch, his strike zone was just about visible to the naked eye. I picked up a ruler and measured it for posterity. It was 1½ inches. Marvelous.

He practiced that crouch for awhile, up and down, up and down, while I cheered him lustily. After a while, he began to test the heft of the bat and glare out toward an imaginary pitcher. He sprang out of his crouch and took an awkward, lunging swing.

"No, no," I said. "You just stay in that crouch. All you have to do is just stay there and take four balls. Then you'll trot down to first base and we'll send someone in to run for you." His face collapsed. You could see his visions of glory leaking out of him.

"Eddie," I said gently. "I'm going to be up on the roof with a high-powered rifle watching every move you make. If you so much as look as if you're going to swing, I'm going to shoot you dead."

The most surprising thing to me, as I moved through the crowd during the first game, was that nobody seemed to have paid any attention to the rather unique scorecard listing "⅛ Gaedel."

Harry Mitauer of the *Globe Democrat* did ask Bob Fishel [the Browns' publicist] about it up in the press box but Roberto was able to shunt the question aside. The next day we had hundreds of requests from collectors, so I suppose there are quite a few of the Gaedel scorecards still in existence.

The press, for the most part, took the sane attitude that Gaedel had provided a bright moment in what could easily have been a deadly dull doubleheader between seventh- and eighth-place clubs.

Vincent X. Flaherty of Los Angeles pretty much summed up the general reaction when he wrote: "I do not advocate baseball burlesque. Such practices do not redound to the better interests of the game—but I claim it was the funniest thing that has happened in baseball in years."

American League president Will Harridge wasn't amused. The next day Harridge issued an executive order barring Gaedel from baseball. A new rule was promptly passed making it mandatory that all player contracts be filed with and *approved* by the league president.

Gaedel's baseball contract was for $100 but, as Veeck had predicted, he became famous and earned an additional $20,000 for television appearances. He died 10 years later, in 1961, at the age of 36, a few days after he was mugged on a south side Chicago street corner. According to a published report, the $11 he had in his wallet was taken from him.

No-Hitters Lost
with Two Outs in Ninth

SEPTEMBER 15, 2001

DON'T FEEL BAD, MIKE MUSSINA. You were not the first nor will you be the last to lose a no-hitter with two outs in the ninth. The Yankees' Mussina was the latest to join Heartbreak Hill, on September 3 in Boston. After retiring the first 26 batters, pinch-hitter Carl Everett broke up his perfect game with a single that parachuted safely into short left field.

As far as can be ascertained, Mussina was the 44th pitcher to lose a no-hitter within one out of glory. This includes Floyd Bevens of the Yankees in the fourth game of the 1947 World Series against the Brooklyn Dodgers and Dave Stieb of the Toronto Blue Jays, the all-time hard-luck champ. Believe it or not, it happened to Steib twice, in successive starts in 1988.

You can look it up. On September 24 a routine grounder by Cleveland's Julio Franco took a bad hop over the head of second baseman Manny Lee for a single. Six nights later, in Stieb's final appearance of the season, Jim Traber of Baltimore destroyed another no-hitter with a bloop single to right field. Both hits came on a 2–2 pitch.

"I just have to laugh," the 31-year-old Stieb told veteran baseball writer Neil MacCarl. "It wasn't a bad feeling. What can you do? I think that sums up my career, the way things have been going for me." Stieb finally got his no-hitter on September 2, 1990, against Cleveland.

The Yankees' Bill Bevens suffered a double whammy. He was the only World Series pitcher deprived with two outs in the ninth and so far as is known the only pitcher to also *lose* the game. Cookie Lavagetto, batting for Eddie Stanky, drove in two runs with a double off the right-field wall that lifted the Dodgers to a 3–2 win.

One game was not played to a decision. In 1942 Al Milnar of the Cleveland Indians was within one out of a no-hitter against Detroit. Doc Cramer broke the spell. This game was scoreless and called after 14 innings. I don't know why it was called. It was the opener of a double-header; the second game was played to completion.

The no-hitters that got away are as memorable as those pitched to completion. In 30 years on the beat I covered only three no-hitters but I must have been a jinx because I saw twice that many broken with two outs in the ninth.

The first one was in 1943 when the Yankees' Joe Gordon ruined Orval Grove's bid for glory in a night game at Comiskey Park. I was in the right upper deck, a 16-year-old fan. Gordon doubled past third baseman Jimmy Grant.

Grove's wife, Katherine, vowed she would never again speak to Gordon. She not only relented but years later the Groves and Gordons became good friends when the Gordons moved to Sacramento.

I have total recall of Billy Pierce's near miss. It was at old Griffith Stadium in Washington in 1958. Pierce had a perfect game going when Ed Fitz Gerald lined an opposite field double to right, fair by no more than two or three feet. Second baseman Nellie Fox, Pierce's buddy, said he should have got his glove on the ball. Fox had no chance. The ball landed almost half way down the right-field line.

The White Sox won their last pennant the next year. Late in that season, in August, they were guests at a luncheon hosted by an Illinois congressman at the old House building. Richard Nixon, then the vice president, was at the door and shook hands with the players as they entered. Nixon was a big fan. When he greeted Pierce he told him he had heard the game on the radio and was rooting for him.

Fifteen years later, in 1973, Stan Bahnsen, also with the White Sox, was denied by Walter Williams, who the year before had been his teammate with the White Sox. Williams drilled a routine grounder past third baseman Bill Melton. The ball stayed down. All Melton had to do was move a step or two to his left and he would have deflected the ball. It rolled by him, untouched.

In 1975 Tom Seaver, then with the Mets, gave up a clean single to the light-hitting "Tarzan" Joe Wallis of the Cubs. This game is often confused with another Seaver near no-hitter, in 1969, when Jimmy Qualls, also with the Cubs, singled in the ninth. But Qualls got his hit with *one* out in the ninth. The Wallis hit was with two outs.

Left-hander Ken Brett, when he was with the White Sox in 1976, was another two-out victim. It was in Anaheim. Jerry Remy of the Angels topped a slow roller to third baseman Jorge Orta, who overran the ball. Orta didn't know Brett had a no-hitter. The ball went under his glove. If Orta had touched the ball, more than likely, he would have drawn an error.

Milt Wilcox of Detroit was sailing along with a 6–0 perfecto at Comiskey Park in 1983 when disaster struck. Jerry Hairston, pinch batting for Jerry Dybzinski, was the spoiler. Hairston singled through the middle.

Since then two other Chicago pitchers, Jose Guzman and Frank Castillo, have suffered a similar fate but I have no memory of either of these games. At that time I was a columnist and no longer traveling with a club as beat writer.

Over the years there probably have been as many as 500 budding no-hitters, perhaps twice as many, lost after the seventh inning. Shed a tear for Mussina and the 43 others who gave up the first hit with two outs in the ninth.

A list of these potential no-hitters and the spoilers follows.

YEAR	PITCHER/TEAM	SCORE	SPOILER/TEAM
1896	Cy Young Cleveland Spiders	7–0	Ed Delahanty Philadelphia Phillies
1899	Doc McJames Brooklyn Superbas	4–0	Hugh Duffy Boston Beaneaters
1904	Bob Rhoads Cleveland Naps	3–1	Chick Stahl Boston Pilgrims
1908	Bill Burns Washington Senators	0–1	Germany Schaefer Detroit Tigers
1909	Bill Burns Chicago White Sox	1–0	Otis Clymer Washington Senators
1911	Nap Rucker Brooklyn Dodgers	1–0	Bob Bescher Cincinnati Reds
1914	Jeff Tesreau New York Giants	2–0	Joe Kelly Pittsburgh Pirates
1915	Herb Pennock Philadelphia Athletics	2–0	Harry Hooper Boston Red Sox
1915	Pete Alexander Philadelphia Phillies	3–0	Art Butler St. Louis Cardinals
1915	Bernie Boland Detroit Tigers	3–1	Ben Paschal Cleveland Indians
1918	Dan Griner Brooklyn Robins	2–0	Gavvy Cravath Philadelphia Phillies
1923	Dazzy Vance Brooklyn Robins	9–0	Sam Bohne Cincinnati Reds
1925	Ted Lyons Chicago White Sox	17–0	Bobby Veach Washington Senators
1932	Tommy Bridges Detroit Tigers	13–0	Dave Harris Washington Senators
1933	Whit Wyatt Chicago White Sox	6–1	Ted Gullic St. Louis Browns
1942	Al Milnar Cleveland Indians	0–0*	Doc Cramer Detroit Tigers

1943	Orval Grove Chicago White Sox	1–0	Joe Gordon New York Yankees
1947	Bill Bevens New York Yankees	2–3**	Cookie Lavagetto Brooklyn Dodgers
1952	Art Houtteman Detroit Tigers	13–0	Harry Simpson Cleveland Indians
1958	Billy Pierce Chicago White Sox	3–0	Ed Fitz Gerald Washington Senators
1967	Billy Rohr Boston Red Sox	3–0	Elston Howard New York Yankees
1968	Blue Moon Odom Oakland Athletics	6–1	Davey Johnson Baltimore Orioles
1973	Stan Bahnsen Chicago White Sox	4–0	Walt Williams Cleveland Indians
1975	Ken Holtzman Oakland Athletics	4–0	Tom Veryzer Detroit Tigers
1975	Rick Wise Boston Red Sox	6–2	George Scott Milwaukee Brewers
1975	Tom Seaver New York Mets	4–0	Joe Wallis Chicago Cubs
1976	Ken Brett Chicago White Sox	2–0	Jerry Remy California Angels
1978	Mike Flanagan Baltimore Orioles	3–1	Gary Alexander Cleveland Indians
1983	Milt Wilcox Detroit Tigers	6–0	Jerry Hairston Chicago White Sox
1983	Chuck Rainey Chicago Cubs	3–0	Eddie Milner Cincinnati Reds
1984	Mario Soto Cincinnati Reds	2–1	George Hendrick St. Louis Cardinals
1986	Walt Terrell Detroit Tigers	3–0	Wally Joyner California Angels
1988	Ron Robinson Cincinnati Reds	3–2	Wallace Johnson Montreal Expos

1988	Dave Stieb Toronto Blue Jays	1–0	Julio Franco Cleveland Indians
1988	Dave Stieb Toronto Blue Jays	4–0	Jim Traber Baltimore Orioles
1988	Mike Scott Houston Astros	5–0	Ken Oberkfell Atlanta Braves
1990	Brian Holman Seattle Mariners	6–1	Ken Phelps Oakland Athletics
1990	Scott Garrelts San Francisco Giants	4–0	Paul O'Neill Cincinnati Reds
1990	Doug Drabek Pittsburgh Pirates	11–0	Sil Campusano Philadelphia Phillies
1993	Jose Guzman Chicago Cubs	1–0	Otis Nixon Atlanta Braves
1994	Paul Wagner Pittsburgh Pirates	4–0	Andres Galarraga Colorado Rockies
1995	Frank Castillo Chicago Cubs	7–0	Bernard Gilkey St. Louis Cardinals
1998	Roy Halladay Toronto Blue Jays	2–1	Bobby Higginson Detroit Tigers
2001	Mike Mussina New York Yankees	1–0	Carl Everett Boston Red Sox

* Called after 14 innings.
** World Series

At Last, Aparicio's Headed for Hall

SUNDAY, JANUARY 8, 1984

THE SO-CALLED PEARLY GATES, the ones in Cooperstown, New York, not up above, should be opening within the next 48 hours for Luis Aparicio, the ballet master in shortstop's clothing who spent most of his career with the Chicago White Sox. Although the votes have yet to be counted, indications are that Aparicio, in his sixth year of eligibility, finally will be elected to the Hall of Fame.

Aparicio put in 10 of his 18 major league seasons at Comiskey Park and in 1959 was, of course, among the principals in winning Chicago's last pennant. But his election will transcend local pride: he will be the first shortstop canonized who carried a golden glove. The Hall has always had an electorate that places the highest value on statistics—home runs, runs batted in, batting average, the usual offensive staples. There are no stats for great plays.

Shortstop is the most vital and demanding defensive position. Yet the 13 shortstops with a plaque in Cooperstown, apart from Walter "Rabbit" Maranville, were elected because of their offensive abilities. "Finally, we're going to get a truly great defensive shortstop," said Jack Lang, the secretary of the Baseball Writers Association of America, who will open the envelopes and count the votes Tuesday.

Maranville, a .258 lifetime hitter, played a good, but not necessarily spectacular, shortstop in a 23-season major league career that ended in 1935. He was enshrined in 1954. It's among the sad chapters of the BBWAA. The Rabbit didn't make it on his ability but because of an enormous promotional campaign by the Hearst Corporation, which in those days had newspapers in many major league cities.

Lang tells the story: "Maranville had been on the ballot since 1937, never came close. In '46, a typical year for him, he got 29 votes, or 11 percent. There were 263 voters that year. And this was from the writers who had seen him play.

"In the early fifties, the Hearst people hired him as the director of their national sandlot program. As soon as he went to work for them, they began promoting him. And then he got some disease and was dying."

In 1979, his first year on the ballot, Aparicio got 28 percent of the vote, far short of the 75 percent needed for induction. He jumped to 32 percent the following year, then dropped to an incredibly low 12 percent. A proud man, Aparicio complained and asked reporters in his native Venezuela, "Didn't they see me play?"

"I saw him play, and he was the greatest shortstop of my time," Ted Williams said last spring in Sarasota, Florida, where he was making a rare appearance at an Old Timers' Day. "I said that 14 years ago when I wrote my book. Joe Cronin was a better hitter, and so was Luke Appling. But in that spot, you take a fielder over a hitter. Tell those guys who vote they should wake up."

There has been a gradual awakening. Aparicio got 42 percent of the vote in 1982 and last year soared to 67 percent, only 29 votes short of election.

Brooks Robinson, probably the best-fielding third baseman of all time, was enshrined in Cooperstown last summer. It was a proud moment for Robby, who was elected in his first year of eligibility. But there was a moment immediately after the induction ceremonies when he seemed somewhat embarrassed. "Looie should have been here, too," Robinson said.

It's difficult, of course, to insist—with total accuracy—that so-and-so was the best at any position. Nonetheless, more than 20 years ago, when

Aparicio was still a young player, the late Donie Bush told Al Lopez, then the White Sox manager: "Mr. Señor, you've got the best shortstop I ever saw." And Bush, a former shortstop and teammate of Ty Cobb, had seen them all, including the legendary Honus Wagner.

Chicago's Lew Fonseca, whose distinguished baseball career spanned seven decades, has been another Aparicio booster. "For years, people have been asking me to pick my all-time team," Fonseca said Friday. "And when I get to shortstop, I tell them, 'There were a lot of good ones, but defensively, Aparicio was the best. And shortstop is a defensive position.'"

In truth, Aparicio's defensive genius was such that it overshadowed his offensive ability. He was a dependable hitter, much stronger at the plate than his .262 lifetime average suggests. And he was the best base runner of his day, leading the American League in stolen bases in each of his first nine seasons and reaching a high of 56 thefts in the pennant season of 1959.

"Looie could have stolen 75, maybe 100 bases," said Ray Berres, the retired White Sox pitching coach. "But it wasn't like it is today. He only ran in clutch situations."

Aparicio's Hall of Fame plaque won't be large enough to list his achievements.

He holds major league records for most career games by a shortstop (2,581) and most career chances accepted by a shortstop (12,564). He also has the major league record for most years leading the league in chances accepted by a shortstop (7). He shares the major league record for most years leading the league in fielding average by a shortstop (8), and holds the American League record for most putouts by a shortstop (4,548). He led A.L. shortstops in putouts four times, assists seven times, and fielding average eight times and has the A.L. mark for most years leading the league in stolen bases (9). He was on 13 All-Star teams.

Those are the stats. They don't show him making the play in the hole, or coming in for a slow roller.

Lights *Were* OK'd
for Wrigley Field

TUESDAY, SEPTMEBER 2, 1984

"IT WAS LIKE A SPY NOVEL. We bought a lot of electric cable, miles of it, under an assumed name. We stored it at the park under the stands. We tried to hide it but you couldn't. The cable was on wooden reels 12 to 15 feet high. The steel was a minor matter. Only about 25 tons."

So begins the story told by James Timothy Gallagher, 80, now retired, and living the life of a country squire in Port Republic, Virginia. Gallagher was a former Chicago sportswriter and, later, the general manager of the Cubs, from 1941 through 1955. It was during his reign that the Cubs won their last pennant.

"We were going to put lights in Wrigley Field. Mr. Wrigley didn't like the idea. He had his quirks. But he had authorized me to go ahead. This was in 1941, right after the season. It was a bad year. We were going over the books, suffering, wondering what the hell we were going to do and so he said, 'All right, we'll put in lights.'

"The word must have gone out. Jack Zeller of Detroit—he was the general manager of the Tigers—called me. Mr. Briggs, the president of the Tigers, he never liked Mr. Wrigley. Mr. Briggs—he made everyone call him 'Mr. Briggs'—had Jack Zeller call me and Jack said, 'What are you and Mr. Wrigley up to?' When I told him, they were very unhappy.

47

By this time most of the clubs had lights. Briggs had been holding out. That's when Briggs decided he'd light up his ballpark.

"By late November we had everything we needed, all the material stockpiled. The first week in December we went to the minor league meetings. They were in Jacksonville, Florida. The meetings wound up on Friday. In those days we had special trains taking us back and forth.

"I almost missed the train coming back. I would have been on time but I had to call Cliff Westcott, he was the president of Westcott Engineering. He handled all the construction at the ballpark. I had to talk to him about getting the program started. The Ryerson Steel Company was going to begin cutting and shaping the steel Monday morning, if I gave them approval.

"My conversation with Westcott lasted quite a while. I was still in the hotel, alone, after everybody had left for the railroad station. Bob Lewis, the traveling secretary—he was my nursemaid—made them hold the train for me. Everybody was madder than hell.

"We got into Chicago about noon Sunday. The Bears were playing the Cardinals, a very important game. I was a great Bear fan for many years. We all were. We had our seats. We went right from the station to Comiskey Park.

"They never did stop the game to announce it, but the news swept through the stands, almost in a whisper. The Japanese had bombed Pearl Harbor. The minute I got home I called Mr. Wrigley. He said, 'Call the War Department first thing tomorrow morning and ask them if they want the material.' It was that simple.

"He always wanted me to call him Phil. But I said, 'Yes, Mr. Wrigley.' That was the only way I could indicate my displeasure with him, my dissatisfaction.

"So Monday, promptly at 8:00 in the morning, I called the War Department. Today they call it the Defense Department.

"I told them we had a few tons of steel and I don't know how many miles of cable. It wasn't against the law but the government didn't want everybody buying steel. And they said, 'Good, we'll take it.'

"I was sick at heart. If the Japanese had waited a few more days, we would have had the steel cut. But, I suppose, even if it had been cut and shaped, I don't think Mr. Wrigley would have gone for it. He was delighted to have an excuse to call the whole thing off. Mr. Wrigley always thought baseball was a daytime game.

"We put a little story in the papers, that the Cubs had given the steel, all the material, to a defense plant. Later, I remember asking where the steel went. I was curious. I never did find out.

"I wouldn't be surprised if it wound up at three or four of those racetracks they were building at that time, in Chicago and in the suburbs, for night racing. While baseball was kowtowing to the government, the racetracks were trying to make money. Jack Zeller called and asked what we were doing with our steel. I think their steel went for a racetrack, too.

"When the season started, in April, Judge Landis [then the baseball commissioner] asked President Roosevelt what we should do. Landis asked if he should close up shop. That's when Roosevelt sent his famous 'Green Light' letter.

"Roosevelt said we should keep on playing ball. This was the best way we could help the war effort. And he said, 'Play more night games' so the people in the factories could get their minds off the problems they have. But, of course, we couldn't play night games. We had given up all our steel. I guess he didn't know that."

A Word for '69: Unforgettable

TUESDAY, OCTOBER 2, 1984

NOW THAT THE CUBS HAVE WON SOMETHING, there have been numerous comments, particularly by Cub players, that "this puts 1969 to rest." Though 1984 is the Orwellian year, this isn't Siberia and there is no need for revisionist history. This is what happened, in part, in 1969, one of the most memorable seasons in Cub lore.

The Cubs were in first place for the first 155 days of the 176-day regular National League season. They opened on April 8 at home with a 7–6 victory over the Phillies. Ernie Banks hit two home runs, but the decisive blow was an eleventh-inning pinch-hit home run by Willie Smith. Phil Regan, who worked the last three innings in relief of Ferguson Jenkins, got the victory.

The Cubs won their next three games, lost one, then won seven in a row, the first of three seven-game winning streaks, their high for the season. They were 16–7 in April, their best month.

The regular rotation starters were Jenkins, Bill Hands, and Ken Holtzman. Groping for a fourth starter, manager Leo Durocher gave Joe Niekro three early starts, none of which Niekro won. Gary Ross, Dick Selma, and Rich Nye each made one April start, also without a victory.

Relievers Regan and Ted Abernathy were outstanding. Regan won four games in April, Abernathy two.

Holtzman, Jenkins, and Selma pitched consecutive shutouts on May 11–13, an achievement that hadn't been accomplished by a Cub team since 1909. Holtzman won 8–0 over the Giants, Jenkins 2–0, and Selma 19–0 over the Padres.

Selma's victory tied a National League record [since broken] for the most runs in a shutout. Hands was knocked out in the seventh inning in the next game, but the Cubs won anyway, 3–2 on home runs by Banks and Ron Santo.

Holtzman followed with a three-hit shutout against Houston, and four days later blanked Los Angeles 7–0, his third shutout in 10 days. Holtzman didn't complete any of his next 12 starts.

A statistical coincidence occurred a week later: Billy Williams hit the 232nd home run of his career on May 24, moving up to number two on the club's all-time home-run list. The next day in the first game of a doubleheader, Santo connected for *his* 232nd Cub home run.

At this point the Cubs were 28–14 and leading their division by seven games.

Two memorable games were played on successive days in New York on July 8 and 9. In the first game, center fielder Don Young was unable to handle two ninth-inning fly balls, both of which dropped for doubles and enabled the Mets to overcome a 3–1 Cub lead. Jimmy Qualls replaced Young in center field the next day and had his moment of glory: a line single to left-center with one out in the ninth that destroyed an otherwise perfect game by the Mets' Tom Seaver.

At the All-Star break, the Mets had narrowed the Cub lead to 3½ games. The All-Star Game came late that season, July 21 in Washington, D.C.

There was ample evidence of the Cubs' success. The entire Cub infield was named to the National League team: Banks at first base (he was used as a pinch-hitter), Glenn Beckert at second base, Don Kessinger at shortstop, Santo at third base, and Randy Hundley at catcher. Red Schoendienst, the National League manager, was criticized for failing to select Williams and Jenkins.

The Cubs opened the second half with gusto. From July 31 through August 6, they won seven in a row. On the morning of August 14 the

Cubs appeared to be a runaway winner; they were 8½ games ahead of the second-place Cardinals and 9½ ahead of the Mets.

But it was the beginning of the Cubs' collapse and the Mets' surge. The Mets were 38–11 the rest of the way; the Cubs were 17–29.

What later was regarded as the pivotal game occurred on September 8 in New York, Hands against Jerry Koosman. Hands knocked Tommie Agee down with his first pitch. Agee retaliated in the third with a two-run home run off a knee-high slider, low and away, a pitcher's pitch.

"When he hit that pitch, I knew we were in trouble," Hundley said later.

The Cubs rallied for a tie in the sixth on singles by Kessinger, Beckert, and Williams, and Santo's sacrifice fly, but the Mets went ahead to stay in the bottom half.

Agee doubled and Wayne Garrett, the Mets' weak-hitting third baseman, followed with a single to right. Hundley went up the first-base line for Jim Hickman's throw to the plate, which came in on one bounce, and whirled backwards. He still insists he tagged Agee.

"I thought I felt the ball going off the end of my mitt," Hundley said. "So I looked to see if it was still there. And it was—in the pocket. I heard a tremendous roar and I said to myself, 'Something's wrong.' Then I saw the umpire giving the safe sign. I knew then and there it was the biggest bloomin' play of the year."

The Mets went into first place two days later, the first time in their history that they had taken the lead. The Cubs finished second, eight games out. Jenkins won 21 games, Hands 20, and Holtzman 17. Santo had his best year with 123 RBIs and 29 home runs. Banks had 106 RBIs and 23 home runs. Williams finished with 95 RBIs and 21 home runs.

Stan the Man:
A Living Monument

WEDNESDAY, APRIL 24, 1985

IT WAS MIDAFTERNOON TUESDAY, and Stan the "Man" Musial, having had lunch at the Stadium Club, was leaving Busch Stadium, home of the St. Louis Cardinals. As he stepped into the sunshine, Musial paused to say good-bye.

Laughing, he waved toward the heroic statue of himself, a 40-foot likeness that stands guard at the main gate.

"So long, Stan," he said, laughing. "See you later."

And Musial laughed again in his unmistakable high-pitched cackle, delighted with the fantasy of talking to himself. And why not? How many men have been cast in bronze and are able to greet themselves when entering or leaving a major league ballpark?

"Jeez," Stan said, serious. "I'm going to be 65 this winter."

He was now speaking to Ralph Kiner, a fellow Hall of Fame slugger who had been among his luncheon companions. "I'm going to be eligible for my social security." Kiner nodded, also aware of the relentless march of time. "I better call my accountant and see if it's feasible for me to take it."

No tag days, of course, will be necessary for Stan the Man. Although his playing career preceded the salary boom, he was among the highest-paid performers of his time.

To maintain contact with him, the Cardinals list him in the club directory as a senior vice president. But Musial seldom goes to the park. He estimates he sees only 20 or 25 games a year.

"I saw the opener," he told Kiner. He had arrived early to watch batting practice. "I saw them [the Cardinal players] take 300 swings," Musial said. "And I only saw one ball go over the fence."

"They're killing hitting," Kiner said, agreeing. "It's the 'Charlie Lau theory.' That's what they talk about today: the inside-out swing."

And Kiner, a broadcaster with the New York Mets, proceeded to demonstrate how hitters now keep their elbows close to the body and as a result seldom have the leverage necessary for power.

It's difficult to believe, but Musial retired 22 years ago, after the 1963 season. When he quit, he held dozens of National League and major league records. Among them was the N.L. record for the most hits, 3,630, since surpassed by Hank Aaron and Pete Rose.

"My last year was Pete Rose's rookie year," Musial said. By coincidence, his last big-league game was against the Cincinnati Reds. "I got two hits," Musial said, laughing. "And Pete Rose got three. He was gaining on me even then."

Rose, of course, is approaching Ty Cobb's major league record of 4,191 hits.

"He'll probably break it; I wish him luck," Musial said. "But it won't be easy. He's 44 years old. It gets tough after 40. I know."

Musial went on to reveal a memorable meeting he and teammate Red Schoendienst had with the great Cobb. It was during the early part of the 1957 season, before Schoendienst was traded to the Milwaukee Braves, and the Cardinals were in New York for a series with the Giants at the Polo Grounds.

"I doubled and scored from second on a single," Musial recalled. Later that night, Cobb called to invite him for breakfast.

"I said, 'Sure, I'll bring Red along.' "

Musial reconstructed the dialogue.

"Cobb noticed that I used cream and sugar. He said, 'Cut one of 'em out. They're not good for you.'

"Then he began asking me questions: 'Would you like to play a few more years?'

"I was 37. I said, 'Yes, I like the game.'

" 'Do you drink?'

" 'Yes, I'm a social drinker.'

"He said that was good; I should be sure to have a glass of wine with my evening meal, that it was a good stimulant."

Musial chuckled at the remembrance.

"And I played five more years."

But the last two seasons, Musial conceded, were near drudgery.

"After you get to be 40, you lose your concentration," he said. "I'd lose my train of thought: I used to have a sixth sense. When I had a pitcher in the hole, I'd guess on the next pitch. This extra sense never deceived me. But once you hit 40, I don't know what it is, but you begin doubting yourself.

"I'd say, 'Be ready. Fastball!' But I'd stand there and take the pitch. The concentration just wasn't there."

It was time to go. But this time Musial didn't bother with a farewell for his statue. He and Kiner shook hands, aging comrades in business suits, fighting the fog of time.

"Funny thing, Ralph," Musial said. "Since that breakfast with Ty Cobb, I never used cream again."

A Crowded Field
of Rose Admirers

MONDAY, SEPTEMBER 9, 1985

RIGHT FIELDER KEITH MORELAND RETRIEVED THE BALL, hurried it back into the infield, and immediately joined in the applause, pounding his bare hand into his glove. In the on-deck circle, Dave Parker dropped his bat and clapped with both hands. Leon Durham, the Cubs' first baseman, moved closer to Pete Rose and said, "Don't move. I want to get the television exposure."

Pete Rose, the indomitable Pete Rose, didn't move. About one minute into the standing ovation, he removed his batting helmet and waved to the appreciative Wrigley Field crowd. Later, he pointed toward the right-field bleachers. Through it all, and the cheering continued for more than three minutes, he kept his foot on the bag. It wasn't the time to get picked off.

It was the fifth inning, Cubs versus Cincinnati, and Rose, a surprise starter, had knocked out his second single in his third at-bat, a line single to right for hit number 4,191 to tie Ty Cobb's record. The ball was already en route to Cooperstown—from Moreland to Ryne Sandberg to Tommy Helms, the Cincinnati first-base coach, to umpire Jim Quick.

When the Reds' half of the inning was over, more cheers washed over Rose as he took his position in the field. John Vukovich, the Cubs' first-base coach, patted Rose on the back as he took his position.

56

"I told him, 'Nice going,'" said Vukovich, who was among Rose's teammates with the Phillies and Reds.

"And he looked at me and said, 'You know I'm going to get another one.' And he meant today, not Tuesday in Cincinnati."

Rose had two opportunities to pass Cobb and become baseball's most prolific hitter. But Lary Sorensen retired him on a grounder to rookie shortstop Shawon Dunston in the seventh. Then in the ninth inning, under darkened skies after a two-hour rain delay, reliever Lee Smith struck him out swinging on a 2–2 fastball.

As he trudged to the dugout, Rose's son Pete Jr. asked him if it was tough to see.

"I told him it sounded like a strike," Rose said later at a crowded press conference.

Rose, in tying the record, needed 2,332 more at-bats than Cobb— 13,761 to 11,429—the equivalent of almost 600 games. He also had a .305 career batting average compared to Cobb's .367, easily the highest in baseball history.

"People who try to knock Pete Rose and say Cobb was better either don't know what they're talking about or they're jealous," said the Cubs' Davey Lopes. "Regardless of the at-bats, regardless of the games, he is going to be the all-time hit leader. And when you do something positive that nobody has done in your field, that's greatness."

Lopes, who is in his 13th major league season, can't think of another player to compare with Rose.

"He's by himself, separate," he said. "He's able to maintain an intensity other players can't match. Nobody reaches his intensity level."

George Scherger, a longtime major league coach and now Rose's "assistant manager," put it another way.

"I've seen Pete go 0-for-4 or 0-for-5 and he's in the dugout yelling at the hitter to get on base so he can get another time at bat," Scherger said. "Most guys—no, not most guys, all guys—when they have a bad day like that they collapse. They want to get away from the ballpark. Pete, he wants to get a hit and start a winning rally."

"For anybody to get that many hits, he's got to be durable," observed Bob Engel, a veteran National League umpire. "Pete's lucky; he's never been hurt. But maybe that isn't just luck. He takes care of himself. And he's always up there swinging. He's getting a lot of walks now, but that's a recent thing."

Rose's achievement, without doubt, is essentially a triumph of endurance. Rose is in his 23rd season; Cobb played 24. Cobb hit .300 or better 23 times; Rose, 15. It's difficult to compare them because the level of play has improved considerably since Cobb's time.

Better coaching and the advent of the relief specialist, who often enters a game fresh as early as the sixth inning, has made it tougher for hitters today. Also, there is no question that the defensive play in Cobb's day was primitive when compared to today's standards. The old-timers should rest easy. Rose is deserving.

Maris Heard
Only the Boos

TUESDAY, DECEMBER 17, 1985

ROGER MARIS WILL BE LAID TO REST Thursday in Fargo, North Dakota, and dozens of his fellow heroes from the baseball community are expected to be there to say good-bye. Mr. Maris will be among friends. There will be no boos.

I was there when he was breaking Babe Ruth's home-run record, and what I remember were the cheers. The cheers were not only for him but also for Mickey Mantle, the other half of the now legendary M&M boys, as they made their heroic twin assault on the greatest single record in the history of American sports.

As Larry Merchant, a former columnist for the *Philadelphia Daily News,* said Monday: "Thirty thousand people could be cheering for Roger, but he only heard the boos."

"After a while he went out looking for boos; he magnified it," acknowledged Til Ferdenzi, who covered the Yankees for the old *New York Journal-American.* Ferdenzi, retired and living in Cape Cod, was a one-time Boston College football star and among the few sportswriters Maris respected.

"But Roger was very sensitive and had reason to be upset," Ferdenzi recalled. "None of the other Yankee players were being booed. Not Mantle.

59

Not [Tony] Kubek. Or [Bobby] Richardson or Yogi [Berra]. Whether it was just a few people who booed Maris, 100 in a crowd of 25,000, the fact is nobody else was being booed. That's what bothered him."

This department didn't major in psychology, but it always seemed to me that Maris was moody but a very decent fellow. Glib he wasn't. He didn't like slick, and he didn't suffer phonies or fools. "He wasn't a ball of joy, especially to sportswriters he didn't know," said Ferdenzi. "And when he was breaking the record, he seldom had any idea who was asking him questions. I know one thing: I was always cheering for the guy. As a person, he had a lot of class."

I was also among those who cheered Roger Maris and was still cheering a year and a half ago when I visited him in Gainesville, Florida. We had breakfast and then went to his office—he owned a beer distributorship—and talked for two or three hours.

It was a pleasant ramble until the finish, when he pulled a newspaper clipping out of his desk.

"Even the sports editor of the paper here in Gainesville took a shot at me," Maris said, puzzled. "He dedicated a whole page to me three years after I got here. He said if I hadn't had that one lucky year, I wouldn't be anything, that I'd be driving a beer truck instead of owning one."

I assured him it was nonsense, that it flew from the typewriter of a sportswriter who had never seen him play, probably some kid trying to be controversial.

"I met him about a year later," Maris said. "He tried to shake my hand. I told him, 'Don't ever bother me again.'"

It was typical Roger Maris. Instead of remembering the millions of good words written about him—there were two books, both laudatory—he was stuck on a smart-aleck column by a small-town sports editor whose experience probably had been limited to the University of Florida.

Had Maris been more sophisticated, more wise to the ways of journalism (which, as has been said, is history written for a 9:00 P.M. deadline), he would have taken the few bad notices and thrown them out with the garbage. Of considerably more importance, wherever he went—and he was with four big-league clubs—he was liked and respected by his teammates. "As good a team player as I ever saw," said Ralph Houk, who managed the Yankees in 1961 when Maris broke Ruth's record of 60 homers.

Some details of the chase have been lost in the fog of time. Mantle, for example, was setting the pace in early August. On August 6, he led 43–41. Six days later, Mantle was still ahead, 44–43. They were tied at 45 on August 14. Maris went ahead to stay the next night when he connected against Juan Pizarro of the White Sox.

It wasn't the first assault on Ruth's record. Hack Wilson hit 56 in 1930; Jimmie Foxx hit 58 in 1932. Six years later, Hank Greenberg was also stopped at 58. Chasing Ruth was not an uncommon occurrence. Willie Mays took aim in 1955 but expired at 51. That winter at the New York baseball writers' dinner, the late Arthur Mann parodied Willie's quest:

> I wonder who's leading me now.
> I wonder if my 60 will bow.
> I wonder if Willie can hold the friends,
> That August brings and September ends,
> For then every muscular youth
> Discovers the secret of Ruth
> That month I was mean, for I hit 17.
> I wonder who's leading me now.

Ruth's 17 September home runs always had been the difference. But Maris and Mantle had an edge. They went into September ahead of Ruth's pace. Maris, with 51, was eight ahead; Mantle finished August with 48, five ahead. Maris tied the record on September 26 in the Yankees' 158th game. Number 61 came in the Yankees' 162nd and final game.

It was the first year the schedule had been expanded to 162 games and Ford Frick, then the commissioner of baseball, ruled that Ruth's record had to be tied or broken within the framework of what had been the standard 154-game schedule. If not, the new record would be noted to show it was achieved in a 162-game season.

What has been forgotten is that Frick made this ruling in mid-July and was legislating against Mantle as well as Maris. Also, there was a frantic reaction by many veteran baseball writers, the so-called keepers of the flame, who expressed concern that, because of the eight additional games, many of the sport's most cherished records would be destroyed.

In the final week, after Maris had tied the record, John Drebinger of *The New York Times,* who covered both Ruth and Maris, was asked to compare them.

"Both great hitters," Drebinger replied. "But if Ruth were alive now, he would have said, 'Why isn't that guy having more fun doing this?'"

Brosnan Pitches
Write Stuff

TUESDAY, FEBRUARY 11, 1986

OF THE THOUSANDS OF MAJOR LEAGUE BALLPLAYERS who have come and
gone, Jim Brosnan is the only former player who became a full-time
sportswriter. No radio or television for Broz. He does his stuff at the
typewriter: hundreds of magazine pieces (many of them for *Boys' Life*),
book reviews, and inspirational and instructional books for kids: *Rookies
of the Year, Techniques of Pitching, From Little League to the Big Leagues*,
and biographies of Ron Santo and Ted Simmons.

"I used to write standing up," Brosnan said, "but I've got a bad knee,
can't stand for more than 10 minutes at a time." He was in the basement
workroom in his Morton Grove, Illinois, home, where he has lived for
the last 29 years. He's one of the few players who worked for both the
Cubs and the Sox and settled in the Chicago area.

The younger set may not know much about Broz, but they should be
assured that he was among the best relief pitchers of his time. He was in
the big leagues for nine years. In 1961, the year Roger Maris hit 61 home
runs, Brosnan was the star of the Cincinnati bullpen and a major force
(10 victories, all in relief, and 16 saves) in helping the Reds win the
National League pennant.

Brosnan also was controversial, a scholarly athlete who, as they say,
marched to his own drummer. Not all of his managers understood him,

63

or approved his bookish manner. There was the afternoon in Des Moines, in 1950, when the Cub farmhand lost a tough 2–1 game on an eleventh-inning home run. Returning to the clubhouse, Broz resumed reading *Time* magazine while his teammates threw their gloves and screamed and hollered, the traditional posture of postgame agony.

"What are you doing reading that stuff?" shouted Charlie Root, his manager.

"The game is over," Brosnan replied. "Nothing we can do about it now."

Root cussed Brosnan and accused him of not having the proper attitude. When he sent in his report to the Cub front office, Root predicted that Brosnan did not have the stuff to make it in the big leagues.

"All it did was puzzle me," Brosnan recalled. "I couldn't figure out the relationship between winning and losing a game and reading a magazine. I was as angry and disappointed as everyone else. Reading was my way of relaxing. Charlie Root's report stuck in the minds of the people in the Cub front office. That's where I got my reputation as being different."

A quarter of a century later, Brosnan was in Bradenton, Florida, doing a piece on Pittsburgh slugger Willie Stargell. Don Osborn, who also had been among Brosnan's minor league managers, was then a coach with the Pirates.

"It was the first time I had seen him in many years," said Broz. "I said to him: 'Oz, why did you stick with me? At times I was such a pain in the butt.'"

Brosnan laughed at the recollection.

"And Oz said, 'Broz, many times I wanted to kick you in the butt. I hated your attitude. But I loved your arm.'"

Today, Brosnan can read without interruption. His den and workroom are clogged with books, including a first-edition copy of his classic *The Long Season*, his irreverent and humorous view of the 1959 season. The baseball establishment reacted with horror. Broz was advised to make a career choice: if he didn't stuff his portable typewriter, he wouldn't be allowed to pitch. He wrote another book in 1961, then stopped writing and pitched for three more years, finishing up with the White Sox.

Unlike most retired ballplayers, Brosnan not only keeps up with the game but is firm in his belief that the players are better than ever.

"It's a more interesting contest today than 20 years ago," Broz insisted. "The players are bigger and faster, and the pitchers, especially the pitchers, are smarter when they come to the big leagues. They know more now. When I was playing, it was more of a power game. People didn't steal the bases at the rate they do now. I only had to worry about one, maybe two guys stealing. Now, half the players on any club can steal."

Still, when it came to selecting the best pitcher of all time, Broz picked a contemporary.

"Sandy Koufax, by far. He was the best."

Brosnan went on to explain that he had done some research for a recent story on the best pitchers in baseball history. For a statistical base, he used the Rickey Ratings, devised by Branch Rickey, the possessor of perhaps baseball's most ingenious and fertile mind.

The Rickey system may seem complex, but it's quite simple. If a pitcher, for example, works 200 innings and gives up 150 hits, he's given 50 points. A point also is awarded for strikeouts in comparison to walks. A pitcher with 200 strikeouts and 100 walks is credited with 100 points. The point total is then subtracted from innings pitched.

"The pitcher's job is to prevent the batter from reaching first base, not giving up a hit or walking him," Brosnan explained. "The strikeout is the most risk-free way of getting an out. The pitcher gets the out by himself. There is no possibility of an error.

"Koufax is the only pitcher to have had more than three-plus seasons in the Rickey Ratings; he had five. [Bob] Gibson had one. [Steve] Carlton had one. Walter Johnson one. Tom Seaver none. Christy Mathewson none.

"I saw Koufax last spring at Dodgertown. He never says much. I told him I had done some research and explained what I found. He said he had heard of the Rickey Ratings but never paid any attention to them, wasn't even sure how they worked."

I asked Broz what Koufax said when he advised him that he had selected him as the best pitcher of all time.

"He just blushed."

Brosnan's next assignment will take him to St. Petersburg, Florida, for a piece on Dwight Gooden, the Mets' young pitching star.

Gooden was the toast of baseball last season. He led the National League in victories (24), earned-run average (1.53), innings pitched (277), strikeouts (268), and complete games (16).

Gooden was a minus-1 in the Rickey Ratings. In 1965, Koufax was a plus-96.

Hank Greenberg
Mixed Religion with Greatness

FRIDAY, SEPTEMBER 5, 1986

The Irish didn't like it when they heard of Greenberg's fame,
For they thought a good first baseman should possess an Irish name.
And the Murphys and the Mulrooneys said they never dreamed
    they'd see
A Jewish boy from Bronxville out where Casey used to be.
In the early days of April not a Dugan tipped his hat,
Or prayed to see a double when Hank Greenberg came to bat.

In July the Irish wondered where he'd ever learned to play.
"He makes me think of Casey!" old man Murphy dared to say.
And with 57 doubles and a score of homers made,
The respect they had for Greenberg was openly displayed.
But upon the Jewish New Year when Hank Greenberg came to bat
And made two homers off pitcher Rhodes—they cheered like mad
    for that.

Came Yom Kippur—holy fast day worldwide over to the Jews,
And Hank Greenberg to his teaching and the old tradition true
Spent the day among his people and he didn't come to play,
Said Murphy to Mulrooney, "We shall lose the game today!
We shall miss him in the infield and shall miss him at the bat,
But he's true to his religion—and I honor him for that!"

So wrote Edgar A. Guest, the American folk poet based in Detroit, whose verse appeared in hundreds of newspapers. This was in 1934, when the Tigers were battling for the pennant in Hank Greenberg's second full year with the club. The power-hitting Greenberg was essential to the Tigers' success—he hit .339 and drove in 139 runs. The fans howled when he said he wouldn't put on a uniform on Rosh Hashanah or Yom Kippur.

An angry fan, in a letter to the editor, insisted that Greenberg shouldn't bench himself. "Rosh Hashanah comes every year, but Tigers haven't won a pennant since 1909."

A Detroit rabbi urged Hank to play on the Jewish New Year, and he responded with two home runs that carried the Tigers to a 2-1 victory over Boston. When he didn't play on Yom Kippur, Detroit lost. Happily, the Tigers went on to win the pennant.

◆

Hank Greenberg, who died Thursday at the age of 75, probably was the greatest of America's Jewish athletes. He played in the major leagues for 13 years, 12 with the Tigers. At the height of his career, he went into the army twice. He was drafted early in 1941, but was discharged on December 5, under a rule allowing those over the age of 28 to cut short their terms. He enlisted after Pearl Harbor. Although he missed the equivalent of four full seasons in the service, he hit 331 home runs and drove in 1,276 runs, averaging almost one run batted in for every game he played the full nine innings. He was the American League's Most Valuable Player in 1935 and 1940 and four times led the league in home runs and RBIs. His 183 RBIs in 1937 were within one of Lou Gehrig's all-time A.L. record. The following year he hit 58 home runs, two shy of Babe Ruth's heroic 60.

Guest's poem had one minor mistake. Hank Greenberg didn't come from Bronxville, a fashionable New York suburb. He was born on New Year's Day, 1911, in Greenwich Village, the third child of David and Sarah

Greenberg, immigrants from Romania who had met in New York. The family moved to the Bronx when Hank was a child.

His parents wanted him to go to college but Hank insisted on playing ball. After listening to offers from the Yankees, the Washington Senators, the Pittsburgh Pirates, and the Detroit Tigers, he signed with the Tigers for a $9,000 bonus.

When he was elected to the Hall of Fame in 1956, he said, "I can't possibly find the words to express how I feel. It's too wonderful for words. This is what every ballplayer dreams about."

Hank Greenberg had a dream season in 1938 when he almost broke Ruth's home-run record.

Eleven times he hit two home runs in one game, still the one-season major league record. He connected for numbers 57 and 58 off Bill Cox of the old St. Louis Browns on September 27, in the Tigers' 149th game.

"It looked like a cinch," Greenberg recalled years later. "I had five games [in those days the schedule was 154 games] to hit three homers and break the record. I figured I had 20 at-bats and even allowing for careful pitching, I'd get at least a dozen good pitches to swing at. But I hadn't counted on the pressure. I found myself swinging at terrible pitches. Other times I'd just freeze. I was so afraid I'd swing at a bad pitch that I wound up letting the few good ones go by."

He went 0-for-3 on September 28. The next day, also against the Browns, he was 1-for-4. The Tigers then moved on to Cleveland for their final three games of the regular season.

At the time, the Indians had two home fields. Most of the games were played in League Park, which had a capacity of about 25,000. Cavernous Municipal Stadium, which had 70,000 seats, hosted games on Sundays and holidays, or whenever a big gate was anticipated. They were the toughest parks in the league for a right-handed batter.

On October 1 at League Park, Denny Galehouse held Greenberg hitless in four trips. The next day, a Sunday, they played a doubleheader at Municipal Stadium. Bob Feller pitched the opener for the Indians and although he struck out 18, Feller lost the game to left-hander Harry

Eisenstat. Greenberg had a double in four trips against Feller. Greenberg went 3-for-3 in the second game, but all of the hits were singles.

Then, and now, there was the unspoken assumption that the opposing pitchers, not wanting Greenberg to break Ruth's record, refused to throw him strikes. But it's not true, according to Eisenstat, a fellow Jew who roomed with Greenberg during the entire 1938 season.

"They pitched to Hank like they pitched to everyone else," Eisenstat said Thursday night in a telephone interview from his home in Cleveland. "What really hurt was moving the games to the Stadium. It was a dark and drizzly day. Everything Hank hit in that last game was a line drive."

Eisenstat said the only time Greenberg didn't get much to swing at was when rookies were pitching. "They couldn't throw the ball over the plate," Eisenstat said. "But it had nothing to do with Hank being Jewish. They were scared to death of him."

A Splendid Pitch
on Art of Hitting

THURSDAY, JANUARY 29, 1987

TED WILLIAMS HAD ASKED FOR A SHOW OF HANDS. "How many of you coaches were pitchers?"

About two dozen hands went up, not many considering that approximately 400 high school and college baseball coaches were in attendance at the annual winter MacGregor Coaches Clinic at the Hyatt Regency O'Hare.

Williams seemed to approve.

"Ordinarily, I think pitchers know the least of anybody in the game," he said. "They play the least because they can't hit or run. It's my experience most of them are dumb."

Everyone laughed, even the pitchers.

Satisfied that the enemy was heavily outnumbered, Williams launched into a dissertation on the art of hitting: 90 minutes of a doctoral thesis, personally delivered by an authentic god of baseball's pantheon. Despite the freezing weather, Theodore Samuel Williams had descended into their midst.

"One of the 10 greatest players who ever played the game," Gordon Gillespie said in the introduction. "And maybe the greatest hitter of all time. He had a .344 lifetime average and was the last of the .400 hitters.

At the end of his career, at the age of 39 and 40, he led the American League in hitting. If he hadn't lost five seasons in the service of his country, only God knows how many records he would have broken. I am thrilled we have him as our speaker."

So was I.

I have never forgotten my first time in Boston's Fenway Park, Ted Williams' home field, and my surprise when I saw how deep it was to right-center, 380 feet. Had he played in Detroit or Yankee Stadium or Wrigley Field, Williams would have broken Babe Ruth's single-season record for home runs, not once but several times.

Ted Williams, 68, still in an open-neck sport shirt, was in his batting stance but having trouble holding both the bat and the microphone. Gillespie hurried onto the stage and curled the cord around his neck.

"Be quick, quick, quick!" Williams explained, demonstrating his swing. "The only way to be quick is to use your hips. The hips must lead the way. You can't do it without good hip action."

He always choked up on the bat, at least a half-inch; with two strikes, sometimes as much as an inch. It was a surprising admission: the Splendid Splinter, who terrorized pitchers and hit .406 in 1941, conceding to the enemy.

"A sculptor was doing a statue of me for the Hall of Fame in Cooperstown," Williams explained. "He said, 'I've studied a lot of pictures of you and you're choked up on the bat.' I did. If you took an inch off everyone's bat, you'd improve every hitter. You don't want too long a swing."

Quickness, bat control, a strong swivel of the hips, and being ready for every pitch are the fundamental requirements.

"What about your eyes?" a coach asked. "I've read that you were able to see the ball as it hit the bat."

Williams laughed.

"Hell no! And I couldn't see the seams. But in the last 20 feet, I could see which way it was spinning. Nothing unusual about that."

When he was in the service, his eyes tested at 20-10, certainly better than normal 20-20 vision. Of necessity, his left eye is stronger. When he was a boy, he was struck in the right eye by a walnut. The right eye is still a problem, he explained. Surgery may be necessary.

Teammates and opponents alike were convinced he had extraordinary eyesight.

"My second or third year in the league, I took a few pitches that were high. And [Hall of Fame catcher] Bill Dickey said to me: 'Ted, how big does the ball look to you? It must look like a balloon.'

"And I told him, 'Same size as it looks to everyone else.' "

Williams also insisted he never considered his hand/eye coordination much better than average.

"Fifty percent of the game is from the neck up. And the nice part of playing in the big leagues is that you're hitting against the same guys. I always felt if I had hit against the pitcher before, I had a better chance.

"When I managed the Washington club, not one or two guys or four or eight but every single hitter on that club had the best years they ever had as a hitter. And I never changed anybody's stance. With only two hitters, I suggested they change their plane, not their swing. The stance isn't important. Jackie Robinson wiggled his bat over his head. Stan Musial. A great hitter and a very unorthodox stance. It's where the bat and hands and hips are when you hit the ball.

"I had a player, Mike Epstein, a big strong guy, 6'3", 220 pounds. Could swing the hell out of the bat. But he missed a lot. Always among the league leaders in strikeouts. One day he came back to the bench and said, 'I can't hit that pitcher.' I said, 'Baloney! Do you think he knows how he's trying to pitch you?' He said, 'Sure.' I told him, 'Get your swing started when he releases the ball.' And the next few times up he crushed it. It's mental."

Few, if any, players studied hitting and pitching the way Williams did.

It is not an exaggeration to say he was to hitting what Einstein was to physics. Williams also wrote a book, *The Science of Hitting*.

He was the first of the big sluggers to use a light bat, 33 ounces.

To be certain of the weight, he went to the post office and bought a scale. His teammates laughed, but even the muscular Jimmie Foxx, the famed "Double X," eventually switched to a lighter bat.

Williams disciplined himself. He almost never swung at a pitch that wasn't in the strike zone. He moved up in the batter's box against sinker-ballers; if he stayed back, the ball would be even lower at contact.

He discovered that when he popped up or missed a pitch, it was because he was late. If he hit the ball on the ground, he was too far in front of the ball, i.e., swinging early.

"I once asked Nellie Fox why he stood so far back," Williams said. "He gave me the perfect answer. He told me: 'I'm a low-ball hitter. I want the ball low.'"

Williams was also a low-ball hitter but preferred the ball high because it gave him a better chance to hit it into the air. "When I put the ball in the air, it could go out. Any pitcher will settle for a line drive, even if it's a base hit, or a bullet to the second baseman or the shortstop."

Unlike some of the modern theorists, such as the late Charlie Lau and Walt Hriniak (the current Boston batting coach), Williams doesn't believe in chopping down on the ball. Ideally, there should be a slight uppercut motion. Arm strength is important, but the hip action is absolutely crucial.

"Thank you, Ted," said Gillespie; and the coaches responded with a standing ovation.

"Good luck to all of you," Ted Williams replied. "Even the pitchers."

Hugh Alexander, a Good Scout, Always Remembers the Ones That Got Away

TUESDAY, FEBRUARY 17, 1987

"MY BIGGEST MISTAKE WAS ON MICKEY MANTLE, but with all due respect to myself, I was one of the few scouts who even knew about him.

"A friend of mine gave me his name. I wrote it on a piece of paper and I went by Commerce, Oklahoma, that spring and talked to the principal of the high school. He told me they didn't have a baseball team, and that Mickey had been hurt in football and had arthritis of the legs.

"Hell, it's hard enough to make the majors if you're healthy, and when he told me that stuff I walked out of the school. When I got to my car, I took that piece of paper and threw it away. I can still see it blowing across the parking lot."

That was 37 years ago, in 1950, but Hugh Alexander remembers it as if it were yesterday—which isn't necessarily surprising. Good scouts never forget. Or to quote Alexander again: "To be a scout, you have to have a good memory. I wasn't blessed with much education, but I do have a great memory. You can name any player you want to, go back as far as you like, and I'm not bragging—I can see that player on the field. I can picture him at the plate, or at shortstop. And if he's a pitcher, I'll tell you about his delivery."

75

In the early and middle fifties, Alexander worked for the White Sox, during the triumphant reign of Frank Lane and Paul Richards.

"Tom Baird—he owned the Kansas City Monarchs—told Frank about one of his players, a skinny kid, a shortstop named Ernie Banks. Frank called me. I was out cross-checking, looking at the top players who had been recommended by other scouts. He said, 'Hughie, get on the trail.'

"I'm sure I was the first scout to see Ernie Banks play. I saw him in Denver, then some town in South Dakota, and in Hutchinson and Salinas, Kansas. I saw him in those four towns.

"When I got through looking at him, Lane said, 'What do you think?'

"I said, 'I'm not sure whether or not he can play shortstop, but he can hit with power.'

"Lane decided he'd take a look for himself. In those days, the American Negro League played its All-Star Game in Comiskey Park. After the All-Star Game, Frank told me, 'I don't like Banks as a ballplayer.'

"I said, 'By God, I do. Why don't you like him?'

"'He made two errors in the All-Star Game.'

"I told him, 'Frank, don't pay any attention to that. He can hit. Anyway, he'll make a good third baseman.'"

Lane told Alexander to contact Baird, the Kansas City owner, and offer him $7,500 for Banks.

"I said, 'Frank, for God's sake, I can't do that. I know he's already had offers for more than $20,000.' So I never got hold of Baird. I wasn't going to embarrass myself."

A year or two later, after Banks had joined the Cubs, Lane and Alexander were together at Wrigley Field.

"I think Frank had forgotten that he'd had me scout him," Alexander recalled, "because he said, 'I wish we had Banks playing third base for us now.'"

"I reminded him that we'd had a chance to get him. And Frank said, 'Oh, yeah. That's right. That's right.'"

Having missed on Mantle and again on Banks, it may appear that Alexander seldom got his man. Not true. He has signed 62 players who made it to the big leagues. It would be possible to play an All-Star Game with his recruits.

More than likely Alexander would have been an All-Star outfielder. He played two years in the low minors, for Fargo-Moorhead in the Class D Northern League in 1936, when he was 17, and the next year for Springfield, Ohio, in the Class C Mid-Atlantic League.

His combined batting average for those two seasons (199 games) was .347, with 60 homers and 192 runs batted in.

"I've got to admit, I was a hell of a good player," Alexander said. "I had all the ability in the world."

But on December 6, 1937, at 11:00 A.M., his left hand was caught in one of the big gears while he was working on an oil rig near his home in Seminole, Oklahoma.

"I was by myself," Alexander recalled. "I went up to a house on the road and borrowed a pillowcase to wrap it up in and then got in a pickup truck and drove 15 miles to the nearest doctor. The doctor gave me two drinks of whiskey and cut my hand off—sawed it off with a saw. And I said then, that day, nothing can ever hurt me the rest of my life. I'm talking about physically."

Hugh Alexander has been a scout ever since, with the Cleveland Indians, Los Angeles Dodgers, Chicago White Sox, and, for the last 15 years, with the Philadelphia Phillies.

Tuesday, he leaves for Mesa, Arizona, and a new assignment: special adviser and assistant to Dallas Green, the president and general manager of the Chicago Cubs.

Campanis Guilty
Only of Not Being Slick Enough
to Escape Koppel's Trap

FRIDAY, APRIL 10, 1987

THE LESSON TO BE LEARNED from the Al Campanis dismissal is this: don't go on the Ted Koppel *Nightline* show unless you're a smooth talker willing to feed the television goat with more pap and what are popularly regarded to be the proper answers.

Campanis was forced to resign under pressure Wednesday as the front office boss of the Los Angeles Dodgers essentially because of his comment that black ballplayers don't have "the necessities" to become big-league field managers or general managers.

He never said they were less intelligent than white players, only that they didn't have "the necessities." Admittedly, Campanis could be accused of poor word usage; "minor league experience" might've been better. I understood what he was saying, but Koppel, sensing controversy, began baiting him. And suddenly, Campanis was no longer a guest with a bag of Jackie Robinson anecdotes, but was forced to defend the small number of black baseball executives.

To acquire "the necessities," a player, almost always, must be willing to take a severe cut in pay and descend into the minor leagues to gain experience, either in the dugout or in the front office. Very few ballplayers, black or white, have been willing to make this sacrifice.

78

This is not to say black ballplayers are always given the same opportunities as whites. I am not privy to all the front-office intrigue that goes with hiring and firing. But this much I do believe: if a black player, having reached the end of his playing career, expresses a desire to manage in the minors, he will receive serious consideration.

I also believe that if a survey were taken, it would reveal that as many white players as blacks have been denied minor league opportunities. Invariably, the bush-league managing and coaching jobs are filled by players who were at or near the bottom of the major league spectrum, fringe players who enjoy the baseball life and are willing to work for $20,000, maybe $25,000, a year.

Campanis' record as a major league executive has been outstanding. I must admit I am prejudiced in his behalf. I have long held the view—which I have written several times—that he is the most astute and most successful of the big leagues' 26 general managers.

A former scout and fringe major leaguer, Campanis worked his way through the Dodger organization. He is truly a disciple of Branch Rickey, who, by signing Jackie Robinson, broke baseball's color line. Campanis was among Robinson's first teammates. He was the second baseman with the 1946 Montreal Royals, then a Brooklyn farm club, and switched to shortstop so Robinson could play second base, which was to become his principal position.

It seems incredible that Campanis was dismissed because of his appearance on the Koppel show, which, in effect, was to be a tribute to the memory of Jackie Robinson. Commissioner Peter Ueberroth, who doesn't miss many bets, has dedicated the 1987 season to the 40th anniversary of Robinson's major league debut.

It has been said by baseball insiders that Ueberroth, who some day may run for high public office, is merely courting the black vote. Before he is finished, Ueberroth may run the ethnic gamut. Next year, a former player of Italian or Polish descent may be similarly honored, and so on.

Campanis was not Koppel's first choice. He was summoned as a late-hour replacement for Don Newcombe, the Dodgers' celebrated black pitcher of the Robinson era. Newcombe, who for many years has worked for the Dodgers in community affairs, was en route to New York but missed a plane connection.

What's unfortunate is that Robinson himself is unable to speak on Campanis' behalf. Still, there are many ballplayers, now with the Dodgers or elsewhere, who can and will testify for Campanis. Bill Buckner, for example, a longtime Dodger now with the Red Sox, expressed sorrow here Wednesday night before taking the field against the Brewers.

"Mr. Campanis just had a bad day at the office," Buckner said. "What else can I say? Of all the people in baseball, he did more for minority players than anybody."

Bob Kennedy, the onetime Cub general manager, also was sympathetic. "What's happened is terrible," Kennedy said from his home in Mesa, Arizona. "I don't care what Al said on television. It was lousy communications. I know the man, and he's not prejudiced against blacks or anyone else."

While Koppel was pressing him because of the absence of black managers and executives, Campanis asked: "How many black executives do you have on a higher level or echelon in your business? How many black anchormen?"

Koppel's reply: "Fortunately, there are a few black anchormen, but if you want me to tell you why there aren't any black executives I'm not going to tell you it's because the blacks aren't intelligent enough. I'm going to tell you it's because whites have been running the establishment of broadcasting, just as they have been running the establishment of baseball, for too long a time and seem to be reluctant to give up power. That's what it finally boils down to, isn't it?"

Yes, Mr. Koppel, that's precisely what it's all about, but it was you who misinterpreted Campanis' usage of the word "necessities" and twisted it to "blacks are not intelligent enough." Those words came from you, Mr. Koppel, not from Campanis.

According to the latest reports from Los Angeles, black leaders not only urged the Dodgers to relieve Campanis from his duties, but to "hire a black executive from among the many capable ones available."

It is to be hoped that ABC will do the same and replace Koppel with a black talk-show host from among the many capable ones available.

Scouting Amateur Free Agents Could Be the Toughest Job of All in Baseball

SUNDAY, MAY 31, 1987

AS YANKEE OWNER GEORGE STEINBRENNER REMEMBERS IT, he was on an American Airlines flight from Chicago to New York. Or it may have been from New York to Chicago. He doesn't recall which way he was going. He was scanning a copy of *Sports Illustrated* and saw a photograph in the "Faces in the Crowd" feature, of an 18-year-old ballplayer from Evansville, Indiana.

Boss George showed it to the stewardess, who earlier in the flight had said she was from Indiana. Remarkably, the stewardess had heard about the boy from her sister who lived in Evansville.

"Kids from the Midwest don't get that much of a chance," Steinbrenner said last Friday, retelling the story. "Because of the cold weather they have a short season. And having gone to Culver [Military Academy], I liked the idea of having a boy from Indiana. So I told Jax Robertson, one of our scouts, to take a look at him. Jax came back with a glowing report."

The major league draft of amateur free agents was held several days later and Steinbrenner remembers sitting at a table with several of his executives and urging them, "Take him now! Take him now!" They told him not to worry.

There was no need for concern.

Finally, on the 19th round, after 493 players had been selected, the Yankees drafted Don Mattingly, who according to the notice in *Sports Illustrated* "had batted .500 and .552 over the past two seasons to lead [Evansville] Reitz Memorial High to a 59–1 record and who in four years with the Tigers had driven in 140 runs, equaling the highest total in scholastic baseball."

Good story.

But Steinbrenner now admits he must have been confused.

The draft began on June 5, 1979, and lasted three days. The Mattingly item appeared five weeks later, in the July 16 issue of *Sports Illustrated*.

Whatever, Mattingly, who was acknowledged as the major league's best all-around player (before the sudden emergence of Cincinnati's Eric Davis), wasn't selected until the 19th round, which merely confirms my belief that of all the men in professional baseball, the free-agent scout has the toughest assignment.

Keith Hernandez, star first baseman of the New York Mets, wasn't chosen until the 42nd round. Ryne Sandberg of the Cubs, like Hernandez a winner of the National League's Most Valuable Player award, went in the 20th round.

Jose Canseco, the 1986 American League Rookie of the Year, was a 15th-round choice; Kansas City's Bret Saberhagen, who leads all big-league pitchers this season with eight victories, 19th round; Dave Parker, Cincinnati, 14th round.

It's possible to field a team of All-Star or near All-Star players who were eligible for the draft but were completely overlooked.

Allan Simpson, editor of *Baseball America* and the foremost authority on the baseball draft, selected the following team: Rich Gedman, Boston, c; Andre Thornton, Cleveland, 1b; Frank White, Kansas City, 2b; Ken Oberkfell, Atlanta, 3b; Kevin Mitchell, San Diego, ss; Brian Downing, California, Jeff Leonard, San Francisco, and Gary Ward, Yankees, of; Larry Parrish, Texas, dh; Rick Mahler, Atlanta, and Bob Ojeda, Mets, starting pitchers; and relievers Dan Quisenberry, Kansas City, and Jeff Reardon, Minnesota.

But this is unfair. The scouts, those hardy, often lonesome souls, have an impossible burden. Putting the finger on raw talent isn't difficult.

The best players, at any level of competition, are easy to spot. But more often than not the best player today is not the best player tomorrow.

The killer is projection.

What will the player look like three or four years later? Will the skinny, 135-pound outfielder sprout into a power hitter, as happened with Harold Baines of the White Sox? Will the kid with an average fastball improve his curve? Or learn how to throw the slider? Or better yet, blossom into a power pitcher?

"I saw Harold Baines when he was a high school senior," recalled Clyde King, the former general manager of the Yankees, a baseball lifer now semi-retired and on special assignment.

There are few secrets in professional baseball. It's dog-eat-dog.

Al Rosen, then the president of the Yankees, discovered that his good friend, the late Bill Veeck, was high on Baines.

By a fortunate coincidence, Veeck, before his second ownership term with the White Sox, was living in Easton, Maryland, near Baines' hometown of St. Michaels.

On orders from Rosen, King went to see Baines. "He didn't show any power, not in the game I saw," King recalled. "He didn't get around on the ball. He flied to left twice, flied to center, and walked."

Obviously, King wasn't impressed but had the disadvantage of seeing Baines only once. Veeck had been watching Baines since he was in grammar school. And, as Veeck thought he would, Baines grew taller and stronger. As his arms and chest widened, Baines became capable of pulling the ball into the right-field seats. The Sox, who had the first choice in the 1977 draft—they had finished with the worst record of the season—selected Baines.

Nick Kamzic, a longtime ivory hunter for the California Angels, understands King's problem. A native Chicagoan, Kamzic hit the first home run and scored the first touchdown for Kelly High School.

"A scout in the Midwest has to be the best," Kamzic insisted. "Sun Belt scouts see a player three or four times. In the Midwest and New England, it rains and snows all spring. We can't stay over. We have too many players to check. We see a kid once and it's *sayonara*."

Kamzic is among the army of some 400 scouts who have been on the free-agent prowl, night and day, since early March. "I'm pooped," Red Sox scout Chuck Koney said Thursday night when he arrived at his home in Oak Lawn, Illinois. Asked how many players he had seen, Koney replied, "I don't know. Too many."

What the scouts look for, essentially, is what they call "tools." Said Kamzic: "I'm a tool scout. A kid's got to have a good arm and good speed. Hitting usually comes later. As for pitchers, if a fellow has a good arm, he'll show it in high school."

A player who can't throw "is just about out of business," according to Gordon Goldsberry, chief of the Cubs' minor league system. Foot speed, Goldsberry explained, is critical because it is the only two-way weapon, essential on offense and defense.

Shawon Dunston, the Cubs' number one choice in 1982, was the fulfillment of Goldsberry's dream. Not only does Dunston have a remarkable arm, but he has exceptional speed. If Dunston couldn't make it as a shortstop, his high school position, he could be shifted to center field. And if he failed to hit, there was the additional possibility he could be converted into a pitcher.

Goldsberry has been criticized because the Cubs, who had the first selection in 1982, could have chosen pitcher Dwight Gooden. Three other clubs, Toronto, San Diego, and Minnesota, had the same opportunity but passed. The Mets, who were next, had an exceptionally good draft that year. Not only was Gooden their first-round choice, but they picked up two more outstanding pitchers, Floyd Youmans and Roger McDowell, in the second and third rounds.

"I would still take Dunston if I had a chance to do it again," said Goldsberry. "We needed an everyday player who could help us on both offense and defense, a player who could play 150 games. Gooden was also very high on our list, but we couldn't get them both."

The Angels' Kamzic agrees. "All the scouts had Dunston number one."

This isn't quite true. The Major League Scouting Bureau, which has a nationwide 50-man staff, had neither Dunston nor Gooden number one. Formed in 1974 as an economy measure that enabled many organizations to reduce their scouting budgets, the bureau services all 26 clubs and provides a computerized ranking of the most promising prospects, from 1 to 800, depending on the quality and quantity of the crop.

The bureau's recommendations for the 1982 draft pegged Dunston number six, Gooden number twenty-eight. How could Gooden have had such a low ranking? Supposedly, because the bureau scout saw Gooden too early in the season, in March and April. Said Dan Duquette, scouting coordinator for the Milwaukee Brewers: "Gooden didn't really blossom until May, toward the end of his high school career."

Bureau scouts also submit the results of eye examinations and do the original paperwork in psychological testing.

There is an extra cost, $4,000 per club, for what is essentially a motivational evaluation.

Fifteen big-league teams, including the Cubs but not the White Sox, currently subscribe to this service.

The test is known as the ISAM and is conducted by the Institute to Study Athletic Motivation, headquartered in Redwood City, California.

There are 190 questions, all simple, supposedly to determine if the young athlete is made of the right stuff. Each question offers a multiple-choice response. Examples:

> Within my league or class I think I can become the best in my sport.
> A) True; B) Uncertain; C) False.

> I lose my temper during competition:
> A) Sometimes; B) Seldom; C) Never.

According to William Winslow, who heads the institute, it isn't as much a test as an "inventory," designed "to give the athletes an opportunity to describe their athletic attitude."

He said more than a million such tests have been given since the institute was founded in 1962.

Less than 1 percent of the athletes refuse to cooperate.

The purpose, said Winslow, is to provide answers on 11 vital attitudes: drive, aggressiveness, determination, responsibility, leadership, self-confidence, emotional control, mental toughness, coachability, conscientiousness, and trust.

Baseball America's Simpson has charted every draft since its inception in 1965, and reports the following findings:

- Approximately 24,000 players have been drafted.
- Fifty-five percent of the high school players chosen in the first round make it to the big leagues, compared to 75 percent of the college players who are also first-round choices.
- Only one of the previous 22 first choices (the first player selected in the first round) did not make it to the big leagues: Steve Chilcott, a left-handed-hitting catcher out of Lancaster, California, chosen in 1966 by the Mets. Chilcott suffered a severe shoulder injury and quit baseball in May 1972.

Reggie Jackson was the number two selection that year, chosen by the then-Kansas City Athletics, and has since insisted he was the victim of racial prejudice—that he, not Chilcott, who is white, should have been the first choice.

Whitey Herzog, currently the manager of the St. Louis Cardinals, was a coach with the Mets in 1966. He said "After it [the draft] was over, I remember our general manager, Bing Devine, going around to the tables and asking the other clubs who they had number one. Nine had Chilcott, ten had Reggie. At that time, you couldn't have gone wrong with either one.

A Bright Future Seen
for Maddux

TUESDAY, JUNE 23, 1987

I ARRIVED AT WRIGLEY FIELD IN GOOD TIME on Monday searching for a column and there he was, rookie Greg Maddux, throwing in the left-field bullpen under the watchful eye of coach Herm Starrette.

"How's the kid doing?" I inquired.

"We're working on everything," Starrette replied. "Especially getting the ball down in the strike zone."

I said it sounded like a good idea and offered the unsolicited opinion that the more I've seen of Maddux, the more he reminds me of Bret Saberhagen, the Kansas City star who two years ago won a Cy Young award and currently leads all major league pitchers with 12 victories.

Starrette, of course, knows considerably more about pitching and pitchers than I ever hope to, and so I was eager to hear if he concurred.

"Little bit," Starrette said. "He does have some resemblance."

Encouraged, I predicted, "Two, three years from now, he's going to be a 20-game winner."

"Definitely," Starrette said. "Very definitely. He's just a baby. He's going to get stronger."

Maddux, 21 last April, was the youngest player in the majors at the start of the season. Obviously, he has much to learn and it may be another year

87

before he's a .500 pitcher. His record—4–6 with a 4.71 earned run average—may not seem impressive, but like shortstop Shawon Dunston, Maddux has the tools: a live, sinking fastball that has been clocked at 91 and 92 miles an hour.

But like many young players, Maddux doesn't always listen to his elders. "The kid's stubborn," said another of his coaches. "We talk to him but he doesn't always listen. There are things we know about certain hitters and we try to pound what we know into his head. But he's reluctant to change. He doesn't always take our word for it."

Maddux, nonetheless, is certain to learn as he goes along. Because his fastball is already first-rate, he's now trying to improve his curve, to give it a sharper break. He is also beginning to throw the slider, which has a short, lateral break and usually is the most difficult pitch to hit.

"From what I've seen to this point," explained third-base coach John Vukovich, "the kid's never, never going to be satisfied. That's what we hope to find in a young player. The desire to get better. And he's very aggressive. We like that."

Vukovich said an example of Maddux's aggressiveness occurred on May 1 here in Chicago against the San Diego Padres. Maddux was inserted in the eighth inning as a pinch-runner and scored the lead run in a 7–5 victory.

"I sent him in from second on a single to left," said Vukovich. "He should have been out by 20–30 feet. I sent him anyway. You never know what's going to happen. He smoked [Benito] Santiago [the Padres' catcher]. And Santiago bobbled the ball. You don't always see that in a pitcher."

Later, after Maddux had finished his workout, I asked if he had been told his pitching style was similar to Saberhagen's.

"I've heard a lot of positive things," Maddux replied. "But I've never heard that. Saberhagen is in an entirely different class. I just hope by the end of this season I'm half as good as he is."

Suddenly, his aggressive nature came to the surface.

"I have no excuse for losing so many games," said Maddux. "I'm capable of winning and I'm not doing it. I've got just as good stuff as the guys I've been throwing against. But I wind up losing."

I mentioned that very few pitchers win as many as 10 games in their rookie season. Besides, he's only 155 pounds; as he fills out and gains 15–20 pounds it would make him considerably stronger. "No," he disagreed. "I'm strong enough now."

He's wrong, of course, but I didn't tell him so. I'm a scribe, a chronicler of events, not one of his coaches.

Because this is his first time around the league, I asked what has impressed him the most, fully expecting the usual response that the hitters are tougher and smarter, etc.

"What's really surprised me," Maddux said, "was going to Jody Davis' house and Rick Sutcliffe's house. And Ryne Sandberg's. Seeing how these guys live, their lifestyles away from the ballpark. That's something I never thought about—what you can get and how you can live once you make it."

The kid's made of the right stuff. No doubt about it.

Babe Ruth's Called Shot

SUNDAY, NOVEMBER 1, 1987

BABE RUTH'S CALLED-SHOT HOME RUN IS A MYTH, a fairy tale conjured from the imaginative spirit of sportswriters who, of necessity, possess a flair for the romantic and dramatic. If it never happened, why then has this fiction taken root? Because people gild lilies and sometimes remember seeing things they didn't see.

The following paragraph taken from a story printed in the *Tribune* magazine by Will Leonard, a distinguished baseball buff and historian, written in 1957, on the 25th anniversary of the occasion, also explains the manufacture and nature of revisionist history:

> A year or two ago a book publisher put out an anthology of sports-page stories describing historic games as reported at the time in the newspapers. The book had a New York writer's account of the "called shot" game of 1932, and when his narrative came to the historic fifth inning, the editor found there was no mention of a pointed finger. So he inserted a paragraph in parenthesis containing the fable, then resumed the actual story of October 1, 1932.

Herbert F. Simons was a Chicago baseball writer, the founder of *Baseball Digest,* and a meticulous editor. Mr. Simons' findings:

90

The first mention in print of a "called home run" that considerable research could find was made by Bill Corum and Tom Meany simultaneously *three* days after the game. In a column on "Men of the Series" for the *New York Journal,* Corum wrote of Ruth: "Words fail me. When he stood up there at the bat before 50,000 persons calling the balls and strikes with gestures for the benefit of the Cubs in the dugout and then, with two strikes on him, pointed out where he was going to hit the next one and hit it there, I gave up. The fellow is not human."

On the same day Meany, in the *New York World-Telegram,* noted:

> Babe's interviewer then interrupted to point out the hole in which Babe put himself Saturday when he pointed out the spot in which he intended hitting his home run and asked the Great Man if he realized how ridiculous he would have appeared if he had struck out.
>
> "I never thought of it," said the Great Man, which is the tip-off on the Babe. He simply had his mind made up to hit a home run and he did.

Fifteen years later, Meany elaborates on the incident in his book, *Babe Ruth,* calling it the most defiant, the most debated gesture in World Series history:

> Root [Cub pitcher Charlie Root] threw a called strike past the Babe and the Cub bench let the big fellow have it. Babe, holding the bat in one hand, held up the index finger of the other, to signify it was indeed a strike. Root threw another strike. Ruth held up two fingers and the Cub bench howled in derision.
>
> It was then the big fellow made what many believe to be the beau geste of his entire career. He pointed in the direction of dead center field. Some say it was merely a gesture toward Root, others that he was just letting the Cub bench know he still had the big one left. Ruth himself has changed his version a couple of times but the reaction of most of those who saw him point his finger toward center field is that he was calling his shot.
>
> Late that winter, at a dinner at the New York Athletic Club, Ruth declared that calling his shot against Root was the biggest thrill he ever had in baseball. As time went on, however, there

was a general move to discount the big fellow's gesture and in the general debate which followed Babe himself grew confused and wasn't certain whether he had picked out a spot in the bleachers to park the ball, was merely pointing to the outfield, or was signaling that he still had one swing to go.

Meany's embellished account is suspect. There were scores of sportswriters in attendance; not one mentioned the called shot in their game stories. Also, if the Babe did call his shot, as he later insisted, and regarded it as his "biggest thrill," etc., why would he subsequently become "confused" and, as Meany admits, "change his version a couple of times"?

Because the entire episode was romantic fiction, fluff designed to enlarge the legend of Babe Ruth. Also, the unusual circumstances in the 1932 Yankee/Cub World Series fed the fable.

This was the setting: the Yankees, managed by Joe McCarthy, had won the American League pennant in a breeze—their 107 victories during the regular season gave them a 13-game bulge over Connie Mack's Philadelphia Athletics, their closest pursuer. The Cubs, lagging behind the Pittsburgh Pirates until Charlie Grimm replaced Rogers Hornsby as their manager on August 2, came on with a furious stretch drive to win the National League flag by four games.

A big factor in the Cubs' surge was the play of their shortstop, Mark Koenig, the Yankees' own shortstop of their 1926–27–28 champions. Rescued from the minors late in the season, Koenig played in only 33 games with the Cubs but nonetheless helped spark the pennant drive. He batted .353, exactly 100 points higher than the wounded Billy Jurges. However, in the pre-Series meeting to divide the forthcoming players' pool, the Cub players placed the emphasis on Koenig's length of time with the club and voted him only half a share. (Hornsby, who managed the Cubs for almost two-thirds of the season, received nothing.)

The Yankees resented this unfair treatment of Koenig, an old pal. A "cheapskate" theme became a principal part of their bench-jockeying, which, in the main, was orchestrated by Ruth.

The Series opened in New York with the Yankees winning the two games 12–6 and 5–2. Then the scene shifted to Chicago. Thousands of people crammed into the LaSalle Street Station to see the clubs arrive. Ruth, accompanied by his wife, Claire, fought his way through the unfriendly crowd to a freight elevator and then to a cab. Motorcycle police had to clear the way for the Yankees. As Ruth and his wife entered their hotel, a woman spat on them.

The anti-Yankee sentiment was also evident at Wrigley Field before, during, and after the third game of the Series. Ruth complained a week or so later that the Chicago press had brought the fans down on him. "They wrote about me riding the Cubs for being tight and about me calling them cheapskates," he said, indignantly.

"Well, didn't you?" he was asked.

"Well, weren't they?" he replied with irrefutable logic.

An overflow crowd of 49,986, which included New York governor Franklin Delano Roosevelt, who was running for president against Herbert Hoover, and Chicago mayor Anton Cermak, jammed Wrigley Field and the temporary stands built outside the ballpark in the streets behind the left- and right-field bleachers.

Whenever a ball was lofted Ruth's way in pregame practice, lemons came out of the bleachers. Each time, the Babe picked up the lemons and threw them back. He was in a cheerful mood. There was a strong wind blowing toward right field and Ruth and Lou Gehrig put on an awesome batting show, far more spectacular than the one in Pittsburgh five years earlier.

Ruth hit nine balls into the stands, Gehrig seven. Ruth yelled at the Cubs, "I'd play for half my salary if I could hit in this dump all the time."

The jockeying between the two teams or, more accurately, between Ruth and the Cubs, became more intense as the game began. Guy Bush, Burleigh Grimes, and Pat Malone were on the top step of the Cub dugout, leading the verbal barrage. Andy Lotshaw, the Cub trainer, yelled, "If I had you, I'd hitch you to a wagon, you potbelly." Afterwards Ruth said,

"I didn't mind no ballplayers yelling at me, but the trainer cutting in—that made me sore."

"The Cub fans simply would not believe how severely or decisively their champions had been manhandled by the mighty Yankees in the East," wrote John Drebinger in *The New York Times*. "The fans roared their approval of every good play made by the Cubs. They booed Babe Ruth thoroughly, even when he homered in his first time at bat. And they howled with glee as Ruth failed in a heroic attempt to make a shoestring catch of Billy Jurges' low liner to left in the fourth inning [a double that lifted the Cubs into a 4–4 tie]. Good-naturedly, the Babe doffed his cap to acknowledge the adverse plaudits."

Richards Vidmer of the *New York Herald-Tribune* described the climactic fifth inning and Ruth's legendary home run:

> As the Babe moved toward the plate with one out in the fifth inning, swinging three bats over his shoulders, a concerted shout of derision broke out in the stands: a bellowing of boos, hisses, and jeers. There were cries of encouragement for the pitcher and from the Cub dugout came a storm of abuse leveled at the Babe.
>
> But Ruth grinned in the face of the hostile greeting. He laughed back at the Cubs and took his place, supremely confident. Charley Root whistled a strike over the plate and the joyous outcries filled the air but the Babe held up one finger as though to say, "That's only one. Just wait."
>
> Root threw another strike and the stands rocked with delight. The Chicago players hurled their laughter at the great man but Ruth held up two fingers, and still grinned, the super-showman. On the next pitch, the Babe swung. There was a resounding report like the explosion of a gun. Straight for the fence the ball soared on a line, clearing the farthest corner of the barrier, 436 feet from home plate.
>
> Before Ruth left the plate and started his swing around the bases, he paused to laugh at the Chicago players, suddenly silent in their dugout. As he rounded first he flung a remark at Grimm; as he turned second he tossed a jest at Billy Herman. His shoulders shook with satisfaction as he trotted in.

Beautifully descriptive stuff from Vidmer who, in a 1972 interview, readily acknowledged he sweetened his prose with wondrous jams. But not one word about a called shot.

The count was even at 2 balls and 2 strikes, not 0 and 2 as Vidmer indicated. Such fuzziness of detail is evident in several contemporary accounts. Westbrook Pegler, covering for the *Tribune,* reported the count went strike, strike, ball, ball, whereas it was strike, ball, ball, strike. Bill Corum said the count was 3 and 2, and so did the play-by-play account in *The New York Times.* Tom Meany's biography and Ruth's autobiography both say, as Root did, that it was 2 strikes and 0 balls. Years later, umpire George Magerkurth insisted he worked the plate and said the count was 3 and 2. Magerkurth didn't have the plate; he was at first base.

Five *Tribune* sportswriters were assigned to the game, including such trained and veteran observers as Pegler, Edward Burns, and Irving "Pop" Vaughan. They didn't see it. Neither did Herbert Simons of the *Daily Times* or Warren Brown of the Chicago Hearst papers. Nor Gordon Cobbledick of Cleveland or Jimmy Isaminger of Philadelphia. Or any of the scribes in the distinguished New York press platoon that traveled with the Yankees: Damon Runyon, Dan Daniel, Bill Corum, Joe Williams, John Drebinger, Tom Meany, Richards Vidmer, and Paul Gallico, a rococo and flamboyant writer who, in his follow-up, wrote: "He pointed like a duelist to the spot where he expected to send his rapier home."

Manager Joe McCarthy, whose Yankees won Game 3, 7–5, on the way to a sweep of the Series, repeatedly refused to confirm or deny. "I'm not going to say he didn't do it," McCarthy said. "Maybe I didn't see it. Maybe I was looking the other way. Anyway, I'm not going to say he didn't do it."

Chicago's Hal Totten, baseball's pioneer broadcaster, was also in attendance. Totten, in 1924, was the first to announce play-by-play directly from the ballpark on a regular basis. He did the home games for the Cubs and the White Sox. In the spring of 1933, as the legend was gaining strength, Totten interviewed the Babe at Comiskey Park. Writing about it later, Totten recalled that he said:

"Babe, people actually now think that when you held out your hand you were pointing to the spot and declaring that's where you were going to hit it. Is that actually a fact?"

And the reply from the Babe—in his true, colorful and picturesque language and unpredictable expletives included—was this: "Hell no, it isn't a fact. Only a damned fool would do a thing like that. You know there was a lot of pretty rough ribbing going on on both benches during the Series. When I swung and missed that first one, those Cubs really gave me a blast. So I grinned at 'em and held out one finger and told 'em it'd only take one to do it.

"Then there was that second strike and they let me have it again. So I held up that finger again and I said I still had that one left. Naw, keed, you know damned well I wasn't pointing anywhere. If I'd have done that, Root would have stuck the ball right in my ear. And besides that I never knew anybody who could tell you ahead of time where he was going to hit a baseball. When I get to be that kind of fool they'll put me in the booby hatch."

Ryan Past Prime,
Still a Cut Above

THURSDAY, FEBRUARY 4, 1988

A BIG TEXAS CATTLEMAN, possessor of three breeding herds of more than 1,000 head and 38 major league pitching records, blew into town Wednesday to talk baseball and inform the middle-aged populace how to stay in shape. He's the ultimate expert in both areas.

"Are young pitchers able to throw faster today?" WGN's Wally Phillips, working the luncheon crowd at Lawry's the Prime Rib Restaurant, asked Nolan Ryan, baseball's all-time strikeout king.

"I don't think so," Ryan replied. "If you talk to the scouts, they tell you there are fewer hard throwers today. The kids are learning to pitch at an earlier stage, but they're not developing their arms. They're throwing sliders and forkballs, easy pitches to pick up."

He is in the midst of a four-city tour on behalf of the National Livestock and Meat Board, advising weekend athletes on how to maintain their youthful posture.

Ryan, 41 last Sunday, will soon open his 21st major league season. He is remarkable not only for his fastball but also for his longevity. Hard throwers, except for Ryan, lose their heaters. The best of them, to prolong their careers, adjust and begin winning with cunning and finesse, with a variety of breaking pitches. Ryan has made no such compromise. The fastball is still his primary pitch.

And how fast is the fastball?

"I don't know," Ryan said. "Maybe 94, 95 [miles an hour]. I'm not sure."

There was a night in Anaheim in 1972 when he knew precisely. Ryan was pitching for the California Angels. The club's promotion wing, in an effort to stimulate the gate, had a contest: the fans were invited to estimate the speed of Ryan's fastball.

"This was before they had radar guns," Ryan recalled. "The people at Rockwell International timed it with beams."

His fastest pitch that night—thrown to the luckless Bee Bee Richard, a light-hitting White Sox shortstop—was 100.9 m.p.h. Maybe Bob Feller or Walter Johnson or perhaps Goose Gossage, in their prime, have been as swift. It's doubtful anybody threw harder.

I asked Ryan when he first became aware of his extraordinary velocity. Was there a magic moment when he knew he had a golden arm?

It was when he was 15, a sophomore at Alvin (Texas) High School. Red Murff, then scouting for the Mets, went to Colt Stadium to watch the Houston Colt .45s play the Cincinnati Reds in a midseason National League game.

That night, after Murff had seen Ryan, he told the Alvin coach: "I saw Jim Maloney and Turk Farrell pitch today, and your kid throws as hard as they do."

"My coach was truly surprised, and so was I," Ryan recalled. "But I don't think my coach was all that impressed. I was tall, skinny, and wild. My coach was more concerned with my control."

Many pitching coaches have since expressed a similar concern. Among Ryan's three dozen big-league records are most lifetime walks, 2,355—an average of five walks for every nine innings of toil. In recent years, however, he has conquered his control problems.

Last season he gave up only 3.7 walks per nine innings, just about average for the course. He also led the National League in earned run average at 2.76 and strikeouts with 271, the only pitcher to lead in both categories and not win a Cy Young award. He was 8–16 and is believed to be the only pitcher with a losing record to win an ERA title. In his 16 losses, the Astros scored only 13 runs while he was on the mound.

Ryan's walks are the only negative. He is the all-time strikeout leader with 4,547 Ks in 4,327 innings, a remarkable ratio of 9.5 strikeouts for every nine innings. In big-league history, Sandy Koufax is the only pitcher who has averaged a strikeout an inning; he had 9.3 for every nine innings. But Koufax went the way of all flesh, fading early, and retired at 31 after a comparatively brief 12-year major league career.

Koufax, Ryan revealed, was his idol.

In 1975, against Baltimore, Ryan pitched his fourth no-hitter, a plateau previously reached only by Koufax.

"I decided then I'd like to pitch another one," Ryan said. "And it took me five years to get number five." By coincidence, it was against the Los Angeles Dodgers, Koufax's old club.

I never thought I'd last this long," Ryan said, laughing. "A lot of baseball people said I'd be burned out at 30."

Power pitchers, almost always, throw the most pitches, especially those with control problems. A winning pitcher going the nine-inning distance will average 115 to 120 pitches. Ryan's average has been about 140. In a 12-inning game against Cleveland, he threw 242 pitches. Tom Morgan, a coach with the Angels, kept a precise count in 1973 or 1974. Ryan doesn't remember the year but recalls that Morgan said he threw 7,400 pitches that season.

"Nolan's always been in great shape," observed Ken Harrelson, a one-time slugger and more recently the general manager of the White Sox. "He has the strongest legs of any pitcher I've seen."

Ryan agrees that keeping the legs in shape is crucial to good conditioning. He emphasized this during several interviews Wednesday.

"Climb stairs, walk, ride an exercycle, jog, do leg curls," Ryan advised. "It will help prevent injuries."

A generous cut of beef, prime or choice, is essential to the renewal process, according to Ryan, who works three spreads in Texas. Tall and slim, with a lean, weathered face crowned by a 10-gallon hat, he is an authentic cowboy, riding the range from October through mid-February.

"Are you the Marlboro Man?" a female fan asked on the first floor at the Merchandise Mart.

Ryan smiled and in his best Gary Cooper manner said, "I reckon so, ma'am. Except I don't smoke."

Durocher Warms Up in the Bull-Session Pen

MONDAY, JULY 11, 1988

OLD BALLPLAYERS DON'T FADE AWAY; they just keep showing up at Old Timers' games. And of course, Leo Durocher, pushing 83, was here with the rest of the geriatric gang and becoming impatient when the Cincinnati Reds' team physician, in a pregame clubhouse meeting, cautioned the old-timers not to exert themselves in the 90-degree heat.

"He was talking like a professor," Durocher explained. "He told us, 'Drink Gatorade! Get plenty of water! Keep the fluids in your body!'

"Finally, I hit the table"—Durocher paused and slammed his hand, palm down, on a table in demonstration—"and I said, 'Damn it, Doc! Take a hike! I never held a meeting this long for a World Series game.'

"And everyone broke up, laughing. And that ended the meeting."

As pleased with himself as ever, Durocher was at Riverfront Stadium Sunday to manage the National League Old Timers' All-Star team against a similar squad of American League ancients managed by Lou Boudreau, a prelude to Tuesday night's All-Star Game. The cast included 23 Hall of Famers, among them Luke Appling of the White Sox; Billy Herman, Ernie Banks, and Billy Williams of the Cubs; and Jocko Conlan, 88, a former National League umpire who broke in with the Sox as an out-fielder and lived for many years in Evanston, Illinois.

"I never held long team meetings," Durocher revealed. "After we beat Cleveland three straight [in the 1954 World Series], we were dressing for the fourth game, and Alvin Dark said, 'Are you ready, Leo?' I said, 'Whenever you are.' And Dark said, 'This is a lousy town. Let's beat 'em and go home.' We didn't need no meeting."

Durocher was drinking milk from a paper cup. Natty as ever, he wore a white polo shirt with blue-gray slacks, his head crowned with a dark blue cap bearing the logo of The Equitable Financial Companies, which sponsors the game and pays the players.

"You should have been on the team bus," Billy Williams had reported. "Leo was sitting next to Jocko Conlan. They were chirping away. All in a good frame of mind."

When Conlan was umpiring and Durocher was managing the old Brooklyn Dodgers and New York Giants, they were at each other's throats and seldom, if ever, had a kind word for each other. One of the famous photographs in baseball history captured Jocko, in retaliation, kicking Durocher in the shin during an argument at home plate.

Durocher acknowledged that he and Jocko had been seatmates. But he wasn't happy about it.

"Look at this," Durocher barked. He held up his left arm, revealing a black and blue mark below the elbow.

"When Jocko talks to you, he's in the habit of grabbing you. Since my quadruple bypass, my doctor told me if I hit anything, I'll get a bruise. I bruise easily. And Jocko has trouble hearing. I kept telling him, 'Jocko, I'm sitting alongside of you. It's me. I can hear.'"

I ask if he had been keeping busy, if he still plays gin rummy.

"No more cards," he replied. "I don't go to the club. I don't monkey around."

What does he do?

"I hang around. Play golf. Take it easy. What the hell, I'm in no hurry to go anyplace. I'm older than dirt: 83 coming up, July 27."

Then, as he always does, he mentioned Dr. Michael DeBakey, the famed pioneer heart surgeon out of Houston. Durocher always prides himself on having the best. He had the best ghostwriter, the best dentist, the best tailor, and, of course, the best doctor.

"I talk to him [DeBakey] all the time," Durocher said. "He told me, 'Stop walking four, five miles a day. Two miles is as good as five.' He said, 'Play nine holes of golf, and if you feel good, take the cart for the last nine. But whatever you do, don't walk 18. Don't walk up and down those hills.' "

Durocher waved his hand, indicating the terrain, the hills and valleys in Palm Springs, California, where he makes his home.

Had he seen the Cubs?

"On television. Once. With that Maddux pitching. Good-looking pitcher. They've got a good-looking young club. Some of those guys can play."

He began walking out towards the field. Tommy Helms, a Cincinnati coach, intercepted him and led him into the Reds' clubhouse.

"Pete wants to see you," Helms said, referring to Pete Rose.

Rose was delighted. As they shook hands, Rose turned to several reporters and said, "He's the greatest. He gave an hour's talk last year in Santa Maria [California]. I had goose bumps. And I had to follow him. They gave him a Cadillac."

Durocher, smiling, revealed that for that single appearance, he had been given a Cadillac with a sticker price of $37,750.

"Everything on it, from bumper to bumper. And in my color. Medium blue. And that wasn't the half of it. They even paid the taxes. It only cost me $42 for the license plates. And the fellows said, 'If you come back in 1939, we'll give you another one.' "

Didn't he mean 1989?

"That's right, 1989."

For Rose's benefit, Durocher repeated the story about the Cincinnati doctor and his lengthy clubhouse speech. As he had earlier, Durocher banged his hand on the edge of Rose's desk.

"That's the way it is today," Rose explained. "You can't play baseball without two doctors, four trainers, and eight certificates."

By this time, most of the old timers were on the field. Ernie Banks, looking good and wearing his No. 14, was his usual effervescent self.

Banks was asked if he had seen Durocher. They seldom spoke during the six and a half seasons Durocher managed the Cubs. More than once, Durocher made it clear he resented Banks' designation as "Mr. Cub."

"Sure I saw him," Banks said. "He said, 'Nice to see you, how things going?'"

Banks smiled.

"He's my friend."

Banks' mouth seemed to be full. I asked if he had taken to chewing tobacco.

He laughed. Then he bent over and whispered in my ear. "I'm chewing Mr. Wrigley's gum."

Santo's Numbers
Hall of Fame Size

THURSDAY, DECEMBER 1, 1988

BILLY PIERCE WON 211 GAMES, more victories than 15 of the pitchers in the Hall of Fame, but never received more than 2 percent of the vote and was dropped from the ballot. Luke Appling, a two-time batting champion, among the greatest players in White Sox history, got in through the side door: a special runoff was held because no players were elected in the original voting.

Billy Williams waited six years. Nellie Fox, up there in Valhalla, is still waiting. In 1985 he received 74.68 percent of the vote. It should have been rounded out to the required 75 percent, but the directors of the Hall of Fame, in a burst of stupidity concealed beneath the umbrella of purity, locked Little Nell out, claiming he missed by 32-hundredths of a percent.

Hack Wilson of the Cubs still holds the major league record for the most runs batted in in one season, 190, but the pearly gates didn't open until 45 years after he had retired as a player. When he became eligible in 1979, Luis Aparicio, possibly the best shortstop of the 20th century, almost didn't make the ballot. Some members of the screening committee scratched him, deeming him not worthy of consideration. Two years later Aparicio received only 12 percent of the vote, barely enough to maintain his eligibility.

When the list of the 1989 candidates was announced Wednesday in New York it occurred to me anew that for the last quarter of a century, with the exception of Ernie Banks (elected in 1971), Chicago players have had to struggle for Hall of Fame recognition. Cooperstown has been cruel to them.

Of the new eligibles, three are likely to be anointed in their first time at-bat: Johnny Bench of Cincinnati, the reigning catcher of his time; Carl Yastrzemski, superstar outfielder with the Boston Red Sox; and pitcher Gaylord Perry, a 300-game winner. Ferguson Jenkins of the Cubs, a seven-time 20-game winner, also is eligible for the first time and worthy of immediate canonization.

Ordinarily I don't pump for Chicago players. It doesn't seem proper. I have preferred to assume it should not be necessary to bang the drum, that the 400-plus voters (10-year members of the Baseball Writers Association of America) constitute an educated electorate.

Then I think of Ron Santo and realize some campaigning is necessary.

A hero Cub in the sixties and seventies, Santo was the best all-around third baseman of his time. Baltimore's Brooks Robinson was, of course, the best-fielding third baseman, but Santo was a much stronger hitter. And he was almost B. Robby's equal in the field.

Santo, nonetheless, was virtually ignored in 1980, his first year on the ballot. It is scandalous to recall that he received only 15 of the 385 votes cast, 4 percent. According to the rules, players with less than 5 percent are automatically dropped from the ballot. From 1981 to 1984, Santo was a nonperson, not welcome in Cooperstown.

The death of Ken Boyer, a star third baseman with the Cardinals, triggered a reexamination of the system. Boyer, too, had been a victim of the 5-percent rule. Bob Broeg, a St. Louis baseball writer, led a movement to reinstate Boyer, insisting Boyer was entitled to another chance.

Boyer's name was restored but with the provision that other worthies, who also had been thrown on the discard pile, would simultaneously be reinstated. Santo was among the players in this group, risen from Boyer's grave. But Santo was to suffer another indignity. The secretary of the

BBWAA apparently had forgotten Santo's first name and listed him as Roy, not Ron. Santo drew 13 percent of the vote in 1985. His percentage has been increasing steadily. He was on 108 of the 427 ballots in the last election, 25 percent.

Probably because he was such a strong hitter, Santo, who for many years was the Cub captain, never received much acclaim for his defensive ability. Through hard work and nothing else (he was originally a catcher), he made himself an acceptable third baseman and soon thereafter was the best defensive third baseman in the National League.

As most fans realize, fielding averages are deceptive. The lumbering galoot who can't move off a silver dollar (once it was a dime, but adjustments must be made for inflation) has an enormous statistical advantage. Errors are not charged for slow fielding; the lead-foot escapes because he doesn't reach the ball. The best index of a defensive player's effectiveness is not fewest errors, but chances accepted.

Brooks Robinson, who played eight more years than Santo, is the all-time career leader in chances with 9,165, including errors. But a closer examination reveals that Santo, who had a 15-year major league career, was the busier third baseman. Santo averaged 457 chances a season compared to B. Robby's 399. Santo averaged more assists, 305 to 270, and more putouts, 130 to 117.

And Santo, of course, was the much stronger hitter with a career total of 342 home runs and 1,331 runs batted in, an average of almost 90 RBIs a season. His power stats (slugging average, home runs, and RBI) compare with those of Billy Williams and Banks, his Cub teammates whose plaques hang in Cooperstown.

"If I'm in, Ronnie should be in, too," Billy Williams said the summer before last, a few moments after he was enshrined.

My sentiments exactly.

Spring Training
a Lousy Yardstick

SUNDAY, FEBRUARY 19, 1989

As THE IRON HORSE WAS PLUNGING ONWARD, through and over the mountains and into the Arizona desert, it occurred to me that whatever happens, I should contain myself and not believe what I see in spring training.

If a rookie pitcher holds a one-run, ninth-inning lead and strikes out the side on nine pitches, I must not pounce on my electronic word machine and trumpet the coming of another Bob Feller. Or rhapsodize about the "new Nolan Ryan." The same applies to the phenom sluggers who tear it up during the exhibition season.

Ideally, there should be two spring-training progress charts: one for the rookies trying to make the club, the other for the established players many of whom, fearing injury, take their sweet time getting into shape. They know they can stand on their records, on previous achievements accomplished during the championship season.

"You don't want to get bombed more than two times in a row," said Jim Brosnan, a wise old head who had a distinguished big-league career as a late-inning reliever and was among the few pitchers to toil for both the Cubs and the White Sox.

"A veteran can take two bombings in a row. You can get away with that. But any time he gets bombed three times in a row, doubt sets in.

The manager and the coaches begin asking, 'Is his arm gone? Has he got the bad attitude? Can we still count on him?'"

Jim Fregosi's spring-training standards are even lower. Fregosi, who managed the White Sox the last two seasons, looks for one good effort from an established pitcher, seven or eight strong innings, preferably at or near the end of the exhibition season.

"That's enough for me to know he's ready," Fregosi said.

Johnny Klippstein, an 18-year major leaguer who pitched on two pennant-winning teams, concurs: "The biggest mistake for a veteran pitcher is to have a good outing, or a couple of good outings in the middle of spring training. He begins thinking he's in shape. Then he really begins coasting. And he's in trouble for the first month of the season."

The objectives are different. When the bell rings (on April 4 for the Cubs and Sox), baseball becomes a team game with only one purpose: to win. In spring training, it's a game of individual performances. As Brosnan said: "The idea is to make yourself look as good as possible, to impress the manager, the coaches, and your teammates. And any scouts who may be looking for a trade."

Klippstein hasn't forgotten his last spring training, in 1967, when he was with Detroit.

"Mike Marshall was a rookie on that club," he said. "He had played winter ball. From the first day, in batting practice, he was throwing 90 miles an hour. He was knocking the bats out of the hands of our best hitters, guys like Al Kaline, Norm Cash, Jim Northrup. The hitters weren't too happy with him. But he didn't care. He was trying to make the club."

Marshall not only made the club but also went on to have a memorable career. An iron man, he still holds the single-season major league record for most appearances, 106, and most innings by a reliever, 208.

Marshall was the exception. Most rookie pitchers, though they have a considerable advantage, don't make the club. They bloom in the spring principally because they report in better shape, especially those who played winter ball. The first time out they not only can throw strikes but their fastballs are hopping, their curves biting as well.

109

It will be at least three and possibly four weeks before the other pitchers catch up. And while the veterans are building arm strength with straight-arrow fastballs, the bushers are in paradise, throwing snakes and writing letters home: "Dear Friend Al: They ain't scored a run off of me yet."

Breaking-ball pitchers are always more effective in spring training and in September, though the latter is true for pitchers in general. There are two reasons: in the spring the hitters are struggling, groping for their timing, and by September, they're tired. Hitters play every day, pitchers once every fifth day. The 1988 cumulative major league batting averages, which I assume are typical, were lowest in April and September.

Orel Hershiser of the Dodgers, baseball's newest glamour pitcher, opened and closed the regular season with matching winning streaks: 6–0 from April 6 to May 4; 6–0 again after August 30. He was 23–8 overall but 11–8 in between. His record-breaking streak of 59 scoreless innings did not begin until August 30. Walter Johnson, who holds the American League "record" of 55⅔ innings, began his streak early, on April 10, Opening Day.

Chances are Hershiser will have a mediocre spring training. And why not? More than likely, he will fool around, test a new pitch, sit for commercials, wait to see what Tommy Lasorda has prepared for dinner; six weeks in the sun, free from the pressure that affects only the rookies and the aging veterans trying to hang on. The rookies, however, will have another chance; if Tommy John isn't effective, it's *sayonara*.

Stack everything together and you can understand why it's impossible to judge a team in spring training, particularly the young pitchers. Even the managers don't know which one they'll keep. They call a press conference and insist: "This is the toughest decision of my life. I've never seen so many good-looking young arms."

But there is one surefire solution: they continue pitching the kids until they pitch their way off the club.

"Dear Friend Al: "They beat me yesterday and I am writing you this so as you will know the truth about the game and not get a bum steer from what you read in the papers. The score was 16–2 when Zimmer took me out in the eighth, but he ought never to of left me in there when he seen how sore my arm was."

"Shoeless"
Was Hardly Blameless

SUNDAY, JUNE 11, 1989

SPORTS ILLUSTRATED HAS JOINED the seemingly popular sentiment for the election of Shoeless Joe Jackson to baseball's Hall of Fame.

Shoeless Joe was among the eight White Sox players banned for life by Judge Kenesaw Mountain Landis, then the commissioner, for participating in the alleged 1919 World Series fix. Jackson departed with a .356 lifetime batting average, third on the all-time list behind Ty Cobb's .367 and Roger Hornsby's .358.

Nicholas Dawidoff, in the current issue of *Sports Illustrated*, offers the opinion: "Excluding Jackson for all these years strikes me as no mean injustice. Short of blatant attempts to undermine the integrity of the game—and I include cheating in that category—good play, rather than good character, ought to be the sole criterion for induction into the Hall. That's why loutish Ty Cobb is there. Jackson meets the standard, too. . . . Jackson was no villain; he was probably more an innocent victim or scapegoat."

Shoeless Joe, an illiterate country bumpkin from South Carolina, is generally regarded with sympathy because he could neither read nor write. But he conquered math. He knew how to count.

For Dawidoff and the other sentimentalists, we are offering a portion of Jackson's 27-page confession, which, so far as I know, has never before been published. The confession was made on September 28, 1920, to a Cook County grand jury and is among the 250 Black Sox artifacts gathered by curator Robert A. Goler of the Chicago Historical Society. The display has been on view for six months and closes Sunday.

Hartley L. Replogle, the assistant state's attorney, asked the questions:

Q. Did anybody pay you any money to help throw that Series in favor of Cincinnati?
A. They did.

Q. How much did they pay?
A. They promised me $20,000 and paid me $5,000.

Q. Who promised to pay the $20,000?
A. Chick Gandil.

Q. Who was Chick Gandil?
A. He was the first baseman on the White Sox club.

Q. Who paid you the $5,000?
A. Lefty Williams brought it in my room and threw it down.

Q. Who is Lefty Williams?
A. A pitcher on the White Sox club.

Q. Where did he bring it, where is your room?
A. At that time I was staying at the Lexington Hotel, I believe it is.

Q. On 21st and Michigan?
A. 22nd and Michigan, yes.

Q. Who was in the room at the time?
A. Lefty and myself. I was in there and he came in.

Q. Where was Mrs. Jackson?
A. Mrs. Jackson . . . let me see, I think she was in the bathroom. It was a suite. Yes, she was in the room, I am pretty sure.

Q. Does she know that you got $5,000 for helping throw these games?
A. She did that night, yes.

Q. You say you told Mrs. Jackson that evening?
A. Did, yes.

Q. What did she say about it?
A. She said she thought it was an awful thing to do.

Q. When was it that this money was brought to your room and that you talked to Mrs. Jackson?
A. It was the second trip in Cincinnati; that night we were leaving [for Cincinnati].

Q. That was after the fourth game?
A. I believe it was, yes.

Q. After the fourth game? Do you remember who won that game?
A. Dick Kerr, I believe.

Q. Cincinnati won that game. Cicotte pitched and Cincinnati won. Do you remember now? Cincinnati beat you 2–0.
A. Yes, sir.

Q. Were you at a conference of these men, these players on the Sox team at the Warner Hotel [in Cincinnati] sometime previous to this?
A. No, sir. I was not present, but I knew they had a meeting, so I was told.

Q. Who told you?
A. Williams.

Q. Who else talked to you about this besides Claude Williams?
A. Claude didn't talk to me direct about it. He just told me things had been said.

Q. What did he tell you?
A. He told me about this meeting in particular. He said the gang was there, and this fellow Attell—Abe Attell, I believe—and Bill Burns is the man that give him the double-crossing, so Gandil told me.

Q. Then you talked to Chick Gandil and Claude Williams both about this?

A. Talked to Claude Williams about it, yes, and Gandil more so, because he is the man who promised me this stuff.

Q. How much did he promise you?

A. $20,000 if I would take part.

Q. And you said you would?

A. Yes, sir.

Q. When did he promise you the $20,000?

A. It was to be paid after each game.

Q. How much?

A. Split it up some way. I don't know just how much it amounts to, but during the Series it would amount to $20,000. Finally, Williams brought me this $5,000, threw it down.

Q. What did you say to Williams when he threw down the $5,000?

A. I asked him what the hell had come off here.

Q. What did he say?

A. He said Gandil said we all got a screw through Abe Attell. Gandil said he got double-crossed through Abe Attell; he got the money and refused to turn it over to him. I don't think Gandil was crossed as much as he crossed us.

Q. You think Gandil may have gotten the money and held it from you, is that right?

A. That's what I think. I think he kept the majority of it.

Q. What did you do then?

A. I went to him and asked him what was the matter. He said Abe Attell gave him the jazzing. He said, "Take that or let it alone."

Q. At the end of the first game you didn't get any money, did you?

A. No, I did not. No, sir.

Q. What did you do then?

A. I asked Gandil, "What is the trouble?" He says, "Everything's all right." He had it.

Q. Then you went ahead and threw the second game, thinking you would get it then, is that right?

A. We went ahead and threw the second game; then we went after him again. I said to him, "What are you going to do?"

"Everything is all right," he says. "What the hell is the matter?"

Q. After the third game, what did you say to him?

A. After the third game, I says, "Somebody is getting a nice little jazz, everybody is crossed." He said . . . Abe Attell and Bill Burns had crossed him. That is what he said to me.

Q. Didn't you think it was the right thing for you to go and tell [Sox owner Charles A.] Comiskey about it?

A. I did tell them once: "I am not going to be in it. I will just get out of that altogether."

Q. Who did you tell that to?

A. Chick Gandil. He was the whole works of it, the instigator of it.

Q. What did he say?

A. He said I was into it already and I might as well as stay in. I said, "I can go to the boss, and have every damn one of you pulled out of the limelight." He said it wouldn't be well for me if I did that.

Q. What did you say?

A. Well, I told him anytime they wanted to have me knocked off, to have me knocked off.

Q. What did he say?

A. Just laughed.

Q. Weren't you in on the inner circle?
A. No, I was never with them. No, sir. It was mentioned to me in Boston. As I told you before, they asked me would I consider $10,000 and I said no. Then they offered me $20,000.

Q. What did he [Gandil] say?
A. Just walked away from me, and when I returned here to Chicago, he told me he would give me $20,000, and I said no again, and on the bridge where you go into the clubhouse, he told me I could either take it or let it alone, they were going through.

Q. What did they say?
A. They said, "You might as well say yes or say no and play ball or anything you want." I told them I would take their word.

Q. What else did you say?
A. Nothing.

Q. After the fourth game, you went to Cincinnati and had the $5,000, is that right?
A. Yes sir.

Q. Where did you put the $5,000? Did you put it in the bank or keep it on your person?
A. I put it in my pocket.

Q. What denominations, in silver or bills?
A. In bills.

Q. How big were some of the bills?
A. Some hundreds, mostly fifties.

Q. What did Mrs. Jackson say about it after she found it out again?
A. She felt awful bad about it, cried about it for a while.

President Holds
a White House Conference
on a Critical Matter: Baseball

TUESDAY, OCTOBER 3, 1989

"MR. PRESIDENT," I SAID, NOT ASKING, "I understand you're rooting for the Cubs."

Apparently, for relief of the weighty problems of government, here and elsewhere, President George Bush, a light-hitting first baseman out of Yale, had invited a dozen journalists to the White House to talk baseball, specifically about the playoffs and World Series.

"The president is a real baseball fan," explained Curt Smith of the White House staff as we were assembling at noon Tuesday at the Northwest Gate. "He'd rather quote Yogi Berra than Thomas Jefferson."

Would Mr. Bush be rooting for the Cinderella Cubs, 44 summers without a pennant, 81 years since their last World Series victory?

"There is something exciting about them," the president replied. "They started off all griping about the lights at Wrigley Field, and they end up having a winner. I don't know what the answer is."

I wasn't sure if he was referring to the players or the fans; more than likely, the fans. I didn't ask.

"You don't read about lights at Wrigley Field anymore," he said. Then, addressing himself to your far-flung correspondent, the president said, "Maybe you do in Chicago."

117

Jack Buck, the Hall of Fame broadcaster out of St. Louis, picked up the baton.

"They're crazy, Mr. President," Buck said. "They hit-and-run with the bases loaded. They start all the runners. [Manager Don] Zimmer's driving all the managers crazy."

The president was a picture of good health and sartorial elegance: dark blue single-breasted suit, with the top button buttoned; white shirt and blue tie, appropriately decorated with a red-and-white stripe. He had weighed in Tuesday morning at 195 pounds, two pounds lighter than usual.

"If I had a choice, I'd love to see a game in Chicago," he said. "It's a great town, anyway. There's something nostalgic about Wrigley Field. But I don't know whether I'll get to go or not."

Phil Pepe of the *New York Daily News,* longtime diamond Boswell and the current national president of the Baseball Writers Association of America, was seated directly across the mahogany conference table from Bush.

Standing, Pepe leaned over and gave the president a bronze lifetime pass. "This will get you in, Mr. President," Pepe said. "It's good for any ballpark in the United States."

Everyone laughed.

President or not, Bush is like all old-time ballplayers and has a recollection of his biggest day: "Three for five against North Carolina State. A triple, double, and a single. [Yale coach] Ethan Allen couldn't believe it."

It was in 1948, when the President was a third-year regular at Yale and captain of the baseball team, a slick-fielding first sacker, with, at best, only occasional power. He batted right-handed and threw left-handed, a rarity. Most players, if not right- or left-handed all the way, swing left and throw right.

"My controlling eye was the left eye," he explained. Then, he added, without finishing the sentence, "If I had batted left-handed from the beginning . . ."

I said it sounded like he was "good-field, no-hit."

118

"Now wait a minute," the president replied, his voice rising in mock anger.

Quickly, he conceded. "But, unfortunately, the record is somewhere out there. I hit .240, .250. I batted eighth. That should tell you."

Dan Shaughnessy of the *Boston Globe* said he had seen a 1948 photograph of the president with Babe Ruth, accepting some of Ruth's memorabilia on behalf of the Yale library. In the photograph, Bush is wearing his Yale uniform. Shaughnessy asked if he would explain the circumstances.

"I was captain of the ballclub, so I got to receive him there," the president said. "He was dying. He was hoarse. He could hardly talk. He kind of croaked when they set up the mike by the pitcher's mound. It was tragic. He was hollow. His whole great shape was gaunt and hollowed out."

The president was asked if he had a baseball hero as a youth.

"Oh, sure. Lou Gehrig. I never met him. But there was something about him. The example he set."

The president insisted sports heroes are role models and because of this have an obligation to the nation's youth.

"I know that's a cliché," he acknowledged. "But I think competitive athletics is a great antidote to some of the bad things out there. When one [player] falls, it breaks the heart of a lot of young people. Pete Rose probably is a good example of that."

Sports columnist George Vecsey, who often doubles in sociology, suggested that athletes aren't always the best role models, that they sometimes have feet of clay.

Replied the president: "I don't think you can judge a whole hero worship by several figures who betray a trust."

It was pointed out that because of television most of the playoff and World Series games would be played at night, when children are asleep.

What did he think about the kids staying up past their bedtime?

The president smiled.

"I would think they can stay up late for a World Series game. I give them my permission."

A Midsummer Classic:
Where It All Began

WEDNESDAY, JANUARY 10, 1990

HOW IT BEGAN ACCORDING TO TOM LITTLEWOOD, author of the recently published *Arch—A Promoter Not a Poet:* "Edward J. Kelly, then the mayor of Chicago, approached his friend, Colonel Bertie McCormick, publisher of the powerful *Chicago Tribune*. Kelly thought it would be appropriate if a sports event could be arranged as an adjunct to the World's Fair.

"'We've got the man you want right here,'" McCormick said.

Five minutes later, sports editor Arch Ward was in McCormick's office.

It was 1933, the Chicago centennial. The city was strangling in the grip of the Depression. Municipal government was on the edge of bankruptcy. Many downtown hotels were in receivership. But a remarkable number of business leaders put up money for a gala "Century of Progress," an exposition that evolved into the famous Chicago World's Fair.

"Arch knew just what he wanted to do," biographer Littlewood explained. "The idea of having a baseball game between the best players of the American League and the best players of the National League did not originate with Arch Ward, contrary to the impression he sometimes left in later years.

"The best teams in each league met every autumn in the World Series, of course. But as soon as the second league [the American, in 1900] was created, there had been fascination with the thought of assembling the

120

best players from all the teams in one league against the cream of the other league."

As early as 1915, F. C. Lane, the editor of *Baseball Magazine,* proposed "an All-Star baseball contest for a greater championship." But Lane met with rejection the several times he discussed this possibility with the league presidents and club owners. The answer was always no.

On April 13, 1933, Arch Ward went to the office of Will Harridge, then the president of the American League. Harridge's headquarters were on Michigan Avenue, just down the street from the *Tribune.*

The office of Kenesaw Mountain Landis, who had risen from a Chicago-based federal judge to become baseball's first commissioner, was four blocks closer to the *Tribune.* But Landis was an autocrat who ruled with an iron fist. More than likely, Ward was in awe of Landis and, like many ballplayers and owners, uncomfortable in his fierce presence. Harridge was a kinder and considerably more gentle soul.

Ward had anticipated some of Harridge's objections. The season had begun, the schedule was set in concrete. If an open date was available, how would the players gather in Chicago on such short notice? Why should the clubs risk injury to their best players in a meaningless exhibition game? Who would pick the teams? Once a precedent was established, wouldn't other cities request future games? And the biggest problem of all: what if it rained on the day of the game?

"Dad never thought the game would go beyond one year," said Thomas Ward, Arch's son. Tom, 66, Ward's only survivor, is a professor at Northwestern University, teaching public relations; for many years he was the press relations officer in Chicago with U.S. Steel.

"Dad felt this was strictly a one-shot promotion," Tom said. "It was the height of the Depression. He believed he could fill Comiskey Park. He was supremely confident it could be done.

"When Colonel McCormick said, 'What happens if nobody shows up?' Dad said, 'You can take the losses out of my paycheck.' And the Colonel said, 'If you're that confident, we'll underwrite it.'"

Convincing the owners was much more difficult. After Harridge agreed to put the proposal on the agenda for the next A.L. owners' meeting, May 9 in Cleveland, Ward went to work on the N.L. He contacted William L. Veeck, the father of Bill Veeck. The elder Veeck, a former Chicago baseball writer, was then president of the Cubs.

Cub owner Philip K. Wrigley was against the idea, arguing that an interleague, midsummer game was likely to diminish interest in the World Series. When Veeck reminded him of the potential harm in antagonizing the *Tribune,* Wrigley had second thoughts. Reluctantly, Wrigley gave his approval.

On May 15, three weeks after Ward's first meeting with Harridge, N.L. President John Heydler polled his owners. St. Louis, Boston, and New York were opposed. Of the three clubs, the Giants had a legitimate complaint. Owner Horace Stoneham contended that if the game were played on July 6, as proposed, it would be a burden on his club. The Giants had doubleheaders in Boston July 4 and 5 and a single game on July 6—five games in three days.

Ward responded to the challenge. Stoneham and Sam Breadon, the owner of the Cardinals, were buried under a blizzard of telegrams and telephone calls, orchestrated by Ward. Stoneham and Breadon wilted under the pressure.

That left only the Boston Braves. According to an unconfirmed report, Ward called the Braves and said: "We're going to announce the game the day after tomorrow. And either we're going to announce there is a game or that we almost had one and didn't because of you."

Contrary to legend, Ward was given a rain date, July 7. The game was played on July 6 in ideal weather and drew a paid crowd of 49,200. Ward selected the managers: Connie Mack of the Philadelphia Athletics for the A.L., John McGraw of the Giants for the N.L. The players were chosen by public ballot conducted by 55 newspapers, which relayed their tabulations to the *Tribune.*

The A.L. won 4–2 on a two-run home run by Babe Ruth.

"That's a grand show," said Judge Landis, who immediately decreed that the All-Star Game should become an annual fixture.

"Dad never thought it would go beyond that one year," said Tom Ward. "He was very surprised."

Archibald Burdette Ward, orphaned at the age of 12, was born on December 27, 1886, in Kankakee County and was the sports editor of the *Tribune* for 25 years.

He died on July 9, 1955, and was buried the morning of the 22nd All-Star Game, which was played in Milwaukee. He also originated the college All-Star football game and founded a professional football league, the old All-American Conference. His detractors described it as the "Arch-America Conference." But that's another story.

Buckner Survives
That Infamous E-3

THURSDAY, APRIL 19, 1990

"WHERE HAVE YOU GONE, BILL BUCKNER?" I was humming that tune en route to Comiskey Park Wednesday night, and of course, there he was: Billy Buck, the original, or what's left of him, age 40, back for a return run with the Boston Red Sox, still with the bad wheels, but as always, exuding good cheer.

I said hello and asked if after 19 full big-league seasons and parts of two others, he was finally relaxed and feeling comfortable.

"I wish I could say yes," Buckner replied. "You'd think someone who has been as successful as I've been could relax and have fun. But whatever I do, or have done, it never seemed like it was enough. If I got three hits, instead of enjoying the three hits, by the time I got home I was always thinking, 'I've got to do it again tomorrow.'"

Buckner chuckled in amusement. He was in the visitors' dugout, waiting to take batting practice.

"Right now, I'm just trying to get three at-bats."

Buckner, of course, has had more than his share of three-hit games. A three-time Chicago Player of the Year when he was with the Cubs, he is now hanging on—hoping for one more season.

"I think I can still hit," he said. "Maybe I'm crazy, just kidding myself. But if I can play every day, get into a groove, I know I can hit."

I believe him. He played enough in spring training to get his rhythm. He appeared in seven Florida exhibition games and batted .386. For his good work, he earned a spot on Boston's expanded roster.

"He's a dedicated ballplayer," said Joe Morgan, Boston manager. "In some ways he reminds me of me. He loves to play, and he plays to win. And there's something else about him that you've got to admire."

And what is that something else?

"It took a lot of guts for him to come back to our town. Lots of players don't have that kind of courage."

Buckner, it will be recalled, allowed a ground ball to roll through his legs at first base in the sixth game of the 1986 World Series. That error helped the Mets come from behind for a tie. The Mets won the Series in the next game.

"It was a bad rap," Morgan insisted. "Everybody blamed Buckner, but what about that wild pitch, or was it a passed ball? They're still not sure what it was, but that was more damaging. And even if he had made that play, there is no assurance we would have won. People forget the next day we had a 3–0 lead with [Bruce] Hurst pitching and we lost the game. We had a thousand chances to win, and all everybody talks about is the one ball that went through his legs."

Buckner was released during the 1987 season, then caught on with the California Angels. Released again, he was re-signed by the Kansas City Royals. When Nick Esasky, Boston's first baseman, fled to Atlanta last winter, Buckner began pounding on the door of Lou Gorman, the Red Sox general manager.

"I told him," Buckner said, "Lou, all I want is to go to spring training and make the club."

Although Buckner made the club, there's no assurance he will remain beyond April 30, when all of the clubs must cut at least two players. Morgan used Billy Buck principally as a pinch-batter. "At this point, I don't know if we can keep him," Morgan said. "It could go either way. There's a chance he might stick."

Buckner has more hits—2,708—than any other active big leaguer. He also possesses an enormous storehouse of valuable information.

"He's great to have on the bench," Morgan revealed. "He gives me advice, inside stuff on what pitches some of the hitters like to hit. No question he's studied the other hitters. And when he tells me something, he's not guessing. He knows what he's talking about."

Remarkably, the Boston fans have also come to know that Buckner's World Series boot wasn't fatal and responded with a standing ovation during the Opening Day ceremonies at Fenway Park.

"I kind of suspected the fans were going to give him a hand," Morgan said. "But I didn't think it would be forever. It was as long as any I've heard."

"It surprised me the way it's turned around," Buckner said Wednesday.

Moreover, the applause has not stopped. The fans have given him a standing "O" every time he has come to the plate. "It's crazy," Buckner said. "It's been great."

It would be better yet for Buckner if he can get more at-bats. He has had only five plate appearances and one hit for a .200 average.

"To me, he'll always be one of the great hitters," said White Sox coach Barry Foote, who was among Buckner's Cub teammates. "He keeps it simple. He has a short stroke and a small stride. He's got it down to the point where very little can go wrong."

Foote also remembers Buckner as a ballplayer with rare perseverance.

"He's had four operations on one ankle," Foote said. "But he never gave up. I remember there was a time when he couldn't even walk. He had to support himself with a cane. But he kept soaking his ankle. For hours and hours. I'd say he's one ballplayer with a lot of courage."

Amen.

Bill Veeck:
An Uncommon Man
Merits the Fanfare

WEDNESDAY, FEBRUARY 27, 1991

MY MOST VIVID MEMORY OF BILL VEECK had nothing to do with baseball.

The man who was voted into the Hall of Fame Tuesday by the veterans committee had gone to Tilden High School on the south side of Chicago to make a speech. Every year, during the 20-some seasons he operated ballclubs, he led the league in speeches—probably an average of two or three a day.

While at Tilden, he fell and slipped in the bathroom. This was some 12 years ago, during his second ownership term with the White Sox. Several nights later, I was among his visitors at Illinois Masonic Hospital. Roland Hemond was also there, and so were Dr. Sid Shafer and Nick Kladis.

And what I have never forgotten is how Bill Veeck propped himself up in bed and wiggled his left knee, the "good knee," which had been fractured in the Tilden fall. He worked it sideways and up and down, a cheerful demonstration of how he had won again and was on the road to recovery.

It then occurred to me that, physically, he was the most courageous person I had ever known. Here was a man with one leg, in pain, but laughing in defiance. Anyone else would have been moaning and whining, "Why did this have to happen to me?"

Not Bill Veeck. He lost most of his right leg at Bougainville, when he was in the marine corps during World War II. Subsequently he underwent at least two dozen surgeries, mostly skin grafts. In the 30 years I knew him, I never heard him complain.

The only time I recall him mentioning his peg leg, the right leg, was early one morning while he was soaking the stump. It was a daily two-hour ritual. Typically, he only saw the benefits, the upside. Because he had to sit, he explained, he had more time to read.

Curious about the world around him, he was a voracious reader. He read probably an average of five books a week, mostly nonfiction, on subjects big and small. Nothing seemed to escape him. He was, in fact, a closet intellectual, but, of course, would never admit it. Once, when Hank Greenberg, for many years his closest friend, chided him for concealing his wide-ranging intellect, Veeck said, "Hank, here's another beer."

There were times when I was convinced that if he had to do it over again, he would go to law school and become an attorney—champion of the people. This may be hard for some of the current owners to believe but it was Bill Veeck who came up with the idea that ballplayers should be "depreciated," just like oil wells.

This was in the early fifties, when Veeck owned the St. Louis Browns. His principal attorney at that time was the late Sidney Schiff, a Chicagoan with a national reputation for vast legal knowledge. Veeck carried his idea to Schiff.

Schiff listened, but according to Mary Frances, Veeck's widow, "had his doubts. He was not convinced it would fly." A couple of years later there was an amendment to the federal tax laws: ballplayers, because they diminished in value, were depreciable.

Veeck had a substantial regard for lawyers and the legal process. He also had an obvious respect for writers. If my memory is correct, his favorite sportswriter was the late John Lardner, who for many years did a weekly column for *Newsweek* magazine.

After he sold the White Sox the second time, Veeck covered the World Series for a national magazine. He approached the assignment with remarkable sincerity: a rookie reporter trying to make the grade. All the sportswriters watched him as he sat in the press box. Veeck did his best to keep a low profile. I can still seem him on the press bus, squirreling under his topcoat, to make himself less recognizable.

Bill Veeck had saved the White Sox for Chicago. In 1975, when the late John Allyn owned the club, there was a genuine threat that the franchise would be moved to Seattle, which was suing the baseball establishment because of the loss of the Seattle Pilots. Andrew McKenna alerted Veeck to the emergency. He urged him to leave his Easton, Maryland, estate and return to Chicago, pronto. Veeck did just that and, in about two weeks, organized a purchase group.

Above all, he was an idealist. He broke the American League color line, during his ownership of the Cleveland Indians, when he brought up Larry Doby. Veeck marched at Selma, Alabama.

When John F. Kennedy was assassinated, Veeck and his son, Mike, flew to Washington, where they were joined by Fred Krehbiel, one of Veeck's nephews, then a student at Georgetown. The three of them got in the long line of people who wanted to view Kennedy as he lay in state in the rotunda of the Capitol. It was a cold night. Veeck was recognized. Because of his celebrity, also because he had been a marine and wounded during World War II, he was told it was not necessary for him to wait, that he and his party would be escorted to the front of the line. Veeck refused. He would wait his turn.

Veeck never pulled rank. He regarded himself as nothing more, or less, than the common man. Mary Frances, who will make the acceptance speech in Cooperstown, selected Aaron Copland's "Fanfare for the Common Man" as the theme music for his memorial Mass.

She also used this quotation from Henry David Thoreau for the Mass card: "If a man doesn't keep pace with his companions, perhaps it is because he hears a different drummer. Let him step to the music which he hears, however measured or faraway."

The midget was the least of his accomplishments.

DiMaggio Still a True Yankee Blue Blood

SUNDAY, MAY 19, 1991

THE SONG LYRIC "WHERE HAVE YOU GONE, JOE DIMAGGIO?/A nation turns its lonely eyes to you" would not have been appropriate Saturday. The often-reclusive Joe D was in Arlington Heights for the unveiling of his statue—a 12-foot heroic bronze that forevermore will guard the main entrance of the National Italian-American Sports Hall of Fame.

The Ferdinand Rebechini sculpture weighs 16,000 pounds and is a remarkably accurate likeness of the great center fielder at the end of his powerful swing. "Very nice," he said after being introduced by Jack Brickhouse.

During the introductions, DiMaggio was hailed as the "Caruso of Baseball," also as "baseball's perfect baseball player," which is precisely what he was.

He excelled in all five areas of play: he hit for average, .325 lifetime; with power, 361 home runs; was the best defensive center fielder of his time; was swift afoot; and had a gun for an arm. His most revealing stat: 369 career strikeouts, only eight more than his career homers.

Today, when many of the big sluggers strike out as many as 150 times per season, sometimes more, DiMaggio had only one season when he struck out as many as 39 times. This was in 1936, his rookie year, when he was adjusting to big-league pitching. From the beginning he used a heavy, 36-ounce bat, and was a line-drive hitter who seldom swung for the fences. He played half of his games in Yankee Stadium, a graveyard for right-handed batters; only three of his home runs cleared in left center, a distance, at that time, of about 430 feet.

The unveiling of "The Yankee Clipper" was timed in celebration of the 50th anniversary of his epic 56-game hitting streak. It is baseball's most enduring record. Fifty years ago Saturday was the fourth game of the streak: 3-for-3 against the St. Louis Browns. In the half century since only one player—Pete Rose with 44 in 1978—has come close.

"I've often said one day the streak would be broken," DiMaggio said before pausing and allowing himself the rare luxury of a small grin. "But I've been saying that for 50 years."

He was, as always, a picture of sartorial splendor: dark gray slacks, a blue sports coat, a white shirt, and a dotted red tie. He has thinning gray hair and a ruddy complexion. At 76, he is an American hero grown to mythic proportions.

"These days I'm as mobile as that statue," he said, his first sentence after the unveiling. He weighs 190 pounds, 5 less than what he carried 40 years ago when he played his last season. Age and arthritis have had a shrinking effect. He has lost two inches from his 6'2" frame.

The arthritis is in the upper part of his arms, his chest, and his back. Most of the pain is in the rotator cuffs, a common ailment for pitchers, not hitters. Another irony: he has no problem with his knees and legs, which gave him the most trouble when he was a player.

"The rotator cuffs are torn from sliding," he explained. "I'd break my slide with my arms. I didn't protect my arms."

Several times he was asked which game, or games, or which hit during the streak did he consider the most important, or the most memorable. He insisted he had no special memory of any one blow. He also indicated he wasn't overwhelmed by the pressure but was irked somewhat when, after he had hit safely in 30 games, he was advised that the all-time record was 44 games by Wee Willie Keeler (set in the 19th century) not 42 by George Sisler.

"I knew sooner or later it had to end," he said. "When it ended I felt bad about it. For a couple of days. I never thought I'd feel that way. That surprised me.

"Winning, winning—that was more important than the streak," he insisted. During his 13 seasons, the Yankees won 10 pennants and nine world championships. "Winning those pennants, those were my biggest accomplishments," he said. "I'm proud of my records but they're just a bonus."

Still, there was one cherished moment during the 1941 season, the moment that provided his biggest thrill.

It occurred after a day game against the Senators in Washington. He and his pal, the late Lefty Gomez, had made dinner plans and had tickets for the theater.

"We were staying at the Shoreham Hotel," DiMaggio recalled. "Lefty said, 'I've got to go up to George Selkirk's room. He's got something for me.'

"I told him, 'Lefty we don't have time. We're late.' But Lefty said no, he had to go up to Selkirk's room. He dragged me along.

"When he opened the door, all the Yankee players were there, all of them holding a glass of red wine. They toasted me and sang 'For He's a Jolly Good Fellow.' This was two or three days after the streak was broken."

Only once did DiMaggio express dissatisfaction during his five hours at this Hall of Fame. This was when someone mentioned he had made a quick exit last Saturday in Boston during a Fenway Park celebration for Ted Williams.

"They booked me in Boston without my approval," DiMaggio said in his defense. As for his hasty departure, he said, "I had to leave. I had an appointment."

DiMaggio, however, more than made up for it Saturday. He submitted to lengthy interviews from three television networks and also spent considerable time with local reporters.

Father of the Hall
Loved His Baby

SUNDAY, JULY 21, 1991

FOR ME, THE STORY OF HOW THE HALL OF FAME BEGAN is of endless fascination. What follows is a 1972 reminiscence of late baseball Commissioner Ford Frick, a one-time sportswriter and the founder of baseball's Valhalla. It is taken, with the author's permission, from the book *No Cheering in the Press Box:*

> The thing I'm proudest of in baseball is the Hall of Fame in Cooperstown. That's my baby. I started it. This was in 1936 when I was still president of the National League and Judge [Kenesaw Mountain] Landis was the commissioner. There's a big portrait of me up there which I didn't like. It says I was the father of the whole thing.
>
> Judge Landis never liked the idea, never warmed up to it, probably because he didn't think of it first. Maybe I shouldn't say that because I loved the judge. He was a great guy but a stubborn son-of-a-gun.
>
> Once the Hall of Fame was established each of the two major leagues would set aside $5,000, a subsidy to help run the place. The owners would get together at the annual joint meeting and every year I'd make the motion to renew our pledge for the $5,000. And every time it came up the judge would say, "What is this god-damned Hall of Fame business?"

Finally, I got mad and said, "Now, listen, Judge, you've been asking that for the last four years, and I've always answered it. If you don't know by now, to hell with it!"

The Judge did go up there, in '39, made a beautiful dedication speech. But he never went back.

I've heard people say it's a publicity man's dream. Maybe it is. But I think of it as more than that, something more substantial. I think of it as tying together yesterday and today. It keeps the continuity and it gives the oldsters a chance to discuss and relive their times. You can compare the moderns with the ancients. I always believed history is important, that we should mark what has come before.

One of the greatest things is the Hall of Fame dinner, when these old guys come back. Every player in the Hall of Fame is invited back to Cooperstown every year, all expenses paid. They participate in the ceremonies and welcome the new players being inducted. Between 20 and 25 Hall of Famers come back every year. They get here about two days early and they sit into the night on that big porch at the Otesaga Hotel, swapping lies and reliving the old days.

Waite Hoyt, Charley Gehringer, Bill Terry, Zack Wheat, Eddie Roush, Red Ruffing, and many others. Cy Young came back year after year until he was unable. Ed Walsh never missed. Even Ty Cobb. He softened in later years. He was always there. I suppose you can say that in the beginning the Hall of Fame was a vision—and it came to pass.

It will always be a happy time for the people who are there, and as people pass on someone takes their place. Other fellows come along. I thought when Cy Young was gone, and Connie Mack, that that would change the atmosphere. But it didn't.

Ed Walsh died. Eddie Collins died, and the Babe died, and Alexander died. It didn't change. Last year it was George Weiss and Heinie Manush. This year three of them won't be there. Two or three die every year. But everybody talks about these guys as if they were still alive. They're just not there, that's all.

The whole thing started with the discovery of the so-called Doubleday Baseball. That was the excuse. The old ball was found on the Graves farm around Cooperstown, in an old trunk. Abner

Graves, supposedly, had played baseball with General Abner Doubleday.

Stephen Clark, a resident of Cooperstown, heard about the ball and bought it for $5. Mr. Clark is a historian, a philanthropist, very museum-minded. He had a baseball collection of his own, old paints and prints. He took this Doubleday Ball—it's all falling apart—had it mounted, and put it on display with his other stuff in the Otesaga Historical Society. And he assigned a member of his staff, Alexander Cleland, to look around and find some other authentic baseball relics.

Mr. Cleland came down to New York, to the National League office, to see me. I had known him from several years before. I'd been up to Cooperstown when I was a sportswriter; I had done a few stories. And he said the people in Cooperstown wanted to have some sort of baseball celebration. They wanted to get some publicity and get the newspapermen up there. He suggested we pick an all-star team and play a game up there—sort of a one-day holiday.

I said, "Hell, why do that? If you're going to do that, why not start a baseball museum—a Hall of Fame—and have something that will last?"

That's the way it started: Mr. Clark was the financial agent. He was a businessman, in Singer sewing machines. That's where the family got their fortune.

I called a meeting with the wire service writers. I can tell you who was there—Davis Walsh of the International News Service, Alan Gould of the Associated Press, and Henry Farrell of the United Press. They picked it up and said they would recommend it to the Baseball Writers Association.

It was Alan Gould who said that 75 percent of the votes should be required for induction. That rule still stands today. Five players made it in the first election—the Babe, Honus Wagner, Cobb, Mathewson, and Walter Johnson.

It's a funny thing about us writers. We build everybody up but we forget ourselves—our own kind, our comrades who through the years made America a great sports nation. One of the reasons I wanted a library at Cooperstown was to take care of all the records and to gather some of the written material of the past.

Now someone who wants to do research, whether for a magazine article or a documented book, can go to Cooperstown and find all the material.

And we have one corner in the museum dedicated to the baseball writers. Lord, that's the way it should be. The names of all the presidents of the Baseball Writers Association are listed. We have some old typewriters and a big, broken-down camera, and Graham McNamee's microphone, the one he used.

Across the way we have a room dedicated to cartoonists, with original cartoons by Tad, Bob Edgren, and Davenport, and all those fellows who started the cartooning business. Willard Mullin gave us his drawing board.

At first, a writer had to be dead before he was elected to the Hall of Fame. But this year, for the first time, two writers will be inducted who are alive—Dan Daniel and Fred Lieb. That's the way it should be. After all, it's nice to smell the roses.

Editor's note: Jerome Holtzman was awarded the J. G. Taylor Spink Award by the Hall of Fame in 1989 and is recognized in the Hall's "Scribes & Mikemen" exhibit.

Tinkering with Cub
Double-Play Legend

THURSDAY, MAY 14, 1992

RYNE SANDBERG STOLE HIS 300TH BASE in Houston Monday night and immediately was linked with two Cub heroes of the gloried past. Four more steals, and Sandberg will tie Joe Tinker for second place on the club's all-time list. After that, Sandberg's target is Frank Chance, who leads with 401 stolen bases.

Whether Sandberg will break Chance's record can be set aside for future debate. But the sudden mention of Tinker and Chance brings to mind that in baseball, as in life, the pen is stronger than the sword. Because of a press-box poet, the Cubs continue to have baseball's most storied double-play combination.

In 1908, when Franklin P. Adams was covering the New York Giants for the *New York Globe*, he wrote one of the most famous poems in baseball history:

> These are the saddest possible words,
> Tinker to Evers to Chance.
> Trio of Bear Cubs fleeter than birds,
> Tinker to Evers to Chance.
> Ruthlessly pricking our gonfalon bubble.
> Making a Giant hit into a double.
> Words that are weighty with nothing but trouble,
> Tinker to Evers to Chance.

137

But how good was this trio of so-called Bear Cubs? More than likely, they were an above-average double-play combination, but not much more.

In 1954, Charles Segar, then the National League publicist, exhumed the box scores and discovered that in 1908, there were only eight Joe Tinker-to-Johnny Evers-to-Frank Chance twin-killings. In scoring parlance, the shortstop-to-second-to-first double play is logged as 6-4-3.

Segar went through the records from 1906 through 1909, when the legendary trio was at its peak. His findings revealed a four-season total of 29 Tinker-to-Evers-to-Chance double plays: eight in 1906, seven in 1907, eight in 1908, and six in 1909.

Segar also checked the reverse, 4-6-3s, started by Evers, not Tinker. The numbers were essentially the same—25 Evers-to-Tinker-to-Chance double plays. So in these four years, the combined total, both ways, was 54. Also, they never led the league in double plays.

For purposes of comparisons, the Cubs' 1969 combination of Don Kessinger, Glenn Beckert, and Ernie Banks, in that one year, completed 36 double plays—20 by the 6-4-3 route, 16 by 4-6-3. Assuming this was an average season, their four-year total would have been almost three times more than the Tinker-Evers-Chance triumvirate.

The numbers for last season were essentially the same: Shawon Dunston, Sandberg, and Mark Grace together turned 35—11 started by Dunston, 24 by Sandberg. Again, the projected four-year aggregate would have been more than three times the 1908 total.

These increases, it can be argued, could be attributed to a variety of changes: much larger gloves, a livelier ball, and the truer bounce provided by artificial turf. Also, in olden times, there were fewer opportunities because of the emphasis on playing for one run, meaning more stolen bases and hit-and-run attempts designed to prevent the double play.

Still, when considering that today's schedule is eight games longer, the degree of change is not as large as would be expected. In 1908, the N.L. average per team was 75 double plays; last year it was 127.

There is this footnote about the Tinker-Evers relationship: one day during the 1908 season, Tinker became upset when Evers (known as the

"Crab" for his surly disposition) took a taxi to the ballpark and didn't offer Tinker a ride. According to published reports, which I don't completely believe, they didn't speak to each other for 22 years—not until 1930, when they met at a Chicago radio station.

Evers was quoted as saying: "At the sight of each other, we had that old feeling again—meaning we wanted to fight. We started toward each other, and what do you think happened? We threw our arms around each other and cried like a couple of babies."

Interestingly, in his 1910 biography *Touching Second,* Evers gives only cursory attention to Tinker. The only time he mentions Tinker at length, he knocks him: "After we had a split a tough doubleheader [late in the 1908 season], the players, returning to their hotel in carriages, were silent and downhearted. Not a word was spoken for a long time. Suddenly, Tinker remarked to Chance, 'Well, Cap, I guess it's all off. Let's break training and make a night of it.'

" 'No,' Chance replied. 'We may win yet.' " Which is what the Cubs did, their third consecutive pennant.

The effect of Adams' poem was apparent 38 years later, in the 1946 Hall of Fame elections, but it took a while.

None of the candidates, including the legendary threesome, received the necessary 75 percent of the baseball writers' vote for canonization. Chance was named on 144 ballots, 8 fewer than required. Evers was second with 130. Tinker had only 55 and was not among the top 10.

A runoff was held, with 197 needed to elect. Again, Chance and Evers finished 1-2 but were short. Chance received 150 votes, Evers 110. Tinker brought up the rear.

Confronted with the prospect of an empty Cooperstown stage, a six-man Hall of Fame committee responded by anointing nine players, including Tinker, Evers, and Chance. In effect, they went in as a unit. Nothing like that has ever happened before or, since.

It's Been a Long,
Deliberate Journey for the Ump
His Colleagues Call "God"

THURSDAY, JULY 2, 1992

HE WAS A ROOKIE, his first time in St. Louis, working his third plate game, the Dodgers against the Cardinals. Ninth inning, two outs, score tied, full count, Don Drysdale pitching and Stan Musial coiled, ready to swing.

Drysdale delivered. Doug Harvey, seeing the ball in flight, raised his right arm, signaling strike three. It was 30 years ago, in 1962, but Harvey has not forgotten. The pitch broke to the outside and missed the plate by six inches.

"And there I am standing with egg on my face, the crowd booing," Harvey recalled. "Musial never looked at me. He told the batboy to bring him his glove. Then, without turning, he said, 'Young fellow, I don't know what league you came from, but we use the same plate. It's 17 inches wide.'"

Immediately, Harvey learned two lessons: "That's when I realized why they called him 'Stan the Man.' And I learned not to anticipate the call."

Harvey estimates it took him five years to slow down. He has been preaching this ever since to the dozens of young National League umpires entrusted to his care. Two things are crucial: to get into the proper position and to wait for the play to be completed.

This is Harvey's 18th season as a crew chief, possibly a record for longevity. But this much is certain: he was baseball's first $100,000 umpire,

140

and including his postseason share, last year became the first $200,000 umpire.

Which is as it should be.

He is held in such awe by his fellow umps that some years ago they began calling him God. Initially, he recoiled at the appellation. Now he dismisses it with a silent smile. For Christmas four years ago, his wife, Joy, presented him with a T-shirt inscribed: "We'll Get Along Just Fine as Soon as You Realize I'm God."

We were having breakfast Wednesday at the Ambassador East Hotel. I asked "God" how many calls he had missed—aware, of course, that Bill Klem, a legendary umpire of long ago, once remarked, "I never missed one in my life, not in my heart."

Harvey neither confirmed nor denied he had missed any calls.

"At the time I made it, it was what I saw," he replied. "But with experience you learn to take a better and longer look at each play and each pitch."

He went on to explain that when he reached the big leagues there was no such thing as timing.

"Everything was called too quickly," he said. "I've got a photograph of Jocko Conlan working first base. Jocko's arm was extended in the out call. But the runner was still short of the bag, and the ball was still in flight. In those days it was common to anticipate the call."

Harvey paused. The waiter refilled his cup.

"I introduced timing to umpiring," he continued. "That's my gift to baseball. My heritage. My legacy. Before, the umpires were always told, 'Be quick! Be decisive!'"

Harvey insists it's better to delay and get it right.

His advice to aspiring umpires: "When you're working first base you watch the ball being thrown well past the halfway mark. Then you leave the ball. The computer in your brain lets you know when the ball will get there. So then you look at the bag, for the feet, and listen for the ball to hit the glove, and you decide who got there first, the ball or the runner. Then you look for the ball to see if the first baseman is juggling it or dropped it. You don't make the call until the runner has run past the bag.

"On a pitched ball, the ball must hit the catcher's glove. Then you make the call.

"On a tag play, look to see if the man stayed on the base, then look to see if the fielder held onto the ball."

The umpire doesn't sit but, of course, has the best seat in the house. He also sees the players as nobody else sees them.

"Willie Mays never complained," Harvey recalled. "Or Ernie Banks. Richie Allen was a sweetheart, loved mankind, loved the umpires. Sandy Koufax never gave me any trouble. Augie Donatelli hated him. Augie had Sandy in his early years, when Sandy couldn't get within a foot of the plate. And when he got one that was close, only six or four inches off, he wanted it for a strike. By the time I came along, he was throwing nothing but strikes.

"One night in Philadelphia, Sandy couldn't get his curveball over. After the first inning he gave it up. I never saw anything like it. The rest of the game he threw nothing but fastballs. It was in '66, the last game of the regular season. The Dodgers had to have it to win.

"Richie Allen came up in the ninth and said, 'I know he's throwing nothing but the heater. But I can hit it.' "

Harvey laughed at the memory.

"It was power against power. Four pitches later Richie yelled, 'Man, he got me.' "

Of all the hitters he has seen, Harvey said there were only two, Allen and Billy Williams, who could make a bat hum.

"I mean a real humming sound," Harvey said. "You could actually hear it."

Unlike most superstars, Williams "griped a little."

"Billy Williams always said that me and Shag Crawford called the inside corner too tight on him," said Harvey. "Later, Shag kidded him and always told him, 'Billy, Doug and I taught you how to hit the inside pitch. You should thank us.' "

Harvey laughed. "In the years since, every time I see him he swings his hand next to his stomach. And I do the same."

Harvey had the plate for the Cubs/Mets game Tuesday night and called the Mets' Chico Walker, the last batter, out on a pitch on the inside corner. After the game, when they were crossing paths, Williams, now the Cubs' batting coach, shouted to Harvey, "You old son of a gun, you're still calling that pitch."

But not much longer. Harvey retires after this season. He will return to Wrigley Field only once more, in August. The Cubs should dig up the plate and give it to him as a memento of his distinguished career.

Marge Schott
and Freedom of
Offensive Speech

THURSDAY, DECEMBER 3, 1992

THE MARGE SCHOTT CONTROVERSY, which has grown into a media circus, presents an interesting legal question of freedom of speech. She is the owner of the Cincinnati Reds and has been accused of making oral slurs against blacks and Jews, the usual targets.

Home-run king Hank Aaron, a vice president of the Atlanta Braves, insists Schott should be forced to sell her team and should be thrown out of baseball. Others, outraged but less militant, contend a one- or two-year suspension would be sufficient punishment.

Nobody knows how it will play out, but there is no doubt she will be reprimanded by her fellow owners, possibly next week in Louisville at the winter meetings, after the report of a subcommittee investigating the charges.

"We are going to fight the good fight," declared Steve Greenberg, baseball's deputy commissioner.

That's good to hear because I, too, have been fighting the good fight, beginning with two years in the U.S. Marine Corps during the big war: gung-ho for the pursuit of liberty and the freedom of speech, including offensive speech.

As I see it, Schott already is the big loser, not the African Americans or the Jews. Despite her denials, her reputation is damaged beyond repair.

144

If guilty as charged, she would be among the millions of similarly unenlightened people who have made unfair remarks about minorities, in private and without consequence.

For example, Reverend Jesse Jackson, the black leader, insulted 2 or 3 million Jews when he described them as "Hymies" and New York as "Hymietown." Jackson used this derogatory term in a personal aside. He apologized after his words were made public.

This was during the 1984 presidential campaign. Reverend Jackson wasn't forced to drop out of the race. And he received millions of votes in primaries.

Jackson has come full circle. A month or so ago he petitioned the commissioner's office requesting he be allowed to speak at the winter meetings. If he speaks, surely he will accuse the owners and their administrators of bigotry. His privilege, of course.

But, according to Greenberg, there is a difference. Baseball has no control over Jackson. Only those employed in the national pastime can be punished for what they say.

So the people working for ballclubs have forfeited their First Amendment rights?

"That is correct," Greenberg said. He also explained freedom of speech does not include "shouting fire in a crowded theater" or "fighting words" that, in essence, are slurs against race or religion.

I agree. Everyone, regardless of origin or religious preference, should be treated with respect.

I called Jay Miller, the executive director of the American Civil Liberties Union, and asked about an incident several years ago when a goon squad of self-proclaimed Nazis marched through downtown Skokie, Illinois, the home of many survivors of the Holocaust. The event was described accurately as "psychological rape."

The ACLU defended the marchers but has been silent on the Schott affair. I asked if the ACLU is planning to come to Schott's aid.

The ACLU supported the Nazi march, Miller said, because federal laws were endangered.

"Mrs. Schott doesn't fall under our purview, because it's not a government action," said Miller.

Still, the attempt to discipline someone for speech, not conduct, would seem to be a significant danger. Schott didn't demonstrate and throw eggs or rocks at the police. She did not inflict bodily harm. Nor is she guilty of theft or general dishonesty.

If true, her alleged crime is stupidity. If she is guilty, so is just about everyone else, blacks and Jews included. Who among us has not voiced prejudices?

Comparisons have been made between Schott and Al Campanis, the former general manager of the Los Angeles Dodgers. Campanis was an employee, not an owner. He was then 70, in his 44th season with the Dodgers.

Asked on national television why there were not more black managers and general managers, Campanis said they "lacked the necessities."

Two days later, Dodger owner Peter O'Malley fired Campanis. Cheers for O'Malley. But what only a few people knew is O'Malley, for several years, had been trying to dump Campanis and was now able to do so without being accused of age discrimination.

I have known Campanis for more than 30 years. He is not a bigot. However wrong, this was his sincere conviction. Happily, it has been proven erroneous. But there is also this to consider: would someone prejudiced against blacks hang a huge painting of Jackie Robinson in his living room?

I asked Greenberg what was the last time an owner was fined for something he said. Greenberg said it may have been in 1983, when then–White Sox President Eddie Einhorn said, "You know how you can tell when George Steinbrenner is lying? When his lips move."

Steinbrenner responded by calling Einhorn and Sox chairman Jerry Reinsdorf the "Katzenjammer Kids."

Bowie Kuhn, then the commissioner, fined all three parties $5,000. So much for history.

Hal McCoy, who covers the Reds for the *Dayton Daily News,* says it's not only African Americans and Jews who are on Schott's sore list.

"She dislikes everybody." McCoy said. "She's anti-human race.

"Last summer at the ballpark we were on an elevator with Bob Quinn [whom Schott recently fired from his general manager position]. And when Quinn got off, she said, "He's Irish Catholic and you know how those people are."

All of us have suffered from the remarks of small-minded people. But as I learned as a young boy, "Sticks and stones will break my bones but names will never harm me."

Schott has her supporters. Robert Kinney and his wife, Hallie, who is employed in the Reds ticket department, are in Schott's corner. "We have been to her house on two occasions," said Robert, "and each time we were treated like a king and queen."

The Kinneys are black.

Mrs. Schott recently fired her field manager, Lou Piniella, who is white, and appointed Tony Perez, a black Latino, to succeed him. At about this time, she approved the hiring of Hall-of-Famer Ferguson Jenkins as pitching coach.

Jenkins, a black, had his best years with the Cubs. The way I see it, Jenkins should be working at Wrigley Field. So should Randy Hundley. If the Cubs are prejudiced against Jenkins, they are equally prejudiced against Hundley, who is white. Fortunately, the Cub executives, as well as those of the other major league clubs, have the freedom of choice.

Understand, this isn't so much a defense of Schott and her privilege of alleged ignorance. Of considerably more importance is the necessity to honor and protect the Bill of Rights against the evils of Big Brother and thought control.

Lasorda's Godson
Could Well Become a Godsend

THURSDAY, MAY 13, 1993

HE WAS THE 1,389TH PLAYER selected in the 1988 summer draft of amateur free agents. The Dodgers picked him on the 62nd round and did it only as a favor to manager Tom Lasorda. He was still unsigned a month later, and so Lasorda had him come to Dodger Stadium for a special workout. The kid hit 15 balls into the bleachers.

"Get me his schedule, and I'll go out and see him play," scouting director Ben Wade told Lasorda.

"If a shortstop or a catcher did that you'd sign him right away, without seeing him play, wouldn't you?" Lasorda asked.

Wade agreed. But the kid was a slow first baseman.

"OK," Lasorda said. "As of right now he's a catcher."

And so began the professional baseball career of Michael Joseph Piazza, a powerfully built right-handed slugger out of Norristown, Pennsylvania. But there is much more to the story. Lasorda is Michael's godfather.

Five years later, and Piazza was at Wrigley Field. He had become the Dodgers' regular catcher, one of the National League's rookie stars.

I asked Brett Butler, the veteran center fielder, for an appraisal. Is the kid made of the right stuff?

"I've been in it 13 years," Butler said, "and I've never seen anybody who hit the ball as hard and as far as he does—consistently."

148

Butler was in the visiting clubhouse, preparing for the series finale against the Cubs.

I mentioned Willie Stargell, the former Pittsburgh slugger. I have seen Stargell hit two 500-foot home runs. The second one may have gone 600 feet. It disappeared into the trees a block beyond the right-field fence at Doubleday Field in Cooperstown, New York. It was against the White Sox in the annual Hall of Fame exhibition game.

"Sure, I saw Stargell," Butler said. "And I've seen Dale Murphy and Bob Horner. They hit the ball hard and far, but I'm talking consistency. This kid's consistent."

I wanted a second opinion.

"He probably does hit it farther than anybody," conceded Darryl Strawberry, 11 years in the big leagues, the author of 289 home runs.

"He hit a ball at Dodger Stadium," Strawberry said. "A line drive out of the park, no more than this high off the ground." Strawberry raised his hand over his head. "Man, it wasn't quick; it was awesome."

Eric Davis, another of the Dodgers' sluggers, joined the Piazza chorus.

"He's outstanding," Davis said. "His whole makeup. He's got an aura about him. It's an aura that says, 'I belong.' He's confident, and at this level you have to be that way."

This isn't Piazza's first visit to Wrigley Field. He was recalled from the minors last September 1 and made his major league debut here: two singles, a double, and a walk in four appearances.

Piazza was in the dugout, drinking in the scene. "I love this park," he said. "I don't know anybody in baseball who doesn't like this park."

Some pitchers would disagree. Still, the wind doesn't always blow out. On Monday, for example, Piazza twice hit the wall, one drive to left, the other to right. If the wind hadn't been blowing in, he would have had two more home runs.

"He has a chance to be something," said Don Drysdale, the Hall of Fame pitcher and a member of the Dodgers' broadcasting crew. "He's a very nice kid, hard-working, the kind of guy you're happy to be around. You hope it never changes."

Drysdale had second thoughts.

"Knowing him and his father, I don't think he'll change."

Mike's father, Vincent, has known Lasorda since he was a boy. They grew up, in modest circumstances, in Norristown. The elder Piazza now owns more than a dozen auto dealerships and was among the frustrated buyers of the San Francisco franchise when it appeared the Giants would be moved to Tampa Bay.

"My father never made it easy for us," Michael said. "He helped us out, but he taught us to appreciate and respect a buck, what it takes to earn it. I remember when I was 14 or 15 I told him I wanted an expensive guitar. He said, 'OK, go to work. Buy it with your own money.'"

When the Dodgers played in Philadelphia, Lasorda allowed one or more of Vincent's five sons to suit up during the pregame practices.

"Knowing Tommy was a big help to me," Mike conceded. "He helped me get the opportunity. But it doesn't help during a competitive major league season. There is only so much he can do. He can't play for me. He can't hit for me."

Piazza won the catchers' job, which was open, during spring training. He hit .450. "It was ludicrous," he said "People were saying he gave me the job because I was his godson."

Lasorda is, of course, delighted with Mike's success. "He worked hard," Lasorda observed. "He didn't get here because of his relationship with me."

"Have I told you about his youngest brother, Tommy?" Lasorda asked "You should see his swing, and he's only 11 years old. I'm his godfather, too."

Cardinals' Smith
Works His Wizardry
to Ward Off Age

SUNDAY, MARCH 27, 1994

IT IS AMONG THE MOST SPECTACULAR PLAYS CAUGHT ON FILM. Jeff Burroughs, a right-handed slugger, hits a ground ball up the middle. Expecting him to pull, shortstop Ozzie Smith is shading Burroughs toward third. Smith makes a long run and dives for the ball, his glove hand extended. The ball strikes a pebble and caroms to the left side of second base. In midair, he realizes his only play is with his bare hand. He makes the grab, scrambles to his feet, and throws Burroughs out.

"It was my best play," Smith said. "I've seen it about a half dozen times. I'll probably watch it a lot more after I retire."

Shortstop is a young man's position. If they don't retire in their mid-thirties they move to third base. But not Ozzie Smith of the St. Louis Cardinals. At 39, he is still their everyday shortstop.

How much longer can he go?

"Probably two or three more years," Smith replied.

He has an unusual contract: automatic renewal at $3 million a year if he makes 400 plate appearances (about 100 games).

I told him he had a pretty good deal.

"I earned it," he said.

Few, if any, players are more deserving. Easily the best fielding short-stop of his generation—the best since Luis Aparicio of the White Sox—

he has won 13 Gold Gloves and has appeared in 13 All-Star Games and three World Series. In a recent *Baseball Digest* poll of National League managers he was named the league's "smartest player."

Which isn't a surprise. Smith went to California State Polytechnic University in San Luis Obispo on an *academic* scholarship. He wasn't chosen in the annual summer draft of free agents until after his junior year in college. Most scouts wrote him off because he was only 5'11" and about 145 pounds.

"I've always had people tell me I'd never make it to the big leagues because of my size," Smith said. "The scouts are always looking for big guys who can hit the ball out of the park."

Smith made his first big-league connection in 1978 with the San Diego Padres, who traded him to the Cardinals four years later. At the time it seemed to be a good deal for the Padres.

But it turned out to be one of the best trades in Cardinals history, second only perhaps to the Lou Brock deal.

"Ozzie's just the best," said Joe Torre, the Cardinals manager. "And he's a good hitter, a lot better than most people give him credit for."

Early on, because he was so spectacular in the field—he was called the "Wizard of Oz"—Smith was typecast as strictly a defensive player. He didn't shake this label until he hit a ninth-inning, game-winning home run in the 1985 National League pennant playoffs. He has a career total of only 23 home runs, but seldom strikes out and has a .273 lifetime average. He is closing in on 2,500 hits.

A natural right-hander, he began switch-hitting as a college junior. "When you are a switch-hitter, it's almost like being two different people," he observed.

Initially, there is enormous difficulty because of the inability to generate power from the other side. But Smith believes that generally the switcher becomes a better hitter from his weak side because "you have to think and concentrate more."

When speaking at clinics, he always has special advice for the smaller players: learn the fundamentals, practice bunting, and always "have your head in the game." And he tells them the primary offensive objective is not the long ball but to hit to all fields and drive in runs. In 1987 he drove in 75 runs.

He also emphasizes the necessity of perseverance and endurance.

He said that people often ask him how much longer he expects to play. "They say, 'What do you feel is changing?'"

Smith concedes his energy level is diminishing.

"It's not as easy to come back for a day game after a night game," he said. "When you're 24 or 25 you never have to think about stealing a base. You run. But when you're 35 or 40 the same energy isn't there, so you might not try to steal."

The second oldest in a family of five, Smith grew up in Los Angeles. He lived across the street from a wood factory and practiced acrobatics in the sawdust. He gives much of the credit for his success to his parents, Clovis and Marvella Smith.

"My father always told me I had to work hard, and my mother emphasized education," he said. "I have been very fortunate."

So has baseball.

Briefing on Nixon:
Fan of White Sox,
Appling, Baseball

TUESDAY, APRIL 26, 1994

RICHARD M. NIXON, BASEBALL FAN, was then the vice president. It was late in the summer of 1959. The White Sox were en route to their first pennant in 40 years. Bob Elson, the late broadcaster, called Congressman John Kluczynski who called Congresswoman Marguerite Stitt Church, also from Illinois. A luncheon in tribute to the Sox players was arranged at the Old House Building in Washington.

The word must have been passed to Nixon because he was there and shook hands with each of the players as they entered the room.

"I remember it very well," Billy Pierce recalled. "He said to me, 'I almost kicked in the television set when Ed Fitz Gerald got that hit off you.'"

The year before, on June 27 in Comiskey Park, Pierce was pitching a perfect game against the Washington Senators—26 batters, 26 outs. Fitz Gerald, pinch hitting, destroyed the dream with a double down the first-base line.

"Gerry Staley was a couple guys behind me," Pierce said. "He told Staley he remembered when he was pitching for the Cardinals."

I was taking notes as Nixon met the players and have never forgotten that he identified Joe Stanka, an obscure right-handed pitcher. Nixon knew that, only a week earlier, the Sox had recalled Stanka from Sacramento in the Pacific Coast League.

I was amazed. Probably half the country's baseball writers were unaware that Stanka had been called up. When I repeated the incident, I was told that, more than likely, Nixon had been "briefed."

Ten years later, in 1969, the All-Star Game was played in Washington. Nixon was the president. Baseball Commissioner Bowie Kuhn arranged a White House reception for the players, managers, coaches, club executives, and some of the baseball writers.

In a rambling discourse in the Blue Room before the reception, Nixon revealed that as a boy growing up in Whittier, California, he was a White Sox fan. He recited the entire 1936 White Sox lineup. Luke Appling, he said, was his favorite player. Later I checked the lineup. He had it right.

It was then Nixon also said: "I like the job I have now. But if I had my life to live over again, I'd like to have ended up as a sportswriter."

This was during the Vietnam War. Nixon was not in full favor. The brash Maury Allen of the *New York Post*, when he met Nixon—there was a long receiving line—said: "It would have been wonderful if you *had* become a sportswriter."

Allen, recalling the incident, later said, "He just laughed and I moved on."

Nixon knew his baseball. When he met Joe DiMaggio, then the Oakland A's batting coach, Nixon mentioned Reggie Jackson, who was threatening the single-season Babe Ruth and Roger Maris home-run records.

"You're doing a good job teaching that fellow how to hit," Nixon told DiMaggio.

"No, I'm not," DiMaggio replied. "He's doing it all on his own."

When Nixon was out of office and in private practice with a Wall Street law firm, he was courted by the two diverse and still warring baseball factions.

In 1965, after Ford Frick's retirement as commissioner, Nixon removed himself from the owners' list of potential successors. According to William

Mead and Paul Dickson, coauthors of *Baseball: The President's Game,*
Nixon was offered a $100,000 salary and an unlimited expense account.
He told the owners not to mention it to his wife.

"Don't tell Pat," he said. "She'd kill me for turning you down."

Soon thereafter, in January of 1966, according to Jim Bunning, Nixon
was asked if he would represent the Players Association, then—as now—
warring with management.

Now a Republican congressman representing Kentucky's fourth dis-
trict, Bunning was then a big-league pitcher and player activist. Bunning
seems to have a vivid recollection of a players' committee meeting with
Nixon, first in Nixon's law office and continuing at lunch in a Wall Street
restaurant.

"He knew more about baseball than anyone we interviewed," Bunning
said. "We wanted him to be our number one horse. He told us he had
other plans."

According to Bunning, also present were player reps Harvey Kuenn,
Bob Friend, and Robin Roberts.

Roberts' memory is at variance. Roberts insists only he and Bunning
met with Nixon and that the meeting took place not before but after
Marvin Miller had been elected the Players' Association's executive director.

"We asked Mr. Nixon to be our legal counsel," Roberts said. "We
thought he and Marvin would make a wonderful combination. Nixon, a
conservative Republican, and Marvin, a liberal Democrat. When we spoke
to Marvin, he said he would rather have a full-time, in-house lawyer and
that's when he brought in Dick Moss."

Many presidents have had a baseball background. Warren G. Harding
was part owner of a minor league club. Herbert Hoover was a Stanford
shortstop. Dwight Eisenhower, a center fielder, played at least one and
possibly two seasons in the minors under the assumed name of "Wilson."
Ronald Reagan was a minor league broadcaster and the elder George Bush
was a first baseman and captain at Yale.

But there is absolutely no question Richard Nixon was the number
one fan.

Billy Sunday Was a Heavy Hitter— When He Preached

THURSDAY, AUGUST 18, 1994

ADVICE FROM A FORMER CUB OUTFIELDER: "I want to say a word to the boys of the diamond, those who are now in their prime. You will not take this as a 'preachment'—you will take the advice of an old timer in the spirit of which this is given, for I am deeply interested in you. Ballplayers, as a rule, are the best class of hale-fellows-well-met that can be found on the face of God's dirt.

"Fellows, listen to me! You will not always be in the spotlight. Your eye will grow dim—you will get a glass arm or a charley horse—down will come the 'is' and up will go the 'was' and you are all in, and pork and beans for yours. You work hard for your money. Get all you can and can all you get. Pass up the booze like a pay car does a tramp, or a WCTU Convention passes up a brewery wagon."

So said the Reverend W. A. "Billy" Sunday, a popular outfielder of modest ability who had an eight-year major league career, the first five (1883–1887) with the Cubs. This was when they were known as Anson's Colts in tribute to manager Adrian "Cap" Anson, the original Mr. Cub.

Sunday was outstanding defensively but, like many of his successors, couldn't hit. He had a .248 lifetime mark and only twice appeared in more than 81 games. He had occasional power: 12 home runs and 170 runs batted in, an average of 21 RBIs a season.

157

"He was as good a boy as ever lived," Anson said, "conscientious, hard-working, and obliging." Before he turned to religion, Sunday would take a glass of beer or wine with the boys, but he avoided hard liquor and the all-night parties.

Sunday retired from baseball after the 1890 season to work full time for the YMCA and, according to Fred Ivor-Campbell, a distinguished 19th century baseball historian, "No one—least of all Sunday himself—could have imagined the fame he would attain and the impact he would have as the foremost Christian evangelist of his day, perhaps of *any* day.

"A whirlwind on the speaker's platform, he brought new meaning and enthusiasm to religion. He often said, 'Enthusiasm is as good a thing in religion as fire in a cookstove.'"

Sunday frequently included his baseball experiences in his sermons. His favorite story was of a catch he made after his conversion. He told it so often that it ranks as one of the great catches in diamond lore. It occurred in Detroit on June 10, 1886.

The Reverend Sunday describing his great catch:

> We were neck and neck [with Detroit] for the championship. I was playing right field. Mike Kelly was catching and John G. Clarkson was pitching. He was as fine a pitcher as ever crawled into a uniform. Cigarettes put him on the bum. When he'd taken a bath, the water would be stained with nicotine.
>
> We had two men out and they had a man on second and third and Charlie Bennett, their old catcher, was at bat. Charlie had three balls and two strikes on him. Charlie couldn't hit a high ball but he could kill them when they went about his knee.
>
> I hollered to Clarkson, "One more out and we got 'em."
>
> You know every pitcher puts a hole in the ground where he puts his foot when he is pitching. John stuck his foot in the hole and he went clean to the ground. Oh, he could make 'em dance. He could throw overhand, and the ball would go down and up like that. He is the only man on Earth I have seen do that.
>
> The ball would go by so fast that the batter could feel the thermometer drop two degrees as she whizzed by. John went clean down, and as he went to throw, his right foot slipped and the ball went low instead of high.

158

I saw Charlie swing hard and heard the bat hit the ball with a terrific boom. Bennett had smashed the ball on the nose. I saw the ball rise in the air and knew that it was going clear over my head. I could judge within 10 feet of where the ball would light. I turned my back and ran. The field was crowded with people and I yelled, "Stand back!" And that crowd opened like the Red Sea opened for the rod of Moses.

I ran on, and said a prayer: "God, if you ever helped mortal man, help me to get to that ball, and you haven't much time to make up your mind." I ran and jumped over the bench and stopped. It was as though wings were carrying me up.

I shoved out my left hand and the ball hit it and stuck. At the rate I was going, the momentum carried me on and I fell under the feet of a team of horses. I jumped up with the ball in my hand. Up came Tom Johnson. Tom used to be the mayor of Cleveland.

"Here is $10. Buy yourself the best hat in Chicago." That catch won me $1,500.

An old Methodist minister said to me a few years ago, "Why, William, you didn't take the $10, did you?" I said, "You bet your life I did."

Billy Sunday preached with fire and brimstone. He was a leading advocate of Prohibition. "I'm trying to make America so dry that a man must be primed before he can spit," he said, "and I'm going to fight the liquor business 'til hell freezes over, and then I'll put on ice skates and fight it some more."

He died in Chicago in 1935 at age 72.

Cubs' "Mr. Wrigley" Made a Difference, but Not Noise

TUESDAY, DECEMBER 6, 1994

PHILIP K. WRIGLEY, WHO OWNED THE CUBS for five decades, was a man of few words. He was never on radio or television and made only two public speeches in his life.

In accepting an award at the Chicago baseball writers' Diamond Dinner, now defunct, he said simply, "Thank you."

Some years later, in identical circumstances, he once again was honored by the Chicago scribes. Before the presentation, he was urged to expand his acceptance remarks. Wrigley complied, saying, "Thank you very much."

Altruistic and *idealistic* were the adjectives often used to describe him. Though born into wealth, the only son of a flamboyant and extroverted father who, associates said, would smile for a photographer at 100 yards, he was the exact opposite, "the best-known unknown man in the realm of sports," *Sports Illustrated* reported.

The anonymity pleased him. He refused to pose for a color portrait for *Fortune* magazine and expressed delight that he was the first competing owner to get through a World Series without being photographed. His biography, written in 1975 by Paul M. Angle, a distinguished historian, was entitled *A Memoir of a Modest Man.*

Mr. Wrigley tried for the common touch. He didn't allow a secretary to answer his phone. I recall him saying that he had regular conversations with a carpenter whom he had never met but apparently was a big Cubs fan.

A poor student in the conventional sense, he had an aptitude for mechanics, how things worked. He was an early expert in aeronautics and was constantly reassembling a fleet of automobiles garaged at his estate in Lake Geneva, Wisconsin.

He overpaid his players, who rewarded him with four National League pennants, but never won a World Series. He was also the only owner of his time who favored abolishing the reserve clause, which held the players in perpetual bondage.

Early on, in the thirties and forties, he was active in league affairs and for many years was vice president of the National League. By the time I caught him he had just turned 60 and seemed to have withdrawn from baseball.

I covered the Cubs for 20 years before his death and saw him only twice at a ballgame, both times in Arizona during spring training. I saw him once at Wrigley Field, in the morning, when he had gone to the ballpark for a meeting.

John C. Hoffman, a longtime diamond Boswell of the previous generation, had a similar recollection. Hoffman could not recall him ever making a road trip, or seeing him in the dugout or in the clubhouse.

A contrarian, Mr. Wrigley was the only holdout against lights and seemed to derive pleasure in surprising baseball writers with unexpected responses. In 1962, when the Cubs hosted the All-Star Game, Jack Kuenster, then with the *Daily News,* called to ask if he was planning to go to the game.

Mr. Wrigley said he didn't want to use two tickets for himself; he preferred they be made available to a fan. He explained further that he would watch on television because it gave him a better view.

Bill Veeck, at that time operating the White Sox and competing for the Chicago baseball dollar, reacted with amusement. Said Veeck: "He's telling the fans to stay home and watch the game on television."

Veeck, 20 years younger, was not among Wrigley's boosters. Veeck's father, William Sr., a former sportswriter who wrote under the name of Bill Bailey, had been the president and general manager of the Cubs. As a boy, Veeck hung out at Wrigley Field. Many years later, Veeck recalled with disdain, "I always called him 'Mr. Wrigley.'"

Bob Scheffing, dismissed in 1959 after three fairly successful seasons as the Cubs' field manager, also was not enthralled.

"He just doesn't think people are very smart, especially if they don't have any money," Scheffing said in an interview three years later. "And at the same time, he is suspicious of other people who have made a million or two. I always shuddered when I saw him with Walter O'Malley [owner of the Los Angeles Dodgers]. I always figured O'Malley would come away with the gum company."

In his later years, when asked about his role with the Cubs, Mr. Wrigley usually described himself as the "balance wheel." He believed in dividing authority. During one stretch, the Cubs had three vice presidents— John Holland, Clarence "Pants" Rowland, and Charlie Grimm. All had equal rank and were constantly competing against each other.

This philosophy was the genesis of his widely ridiculed no-manager policy. Weary of firing managers, Wrigley inaugurated an unprecedented system of rotating head coaches. Like the vice presidents, it became a tournament, each head coach trying to outdo the other.

In explanation, Wrigley said, "When the bulldozer breaks down, it's time to change the driver." What he didn't realize, or refused to acknowledge, was that it was the bulldozer that required repair.

"Phil was the most visionary owner we ever had," said Gabe Paul, who was among his contemporaries, long since retired and living in Tampa. "He was the only owner who would vote against his best interests if he thought it would help the league."

Mr. Wrigley died in 1977 at the age of 82. Sunday was the 100th anniversary of his birth.

Worst Deal Ever?
Principals Deny It—
and They Should Know

SUNDAY, JANUARY 22, 1995

I WAS TALKING TO ERNIE BROGLIO when Lou Brock walked in and sat down at the table.

"Do you know why I'm here?" Broglio asked Brock. Then, without waiting for a reply, Broglio said, "I'm here because of you."

"History put us together," Brock acknowledged. "We're joined at the hip."

This little dialogue occurred Friday at the Hilton Hotel when the Cubs were opening their annual winter fan convention. As an added attraction, John McDonough, the Cubs' marketing director, had the inspired idea of bringing Brock and Broglio together.

It was perhaps the most disastrous deal in Cubs history: Brock to the Cardinals for Broglio, nearly 31 years ago, on June 15, 1964. Brock went on and had a Hall of Fame career with the Cardinals. Broglio won a total of seven games for the Cubs.

In the years since, they have been together on five or six occasions, usually at old-timers games. Broglio recalled his last Wrigley Field appearance: "It was an old-timers game. I got a standing ovation; 40,000 people booed me. Leo Durocher brought me back. But he was so mad he didn't pitch me."

When the deal was made, the unanimous reaction, here and in St. Louis, was that the Cubs had pulled a major coup.

The report in the *Chicago Daily News* began, "Thank you, thank you, oh, you lovely St. Louis Cardinals. Nice doing business with you. Please call again any time."

Bill White, later the National League president but then the Cardinals' first baseman, remembers that none of the St. Louis players liked the deal. Some fans carried a banner reading: "Broglio for Brock. Who could make such a deal?"

While visiting with Broglio, Brock admitted that he was also surprised.

"Here's a young gun with two left feet who doesn't know where he's going and I was traded for a 21-game winner," Brock said. "I knew the kind of quality pitcher he [Broglio] was. Until the trade, I had no idea of my value in baseball, what my stock was worth.

"It gave me some indication how good I might be. It solidified my confidence. The day before the trade I hit a two-run homer to win a ballgame 3–2. So I was feeling pretty good. But most of the time I was worrying, thinking I might get sent back to the minors."

That changed the day he reported to the Cardinals. As soon as he suited up, manager Johnny Keane put his arm around Brock's shoulder and told him, "We traded for you because we think you can play. You're in right field."

Keane was right, of course.

Brock, who had been hitting .251 with the Cubs, batted .348 with 33 stolen bases the rest of the season to lead the Cardinals to the pennant. Broglio, in the meantime, had nothing but woe in his maiden season here, winning only 4 of 18 starts.

What the Cubs brass apparently didn't know was that Broglio had suffered a minor arm injury a month before the trade. "At the time, it wasn't very serious," Broglio said Friday. "It kept getting worse."

Broglio won one game for the Cubs in 1965 and two the next year. He was then traded to the Cincinnati Reds and never appeared in another major league game. Lifetime he was 77–74. In 2½ seasons with the Cubs, he was 7–19.

Brock had a blockbuster career. He finished with 3,023 hits, a .293 lifetime average, and a major league–record 938 stolen bases, since broken by Rickey Henderson.

"I don't agree with the people who say it was the worst deal in history," Broglio said Friday. "Brock made himself. He would have done the same thing here in Chicago if they had let him play. I'm happy that he got into the Hall of Fame. And I'm happy that I got to play in the big leagues as long as I did." Brock was a bit player during his 2½ years with the Cubs. He was Mr. Anonymous except for one day, June 17, 1962, when he became only the second player to hit a ball into the center-field bleachers in the old Polo Grounds in New York, then the home of the Mets.

As could be expected, Brock has total recall of that memorable moment:

> The pitch was over my head, fastball with a lot of backspin. I chopped down on it and began running as fast as I could. Bill Jackowski, the second-base umpire, gave me the home run sign. I thought he meant if I kept on running I'd have an inside-the-park homer. I came around home plate as fast as I could.
>
> Nobody shook my hand. All the Cubs were looking out to the outfield. [Ron] Santo then began pounding me and said, "Did you see where the ball went? Did you see the ball? Way up there."
>
> I looked to where he was pointing. I remember saying to myself, "I need binoculars."
>
> Hank Aaron hit a grand slam up there the next day. He really took the thunder out of my home run.

But nobody took the thunder out of Brock's career. As for Broglio, he was and presumably still is a good fellow. "I knew I was going to be traded," Broglio said. "I was in Johnny Keane's doghouse."

Anyway, he was traded for the right guy. Otherwise, he would have been forgotten in the fog of time. As he told Brock, "I'm here because of you."

In '45, a Warm Body
Could Get a Man
in the Major Leagues

SUNDAY, FEBRUARY 19, 1995

I WAS DISCUSSING REPLACEMENT PLAYERS with Steve Hirdt, a ranking base-
ball historian with the Elias Sports Bureau in New York, and he asked if
I remembered the following players: Bud Metheny, Hersh Martin, and
Tuck Stainback.

The only one I could identify was Stainback, who was with the Cubs
in the middle and late thirties.

"They were the regular outfielders for the New York Yankees in 1945,"
Hirdt said.

What was so significant about that?

"They were replacement players," Hirdt explained. "They replaced
Tommy Henrich, Joe DiMaggio, and Charley Keller."

So it has happened before?

"That's right," Hirdt replied. "Replacement players have been used
before."

But there was a considerable difference, of course. It was in 1945. The
players were not on strike. They were in the service of their country, fighting in World War II.

The manpower shortage was so acute that Pete Gray, a one-armed
outfielder, batted .218 in 77 games with the defending American League –

champion St. Louis Browns. There was also a one-legged pitcher, Bert Shepard of the Washington Senators.

Whereas Gray lost his right arm in a boyhood accident—he fell off a wagon and the arm got stuck in the spokes of the wheel—Shepard's loss occurred while his plane flew low over a German airfield on his 34th mission. A bullet shattered his right leg, which was amputated.

Shepard, who had pitched in the minor leagues before entering the service, was fitted with a wooden leg and made starts for the Senators in a war bond exhibition against the Brooklyn Dodgers and in several games against service teams.

Shepard made his first and only American League appearance August 14 against the Red Sox: 5⅓ innings on a yield of one run and only three hits. "Gee," he said, "maybe I'll be able to make the club next year." He didn't.

In Cleveland, the Indians hired a player with size 17 shoes, which kept him out of the armed forces. Howie Schultz, a first baseman with the Dodgers who also played professional basketball, was rejected as too tall.

Pitchers John Rigney of the White Sox and Hal Newhouser of the Tigers, who won 25 games and, for the second year in a row, the American League's Most Valuable Player award, were declared unfit because of heart murmurs. The St. Louis Cardinals were able to keep third baseman Whitey Kurowski because he had a mangled arm.

Jimmie Foxx, the old "Double X" whose 58 home runs in 1932 were second to Babe Ruth's historic 60, returned at the age of 37 as a pitcher with the Philadelphia Phillies. Throwing almost nothing but knuckleballs, Foxx got into nine games and had a 1.59 earned run average. He also hit seven home runs.

Yankees third baseman George "Snuffy" Stirnweiss, afflicted with ulcers that defied army chow, led the A.L. with a .309 batting average. It was the lowest average for a league leader until Carl Yastrzemski's .301 in 1968.

The batting race was the closest in A.L. history. Tony Cuccinello, the White Sox third-base coach of fond memory, was second to Stirnweiss. Stirnweiss hit .30854. Cuccinello, 37, and in his 15th and final season, batted .30846, a difference of .00008. Cuccinello lost a hit in the final week because of a rainout. If it had been an official game, he would have batted .31017.

The Dodgers had a 16-year-old second baseman, Tommy Brown, but he wasn't the youngest major leaguer to appear during World War II. The year before, a 15-year-old pitcher, Joe Nuxhall of the Cincinnati Reds, the youngest player in big-league history, not old enough for a driver's license, worked two-thirds of an inning against the St. Louis Cardinals.

"We searched everywhere for guys who had a hole in their ear or who were 4-F [unsuitable for the draft] because of flat feet," recalled James T. Gallagher, then the general manager of the Cubs. "In those days most players were through when they were in their mid-thirties. This was before 40-year-olds were supposed to play professional sports."

Among the baseball elderly summoned during the emergency was Hod Lisenbee, a right-handed pitcher out of Clarksville, Tennessee, who was born before the turn of the century. Lisenbee broke in with the 1927 Washington Senators when Ruth hit his record 60 home runs. Numbers 26 and 58 were off Lisenbee.

Lisenbee was sent down after the 1932 season. He reappeared for one major league season, in 1936, and nine years later, in 1945, when the clubs, then as now, were seeking replacements, was signed by the Cincinnati Reds. He was 47, almost old enough to be Joe Nuxhall's grandfather. Lisenbee, working 80 innings, had a 1–3 record and a 5.49 ERA.

The old St. Louis Browns, who won their only pennant in 1944, had 16 4-Fs on their 1945 club. Denny Galehouse, who was one of their best pitchers, worked in a war plant in Ohio and appeared only in weekend games. The Browns started some of their games at 11:00 A.M., others at 10:00 P.M.

There was no All-Star Game in 1945 because of the restrictions on travel. The season also began without a commissioner. Judge Landis, baseball's first czar, died on November 25, 1944, after a 24-year reign. Happy Chandler succeeded him on April 24, 1945.

Also not to be forgotten: 1945 was the last year the Cubs won a pennant.

Nice Try, Mike,
but You Belong in Basketball

SUNDAY, MARCH 12, 1995

SO LONG, MICHAEL. Don't let the door hit you on the way out.

Still, I must admit you exceeded my expectations. I didn't think you would hit .200 in a Class A league. I was wrong. You hit .202 in Double A but, as I recall, you had to sit out the next-to-last day of the season to protect your .200 average.

I shouldn't be taking a bow for my pessimistic prediction.

I ran into Joel Horlen at Scottsdale Stadium Friday and asked him if he thought Jordan would make it to the big leagues. Horlen is a former White Sox pitching star now employed by the San Francisco Giants as a minor league pitching coach.

Said Horlen: "It might be the only time in baseball that everybody was right."

Except for his White Sox tutors, who hewed to the party line, I can't recall anyone with more than marginal big-league experience who believed Jordan had a Comiskey Park future.

Or as Bing Devine said here Friday: "Nobody thought he'd make it to the big leagues unless it would be for show. He didn't have that kind of talent." Devine is the former general manager of the St. Louis

Cardinals and currently scouting for the Philadelphia Phillies. He is the fellow responsible for the Lou Brock heist.

Devine says Jordan should be commended. "Not many people his age could have done as well as he did."

In his youth Devine was an outstanding basketball player. I mentioned to him that basketball must be an easier game to play than baseball. The only evidence I can offer is that professional baseball players have had much more success after they switched to basketball.

"I'll tell you why," said Devine. "They don't have to worry about hitting a baseball."

There have been a half dozen examples of failed baseball players who went on and had outstanding basketball careers: Danny Ainge, a weak-hitting infielder who has been a longtime NBA star; Dave DeBusschere, who flopped as a pitcher with the White Sox but had a brilliant career with the New York Knicks. Also, Howie Schultz, Ron Reed, Bill Sharman, and Gene Conley.

The only exceptions I can recall are Dick Groat and Lou Boudreau, college hoop stars who also excelled in baseball. Both were shortstops, outstanding in the field and exceptional situational hitters, especially on the hit-and-run.

It has always seemed to me that the old-style playmaking basketball guards such as Boudreau and Groat, endowed with peripheral vision and lateral quickness, had the best tools to play shortstop. Also in their favor was that the playmaking guard, in those days, was of average size.

"The odds were pretty tough against Michael Jordan making it in baseball," observed Marcel Lachemann, manager of the California Angels. "I definitely would have tipped my hat to him if he had made it to the big leagues—especially as big as he is, 6'6" or 6'7". They're so big they can't cover their strike zone. There is just too much strike zone to take care of."

Dick Pole, the Giants' pitching coach, insists Jordan made the correct decision in returning to basketball.

"It was like Van Gogh giving up painting to become an architect," Pole said. "Basketball and baseball are just different games. If he had started playing baseball at a younger age, he would have had a better chance.

"Hitting a baseball is the toughest thing in the world to do. They throw a round ball and give you a round bat. And they tell you to hit it squarely."

Mike Krukow, a former Cub pitching star, admits that in the beginning he wasn't cheering for Jordan.

"I was insulted that he believed he could get into the baseball world and be successful," Krukow revealed. "But then when I watched him work as hard as he did, I started rooting for him. He gave it a really good shot. He longs for that competition at the top level and that's probably why he's going back to basketball. I wish him well."

I also wish him well, especially now that he is leaving baseball. His presence with the White Sox has been somewhat pleasurable for some but certainly not all of his White Sox teammates. To put the knock on Michael, publicly, would have been heresy. Still, if a poll taken were taken, I would guess that the majority of White Sox players would agree that Michael was an annoying distraction. There was nothing he could have done to help them win a flag. His farewell to baseball is a boon to the White Sox.

His return to basketball could also be beneficial to the Bulls if he would agree to be traded to the Houston Rockets in exchange for Hakeem Olajuwon. What the Bulls need most is a hard-working center, a team player who can clog the middle, with outstanding scoring and rebounding skills.

What the Bulls don't need is another Scottie Pippen—unless the rules have been changed and two balls are in play instead of one.

Gehrig's Legacy Far Surpasses 2,130-Game Streak

TUESDAY, SEPTEMBER 5, 1995

IT WAS A HOT, STEAMING DAY IN NEW YORK, June 2, 1925, and Wally Pipp, the Yankees' regular first baseman, asked the clubhouse boy to bring him two aspirins. Pipp gulped them down with a glass of water and stretched out on the dugout bench.

Miller Huggins, the Yankee manager, asked Pipp what was wrong. Pipp explained that he was bothered by the oppressive heat. "Hug," he said, "I have a terrific headache. It's killing me."

"Take a few days off," Huggins advised. "I'll take a look at this kid from Columbia."

Lou Gehrig went in at first base and didn't come out of the lineup for the next 14 years, not until May 2, 1939. The popular belief is that Pipp never got back in the lineup, and that Gehrig's iron-man streak—2,130 games without a miss—began the day he replaced Pipp. Neither is true.

Gehrig's streak began the day before, when he made his big-league debut as an eighth-inning pinch hitter for Pee Wee Wanninger. As for Pipp, he played first base five times during the first month of the streak—as a late-inning defensive replacement for Gehrig.

If all goes according to plan, Baltimore's Cal Ripken Jr. will break Gehrig's record, once thought unbreakable, on Wednesday night.

Unlike Ripken, Gehrig had only one season when he played every inning. Ripken has had six, in succession, a remarkable streak of 8,423 innings.

Gehrig was taken out eight times for a pinch hitter, four times for a runner. Umpires ejected him on six occasions. According to Ray Robinson, his last and most thorough biographer, he didn't finish 66 games and made token appearances in as many as a dozen games, possibly more.

The biggest threat to his streak came on July 13, 1934, when the Yankees were in Detroit. Gehrig was suffering from lumbago. After rounding first base on a single off Tommy Bridges, he had to be helped off the field. His streak had reached 1,426 games and appeared to have come to an end.

But the next day he was in the lineup, leading off and listed at shortstop. Barely able to stand, Gehrig singled and played the bottom half of the inning in the field. He was replaced in the lineup by Jack Saltzgaver in the second inning. A cab was waiting and he returned to his hotel room.

During the streak Gehrig suffered a succession of injuries: broken toe, broken rib, broken thumb, a series of lumbago attacks, numerous colds, and a variety of other ailments. He became known as the "Iron Horse" because of his durability.

It took an incurable disease to fell him, one that now bears his name—amyotrophic lateral sclerosis, or Lou Gehrig's disease. It affects the spinal cord and lower brain stem and inhibits the brain's ability to start and control muscle movement. The cells in the spine harden and the muscles eventually become paralyzed.

Gehrig decided to take himself out of the lineup on May 30, 1939, after a game against Washington. He fielded a grounder, then flipped the ball for the putout to pitcher Johnny Murphy covering. When the Yankees returned to their dugout, Murphy and several other of his teammates "congratulated" him for the simple play he had made routinely hundreds of times before.

The next day, a Monday, was a travel day. That night Gehrig made his decision and talked at length with manager Joe McCarthy.

He was replaced at first base by Babe Dahlgren.

"I didn't want to play that day," Dahlgren recalled many years later. "There were tears in my eyes as we looked at each other and I heard myself saying, 'C'mon, Lou, you better get out there. You've put me in a terrible spot.'

"He slapped me on the back and said, 'Knock in some runs.'"

Knocking in runs was Gehrig's specialty. A powerful left-handed hitter, he batted in the cleanup spot behind Babe Ruth and drove in 100 or more runs in each of his 13 full seasons, five times leading the American League. His 184 RBIs in 1934 is still the league record. He hit 493 home runs, including a major league record 23 grand slams, and had a career .340 batting average.

On July 4, 1939, Lou Gehrig Appreciation Day was celebrated at Yankee Stadium between games of a doubleheader against Washington. More than 62,000 fans, dignitaries, and Yankee players of the past turned out. Standing at home plate in front of a microphone, Gehrig uttered a memorable and simple message of courage.

"You've been reading about my bad break for weeks now," he said. "But today, I consider myself the luckiest man on the face of the earth."

His fellow players presented him with a silver bowl engraved with a verse by John Kieran. It read in part:

> Idol of cheering millions,
> Records are yours by the sheaves;
> Iron of frame they hailed you;
> Decked with laurel leaves.
> But higher than that we hold you,
> We who have known you best;
> Knowing the way you came through
> Every human test.

The son of German immigrants, Henry Louis Gehrig grew up on the east side of New York and went to Columbia University, where he became a baseball star. Following his sophomore year in college, "Columbia Lou" signed with the Yankees. He died on June 2, 1941. He was 38.

Sosa Destined to Enter
Game's Elite Territory

THURSDAY, JANUARY 20, 1996

SAMMY SOSA, SUPERSTAR! It has a nice sound to it, and Cub fans can begin practicing those three little words in front of a mirror.

Sammy isn't quite there yet—he must get his average up—but he is on his way and should be checking in, pronto.

"He's a five-point player right now," Tom Lasorda, manager of the Los Angeles Dodgers, said Wednesday at Wrigley Field.

"Do you know how many five-point players are in the major leagues?" he asked.

Before an estimate could be offered, Lasorda jumped in.

"Not many."

Lasorda went on to explain the necessary qualifications: "He has to hit with power; hit for an average; [have] outstanding speed; [have an] outstanding throwing arm; and be very good defensively."

Lasorda was guilty of a slight exaggeration. Sosa doesn't hit for much of an average—around .250 this season, .268 last year, .256 lifetime. But Cub coach Billy Williams, certainly an expert on hitting, says Sosa soon will become a reliable .300 hitter.

"He's getting there," Williams said. "He's learning how to hit the pitch on the outside to right center. That, right there, can give him 30 points."

175

Otherwise, Sosa qualifies in all areas of play. He leads the National League in home runs with 23, is seventh in total bases, and among the leaders in runs batted in with 53. These numbers, projected over the full 162-game schedule, translate to a huge season: 52 home runs and 119 RBIs.

This, of course, is assuming Sosa can maintain his pace. It seems a likely possibility. The hitters are usually at their best during the steamy months of July and August.

So, barring injury, Sosa can be expected to have his third 30/30 season—30 or more home runs and 30 or more stolen bases. He has only 12 steals but can turn on the heat whenever necessary.

Only three players have had three or more 30/30 seasons: Bobby Bonds, who had four; his son, Barry, who has three; and Howard Johnson, also with three. Sosa is the only Cub in the 30/30 club.

Sosa concedes it's nice to belong to such an exclusive group but insists he isn't overly concerned.

"I don't worry about it," he said. "If it happens, it happens."

He also doesn't worry about his high strikeout ratio, aware that strikeout leaders are often power hitters as well.

In the ideal scenario, the Cubs would have another genuine power hitter batting behind him. Without this protection, rival pitchers can keep Sosa on a steady diet of pitches out of the strike zone.

But Sosa has a hyper persona, a desire to excel and carry the club on his back. Instead of exercising patience, as he should, he sometimes whales away, to his and the team's disadvantage.

Tony Muser, the Cubs' third-base coach, offered an interesting observation.

"Sammy is so intense and aggressive once the game begins, who's batting behind him is not a factor. I've seen him for four years and I'm convinced he's out to prove he has a chance to be the best ballplayer who has ever lived."

And Muser believes Sosa could succeed.

It has been obvious almost from the beginning of his professional career that Sosa was possessed with extraordinary ability. The Texas Rangers signed him off the sandlots of the Dominican Republic four months before his 17th birthday.

After only 25 games with the Rangers, he was traded to the White Sox in July 1989. Larry Himes, then the general manager of the Sox, swung the deal.

Ron Schueler, who had succeeded Himes, traded Sosa to the Cubs for aging slugger George Bell before the 1992 season.

None other than Larry Himes was again on the receiving end. By this time, Himes had resurfaced as the Cub general manager, the only person to be GM of both of Chicago's big-league clubs.

"I'll never forget Larry Himes," Sosa said Wednesday. "He traded for me twice. That was very good for me. It gave me confidence."

It has been more than a year since Sosa saw Himes, now working for the Cubs out of Arizona.

"I'm sure he's very proud of me," Sosa said.

At 65,
Being Mr. Cub
Still Fits Banks Perfectly

TUESDAY, JANUARY 30, 1996

ERNIE BANKS, MR. CUB, will be 65 on Wednesday and is as joyful as ever. He has no regrets or envy—except for a fleeting moment during the 1977 World Series when Reggie Jackson crashed three home runs on three consecutive pitches, all off different pitchers.

"I used to dream about playing in the World Series," Banks said Monday in a telephone interview from Los Angeles, where he was visiting with his three children. "It was always the seventh game. When Reggie Jackson hit those three home runs, it was me doing that."

Banks still sees Jackson at banquets and at celebrity golf tournaments. Banks laughed, "I tell him, 'Reggie, that was me.'"

But it wasn't. Reggie was Mr. October. Banks holds the all-time record of 2,528 games from 1953–1971, 19 seasons with the Cubs without appearing in a World Series.

"I'd rather be Mr. Cub," Banks said.

He hung it up after the 1971 season, two years before the inception of the designated hitter.

"I would have liked to be a DH," Banks said.

"I'll tell you something I've never told anybody before. In '69, when I was 38, I thought about playing only home games, not going on the road, like Harry Caray does now. A couple of times I started out to see [team owner] Mr. [Phil] Wrigley. But I always got cold feet. It would have created too much tension for him. There couldn't be one rule for me, and another rule for the other 24 players."

There should have been.

Without question, Banks was the best and most productive hitter in Chicago baseball history: 512 career home runs; five seasons, including four in a row, with 40 or more home runs; eight seasons with 100 or more runs batted in; winner of the National League's Most Valuable Player award two years in succession, the first player honored twice from a second-division club; five grand-slam home runs in one season, a record since broken by the Yankees' Don Mattingly.

Most fans may not be aware but Banks also set the one-season fielding record for shortstops: fewest errors, 12, and highest fielding percentage, .985. He was also an iron man. He has the record for most consecutive games from the start of a major league career, 424, and later, a streak of 717 games, longest for an active player at that time.

Probably because he was on an optimist beyond compare, always predicting a Cub pennant, often in verse, he seldom was acknowledged as a tough competitor. But behind his cheerful manner lurked a ferocious desire. During 1958, after he either was hit or knocked down by Bob Purkey, Don Drysdale, Jack Sanford, and Bob Friend, he hit the next pitch for a home run.

"I didn't think anybody remembered that," Banks said, pleased with the recollection. "Alvin Dark [then a teammate] talked about it a lot. He'd say, 'Knock Ernie down and he'll kill you.'"

Banks hit three home runs in a game four times. In 1962, Moe Drabowsky, a former teammate then with Milwaukee, hit him on the back of the head. For the first time, Banks decided it was time for him to wear a batting helmet. When he returned four days later, he hit three home runs and a double.

He was also a favorite target of Don Newcombe, the Dodgers' hard-throwing right-hander.

"He used to hit Gene Baker and me," Banks recalled. "Campy [Roy Campanella, Newcombe's catcher] would sit behind the plate and warn us. He would say, 'Watch out; the next one's coming at your head!'"

Banks seldom complained. So far as I can recall, the only time I saw him upset was when Sandy Grady, a Philadelphia sports columnist, described him as having "pencil-thin" shoulders. For days Banks walked around saying "pencil-thin shoulders," sometimes with a smile, sometimes not.

It peeved him because there were many references to his slender build. Meeting him for the first tune, many people were surprised that he wasn't bigger, with bulging muscles. But his power was generated by his hips and legs.

He will celebrate number 65 with his twin sons, Joey and Jerry, both of whom live in the Los Angeles area. His daughter, Jan, and her husband have flown in from Las Vegas.

"Just a quiet family dinner," Banks said. "When I'm with my kids we evaluate ourselves, where we are, what he want to do, how to become a better person. How to help, how to share. Jan is kind of the leader."

Banks doesn't think about retirement. He has his own sports marketing firm in Chicago, Ernie Banks International, and is employed by World Van Lines moving company, a job he has had for almost 20 years.

Banks' 65th birthday may depress many Cub fans and remind them that they, too, are growing older, especially those who saw him play in their youth. But he doesn't see it that way.

"I want them to grow old with me," Banks said. "I'm going to live until I'm 100. I want them to be centenarians, just like me."

When the time comes, what epitaph would he like?

"Actually, I want to be cremated," he advised, "and have my ashes spread over Wrigley Field—with the wind blowing out."

Andre Dawson:
The Mantle of His Time

TUESDAY, AUGUST 20, 1996

ONLY TWO BALLPLAYERS, SO FAR AS I COULD TELL, were held in awe by their teammates: Mickey Mantle and Andre Dawson.

And it wasn't only because they hit home runs and were superb in the field. The principal reason their teammates regarded them so highly was because they played in pain. And never complained.

Dawson, who had a glorious six-year career with the Cubs, last week announced his retirement at season's end. He was at Wrigley Field Monday night for his last hurrah here. He has finished his career with the Florida Marlins after being used sparingly: 40 at-bats, a .300 average, with only one home run. As expected, he was engulfed by reporters.

The Cubs were in the midst of batting practice and manager Jim Riggleman, watching from a distance, offered the best summation: "When you see how his teammates feel about him, the other team starts looking at this guy, and they're thinking, 'He must be something special to command so much respect.' This feeling transcends into the other dugout. And the next thing you know, both teams idolize the guy."

Like Mantle, Dawson will be a first-ballot Hall of Famer: 21 major league seasons, 437 home runs, 1,587 runs batted in, and 314 stolen bases. The numbers are staggering. Few players have possessed this uncommon combination of speed and power.

Don Zimmer, the former Cubs manager, was among the first to express the Mantle and Dawson similarities. "We'll never know how good Mickey Mantle would have been because he played on bad knees," Zimmer said. "In my time, Andre Dawson was Mickey Mantle. If Andre hadn't had all those knee operations, he would have had 600 home runs and 500 stolen bases."

The Hawk underwent his 12th knee operation last May; he's had 7 on the right knee, 5 on the left. "I took them as far as they let me go," Dawson said Monday. "With better knees I could have played three or four more years. But I was lucky to play as long as did."

Rusty Kuntz, one of the Florida coaches, said, "I told Hawk the other day that I would be glad to give him [Dawson] my knees. It's a big loss."

Dawson said earlier that if and when he was elected to the Hall of Fame, his bronzed plaque would show him in the cap of the last team for which he played. He since has changed his mind. He will be enshrined as a Cub.

Dawson said the best of his baseball days were with the Cubs. He broke in with the Montreal Expos in 1976 and joined the Cubs in 1987. The circumstances of his signing bordered on the bizarre. A free agent, he stalked the Cubs, showing up at their Arizona spring training camp and signing for $500,000, half his previous salary.

"It was like a rebirth for me," Dawson said. "I really enjoyed playing here."

His career year was 1987, his first season with the Cubs, when he led the National League with 49 home runs and 137 RBIs, a landslide winner of the N.L.'s Most Valuable Player, the first MVP selected from a last-place club.

The fans in the right-field bleachers, in appreciation and devotion, salaamed before him every time he returned to his position. Dawson has not forgotten. "From the first day, the reception was so warm," he said. "I was always anxious to get to the ballpark."

His most memorable Wrigley Field moment was his final 1987 at-bat: home run number 47, off Bill Dawley.

But Dawson was much more than a batting star. Quiet in manner, he was a comparatively silent hero who led by example, the first player at the ballpark and the last to leave. He arrived at 8:30 in the morning before a day game. When he departed he always stopped to sign autographs.

"I used to laugh at the Hawk because he spent so much time in the training room," recalled Shawon Dunston, the former Cubs shortstop now with the San Francisco Giants. "And he'd say to me, 'Wait until you're 30.' And now I'm in the training room every day.

"He never complained. He never wanted a day off. He'd be diving for fly balls when he shouldn't have. They talk about Ernie Banks, but Andre and Ryne Sandberg were the greatest players in Cub history."

Aware that Dunston was a frightened young player, Dawson made him his constant dinner companion.

"He never let me pay," Dunston recalled.

When Dunston got his first million-dollar contract, Dawson still insisted on picking up the check. When Dunston got to $2 million, Dawson told him, "Now you can leave the tip."

"I only have one father," Dunston said. "But if I had to pick anybody else to be my father, it would be Andre."

It will be Andre Dawson Day at Wrigley Field Wednesday. Be there!

Courageous Flood
Staked Career on Free Agency

TUESDAY, JANUARY 21, 1997

TWENTY-TWO PLAYERS AND OWNERS, eleven for each side, testified during the 1970 Curt Flood trial, which opened the gates for free agency. Among those who spoke for Flood was Jim Brosnan, who pitched for both the Cubs and the White Sox.

Brosnan's testimony brought laughter to the courtroom. He told of the time his contract had been transferred—i.e., he had been traded—and went home to tell his wife, Anne, that they had to pack their bags.

"My wife threatened to divorce me," Brosnan recalled. "She had just bought two weeks of steaks to put in the freezer. She wanted to know what to do with the steaks."

And, asked counsel, could Brosnan say what she finally did with the steaks?

"She gave them to the player who reported in my place," Brosnan said.

This is but an amusing anecdote but one nonetheless relevant to Flood's suit against baseball and his contention that players should not be traded or sold without their approval. Though Flood, who died Monday of throat cancer at 59, lost in court, the litigation loosened the bondage of the reserve system, in which a club held title to its players until they were sold or traded—and then they became the chattel of their new employer.

184

Flood, in a subsequent interview, told how he contacted Marvin Miller and told of his desire to challenge the reserve clause. Miller was then the executive director of the players association.

"Right from the start, Marvin tried to discourage me," Flood revealed. "He said, 'If you go ahead with this, forget any idea of ever being the first black manager. Or even a coach or a scout. Forget it!'

"He talked about blacklisting and how long the legal proceedings could take—two or more years—and how much the legal fees would cost. He emphasized how much I could lose in salary—maybe $200,000 or more."

Flood also recalled, "One of the players, I've forgotten who, asked me, 'If, after you start this suit, someone comes knocking at your door and offers you $1 million to withdraw the suit, what will you do?'

"I looked at the man and said, 'I can't be bought.'"

Flood also had to convince the union of his sincerity to follow through. Miller had recommended that the union pay all of Flood's expenses.

"I walked into the annual winter meeting of the player reps at the Americano Hotel in San Juan," Flood said. "I had to tell them why I planned to challenge the reserve clause in a case that could revolutionize the structure of baseball and stop 24 millionaire owners from playing God with thousands of ballplayers' lives."

Miller, reached at his Manhattan apartment Monday night, spoke of Flood with the highest praise.

"That kind of integrity and courage he had was so rare," Miller said. "At the time, most people couldn't understand it. I told him he should give it a lot of thought—there were many kinds of repercussions. He came back a few days later and said, 'If a principle is right, you've got to do it, regardless of the cost.'"

Miller kept in touch with Flood and was aware he had been ailing for the last year.

"He was unable to speak the last few months," Miller revealed. "When I called, his wife would put his speaker-phone on so he could hear me. He would write his responses on a blackboard. We lost a great human being."

How Wendell Smith
Helped Robinson's Cause

MONDAY, MARCH 31, 1997

IT BEGAN IN MARCH 1945.

Wendell Smith telephoned Isadore Muchnick, a Boston councilman who was campaigning for reelection in a predominantly black area. Smith was a young sportswriter with the *Pittsburgh Courier*, the nation's largest African-American newspaper, and suggested that to increase his popularity in the community, Muchnick should help arrange a tryout with the Boston Red Sox and the Boston Braves for several black players.

Muchnick agreed, and Smith chose three players: Marvin Williams, a second baseman for the Philadelphia Stars; Sam Jethroe, a speedy out-fielder and .350 hitter for the Cleveland Buckeyes; and Jackie Robinson, a shortstop with the Kansas City Monarchs.

In an interview many years later, Smith acknowledged Robinson "wasn't the best player." He picked him because he had played on an inte-grated team and was a college man—among the greatest all-around ath-letes at UCLA, where he had excelled in all the major sports.

"He was the best player at that time for this situation," Smith explained.

Because of a scheduling conflict, the tryout with the Braves wasn't held. The Red Sox fulfilled their commitment but the tryout was a farce. Young pitchers from their lower minor league clubs threw to the black stars, who

186

rattled the left-field fence with line drives. It was not a real test. When it was over, Duffy Lewis, the Red Sox's traveling secretary, who had been a star player many years before, told Smith, "They look like pretty good ballplayers. You'll hear from us."

A call did come, but not from the Red Sox. It was from Branch Rickey, the general manager/president of the Brooklyn Dodgers. Rickey asked Smith to stop in at his Brooklyn office. Smith obliged and told Rickey what had happened in Boston.

"When I said, 'Jackie Robinson,'" Smith recalled, "Mr. Rickey raised his bushy eyebrows and he said, 'Jackie Robinson! I knew he was an All-American football player and an All-American basketball player. But I didn't know he was a baseball player.'"

"He's quite a baseball player," Smith replied. "He's a shortstop."

Rickey called Smith a week later and advised he was sending Clyde Sukeforth, one of the Dodgers' scouts, to follow Robinson. Like others in the Brooklyn organization, Sukeforth assumed Rickey was interested in signing him for the Brown Dodgers, supposedly an anchor team in a third Negro league.

Smith knew better and asked Rickey, "Is there any chance of this ballplayer ever becoming part of the Brooklyn ballclub?"

When Rickey hedged, Smith realized history was in the making. He also understood there was no need to divulge these thoughts to Robinson. It would only add to the pressure.

Sukeforth followed Robinson for almost the entire season. Pleased with Sukeforth's reports, Rickey signed Robinson to a contract with the Montreal Royals, the Dodgers' top farm club. At the same time he asked Smith if he would be Robinson's companion on the road. Rickey put him on the payroll for $50 a week, the same wage he was receiving from the *Courier.* Smith was listed on the official club directory as a scout.

Smith always considered himself as a member of the Brooklyn press corps and wrote daily dispatches for the *Courier,* chronicling not only the rejections encountered but the few welcome receptions. He also recommended several other stars from the Negro leagues, including Monte Irvin, Larry Doby, and Roy Campanella.

"Leave them alone," Rickey said. "I want some of the other ballclubs to take them."

The New York Giants signed Irvin and Bill Veeck, then operating the Cleveland club, corralled Doby, the American League's first black player. But Rickey couldn't resist and signed Campanella, one of baseball's greatest catchers.

"When I think back, it was absolutely fantastic, all we went through," Smith recalled. "It's hard to conceive. Going into a town and finding a decent place to stay was not easy in those days. Eating in the places we ate, second- and third-rate. Always having this stigma hanging over your head. But I knew Jackie would make it. And I knew if he made it, things had to open up."

Wendell John Smith finished his career in Chicago. He joined the sports staff of the *Chicago American* after the 1947 baseball season, later wrote a weekly column for the *Sun-Times*, and was an announcer for WGN. Smith and Robinson went to their graves together. Smith died at the age of 58, a month after Robinson's death. A Chicago elementary school was named in his honor in 1973.

Stealing Signs:
Grand Larceny
a Part of the Game

SUNDAY, JUNE 1, 1997

THE 1959 WORLD SERIES between the White Sox and the Los Angeles Dodgers is long since gone, but some memories remain. Among them is the rhubarb between the rival third-base coaches, Tony Cuccinello of the Sox and Charlie Dressen of the Dodgers.

After the Dodgers won the Series in six games, Dressen claimed credit for the victory with the assertion that he had stolen the White Sox's signs.

Ordinarily a peaceful sort, Cuccinello responded with uncharacteristic anger.

"That's Dressen," Cuccinello said. "Always bragging. The truth is Dressen was tipping off their signs. We figured them out after the first game."

This came to mind last week when San Francisco manager Dusty Baker chastised Montreal manager Felipe Alou and accused the Expos of stealing the Giants' signs. This dastardly deed, Baker insisted, gave the Expos an unfair advantage.

Espionage has been part of big-league baseball since the beginning of time. According to diamond historian Fred Lieb, the practice surfaced in 1898 when Tommy Corcoran of the Cincinnati Reds got his spikes caught

189

at third base. Initially, Corcoran thought they were snagged on a thick vine but, upon closer inspection, he discovered it was a wire. According to Lieb:

> Corcoran kept tugging at the wire and, with the umpires and players from both teams at his heels, traced the cable across the field to the Phillies' clubhouse. There they found Morgan Murphy, the Phillies' second-string catcher, with a telegraph instrument. Morgan also was equipped with spyglasses and, via the wire, relayed his findings to the Phillies' third-base coach. One buzz for a fastball, two for a curve, and three for a change-up. The coach then signaled this information to the batter.

This was, of course, when sign stealing was in its infancy. With time, the practice has become considerably more sophisticated. It has been accepted as part of the game and so it was a great surprise when Baker shouted foul, indicating it was a violation of baseball etiquette.

Etiquette or not, there are no rules against sign stealing. It has been and presumably still is part of the game. Just to be sure, a call was put in to acting commissioner Bud Selig for his views.

"The dispute is nonsense," Selig replied. "The object is to win."

Does he approve?

"Why not?" he said. "It has been going on for years."

Selig went on to explain that Dressen, when he was a coach with the Milwaukee Braves, was always tipping off the Milwaukee hitters. Among the principal beneficiaries was slugging first baseman Joe Adcock.

Later, in a conversation at Wrigley Field with Cubs coach Billy Williams about sign stealing, Adcock's name was mentioned. He is among the few players who has hit four home runs in one game.

"When Joe Adcock knew what was coming," Williams said, "he'd knock the cover off the ball."

Like many other old pros, Williams had no objections to this, but he maintained he never wanted any advance notice, "especially when I was going good." He indicated Ernie Banks had the same approach.

Joel Youngblood, a former hard-nosed infielder now a coach with the Cincinnati Reds, insisted sign stealing is an extension of aggressive play.

"If a team doesn't try to steal signs, it means it doesn't care, it's not looking for an advantage," Youngblood said. "I'm not that good at it, but I'm always looking."

Every time a player is traded, it is necessary for his former club to change its signs.

"Whenever we get a guy, the first day he's with us, we always ask about the signs," Youngblood said. "You can't wait a week or two. After a couple of days, he has forgotten. You have to get to him right away."

Youngblood maintained, correctly, that sign stealing is in the same family as scouting and watching films.

"If you watch [a third-base coach's] every move long enough, chances are you'll pick up something," Youngblood said.

As for Baker, he is so concerned about tipping off his signs that a partition has been erected in front of the corner of the dugout where he dispenses the signs.

"He hides in San Francisco," Youngblood said. "But we can get him on the road."

Interleague Play
Validates Veeck's
75-Year-Old Vision

THURSDAY, JUNE 5, 1997

LIKE A GLACIER, big-league baseball moves slowly and so it has taken a while—75 years—but William L. Veeck's idea of a round robin of interleague games will begin a week from Friday. Only a few old-timers are likely to remember him, but he was among baseball's premier executives and president of the Cubs for 14 years—from 1919 to 1933, when he died at the age of 56.

His son, the late Bill Veeck, who operated four major league clubs, including two terms with the White Sox, is much better known and now resides in the Hall of Fame. It isn't likely that the father will make it to Cooperstown but he is a worthy candidate for the Veterans Committee, which often rescues some of the forgotten heroes who have been lost in the fog of time.

Veeck was born in Booneville, Indiana, in 1877. He worked as a newsboy, messenger, druggist's helper, printer's devil, printer, and, finally, a reporter on the *Louisville Courier Journal*. He came to Chicago to cover the 1893 Columbian Exposition and eventually hooked on with the *Chicago Inter Ocean* newspaper, which soon folded.

With its collapse, he moved to the *Chicago Evening American*, continuing as a reporter and rewrite man. When an opening developed in the sports department, Ring Lardner recommended him for the baseball assignment. Writing under the name of Bill Bailey, a stock byline, he covered the Cubs for eight seasons.

Interestingly, he was the inspiration for the song "Won't You Come Home, Bill Bailey?" It has been my belief that his wife was urging him to quit the road. But Mary Frances Veeck, the widow of Bill Jr., maintains it was the plea of his Louisville colleagues.

Whatever, the elder Veeck knew his stuff and soon came to the attention of William Wrigley, Philip's father, who founded the gum company. Wrigley recently had taken over the Cubs as the majority owner, and had been scouting for someone to head the organization.

The prevailing belief is Veeck, in a series of articles, had been scorching the club, but the junior Veeck, in his memoir, *Veeck—as in Wreck,* writes, "The story is not really inaccurate but overstated. He did not blast the Cubs, he wrote a sane and thoughtful series telling what changes he would make if he was running the club. It was constructive criticism without any attempt to be either colorful or clever."

Wrigley invited Veeck for dinner and asked, "Could you do any better?"

"I certainly couldn't do any worse," Veeck replied.

"We are going to put together a winning team," Wrigley said at the time. "And Veeck knows how to do it."

During his incumbency, he engineered the biggest deal in baseball to that point: $200,000 and six players to the Boston Braves for Rogers Hornsby. The Cubs won two pennants under Veeck's command, in 1929 and again in 1932. He died the next year during the World Series.

"If you asked anybody who knew my daddy to describe him in a word, that word undoubtedly would be *dignified*," Veeck wrote. "And then they would be constrained to add 'dignified without being stuffy.' He had a good sense of humor and was always scrupulously fair. I can say, without any fear that I might be a little prejudiced, that he was the most popular fellow in baseball.

"One of the differences between me and my father is that he was always 'Mr. Veeck' to everyone who knew him and I am always 'Bill.' Not even the members of the Cubs staff, all of whom remained throughout his career with the Cubs, would have dreamed of calling him by his first name."

The father was not a prude but he never swore. Once, when young Veeck was in his teens, he let loose a string of cusswords.

"My father cured me," he recalled. "He told me, 'If you want to show people you're stupid, that's up to you.'"

Unlike the son, the elder didn't believe in promotional stunts. But he was among the greatest innovators of his time. He initiated Ladies Day, was the first big-league mogul to allow his games to be broadcast, which many league officials criticized heavily, and, in a National League meeting in 1922, proposed a schedule of interleague games at the midpoint of the championship season. So far as is known, it was dismissed out of hand and never came to a vote.

He Had Many Loves:
People, Baseball, Chicago—
and Life

THURSDAY, FEBRUARY 19, 1998

ORPHANED IN CHILDHOOD, Harry Caray had the usual quiver of poor-boy stories. The one he seemed to enjoy telling the most was the day of his grammar school graduation in St. Louis.

All the boys were supposed to be in white pants. Harry didn't have enough money to conform to the dress code and wore his everyday gray pants.

"My classmates ridiculed me," Harry recalled. "I was very hurt and embarrassed. I was crying when I went to sleep that night and I vowed that someday I would have enough money to buy 100 pairs of white pants."

Other than that, I can't recall him ever feeling sorry for himself. He was always up and at 'em, eager for the sun to shine and for the next game. He took it one day at a time and squeezed the life out of it.

I knew him for many years. I was never among his regular drinking buddies, but we were constant gin rummy companions on the road, on the charter flights, and in the hotels after night games.

Harry was a good gin player—not the very best, but good enough. What I remember most about these games, which usually lasted until 3:00 or 4:00 A.M., is that every time he was about to win a hand, he would shout, "What do you make a martini with?"

And then he would answer his question with the declaration, "Gin!" After 25 years in St Louis and another season in Oakland, he came here in 1971 to broadcast White Sox games. He succeeded Bob Elson. Both were Hall of Famers. But you couldn't find more disparate personalities.

When the White Sox arrived on their chartered plane and a crowd was waiting to greet them, Elson ran the other way. He couldn't escape fast enough. Harry was just the opposite. He would quicken his pace and stride into their midst.

"He just loved people," said Pete Vonachen, his friend for a half century who is in his second term as owner of the minor league Peoria Chiefs. "It was tough to get him to go home. But Harry was never the big drinker some people think he was. He drank, sometimes he drank a lot, but he always had control of himself."

Vonachen told of a day he was with Harry in the booth at Wrigley Field.

"He was dead tired and said we had to make a quick getaway," said Vonachen. "When he got to his car he stopped to sign an autograph. And within a minute there were 50 or 60 people lined up. And he was there for an hour signing for everyone.

"I said, 'Harry, I thought you wanted to get going.' And he said, 'How can I turn down these kids?'

"That didn't happen one day. It was an everyday thing."

Vonachen owned a restaurant in Peoria. Harry stopped in whenever possible.

"I always told the manager, 'Keep the people away when he's eating. Give him and his party some privacy.' One night a pretty girl approached his table. She wanted her picture taken with him.

"He said, 'C'mon over, honey, sit on my lap.' And everyone in the restaurant hurried to his table. His dinner got cold. He didn't care. He enjoyed being with people and talking to them."

I know, from my own experience, that Harry loved Chicago. One night, when my wife and I were out with him on Rush Street, he couldn't take two steps without being stopped. People also shouted greetings from across the street and from second-story windows. Everyone was delighted. The king was in their presence.

Harry always insisted Chicago was his kind of town.

As a young announcer in St. Louis he was brash and energetic, quick to criticize and state his opinion. The St. Louis sportswriters, envious of his growing popularity, tuned him out.

"They got back at me by never mentioning my name," Harry said. "I had to get run over by a car to get my name in the paper."

He wasn't kidding. Harry was injured when struck by a car shortly before he left St. Louis.

The Chicago sportswriters embraced him in an enduring bear hug. Once he joined the Cubs he became the country's most popular announcer, the best known of any of the breed, past or present. His popularity easily exceeded that of the Cubs players, including Ryne Sandberg.

Above all, Harry loved baseball. Steve Stone, his longtime broadcast partner, is still amused by an incident in 1987 when Harry returned to the booth after suffering a stroke.

"President Reagan called to extend his best wishes," Stone recalled. "They talked for a while and Harry said, 'Bobby Dernier just bunted for a single. I've got to get back to the game.'

"I doubt that the president ever had anybody hang up on him before. It was an example of Harry's priorities and really showed his love for baseball."

So long, Harry. There never will be another one like you.

For Baseball's Real First Black, Fame Wasn't Even Fleeting

WEDNESDAY, APRIL 15, 1998

LEONARD J. JACOBS OF OREGON, ILLINOIS, a constant reader, has registered what on the surface seems to be a legitimate complaint. What is it, he asks, that discourages sportswriters from acknowledging that Jackie Robinson and Larry Doby were not the first African Americans to play major league baseball?

"Is it discrimination, or is it that the scribblers don't want to rock the boat? I don't understand," he writes. "It's like saying John Adams and not George Washington was our first president. It's time someone wrote about the Walker brothers and gave them their due. They were the first black players."

Reader Jacobs is correct but should be advised there has not been a conspiracy of silence. The Walkers are listed in all the encyclopedias and prominently mentioned in most baseball histories. The problem is that they played in the major leagues only one year, 1884, before baseball's so-called modern era began in 1900.

Moses Walker, also known as "Fleet" or "Fleetwood," was the first to break the color line. A catcher, he appeared in 42 games with Toledo. Welday Walker, a reserve outfielder, also with Toledo, played in only five games: 18 at-bats, a .222 average. Fleetwood, three years older, batted .263. They never played in the same game.

Raised in Steubenville, Ohio, the sons of Moses Walker, Steubenville's first black physician, they both enrolled at Oberlin for prep school and college. They were on Oberlin's first intercollegiate baseball team in 1881. Neither graduated from Oberlin; both transferred to the University of Michigan.

According to Jerry Malloy of Mundelein, the ultimate expert on the Walkers, there was much speculation that Michigan recruited Fleetwood due to his baseball ability. "Welday tagged along," Malloy said. "Fleet was the major character."

They began their career in organized baseball in 1883 with Toledo in the Northwest League, then a minor league. The next season, Toledo joined the American Association, at that time of major league status.

Tony Mullane, Toledo's star pitcher, many years later recalled that Fleetwood "was the best catcher I ever worked with, but I disliked a Negro and whenever I had to pitch to him I used to pitch anything I wanted without looking at his signals."

According to biographer Malloy, Toledo fans and the sporting press received Fleet warmly. Despite facing hostility in a few southern towns, he was popular in other league cities. Malloy characterized him as "a dependable catcher with a good arm and an aggressive base runner . . . a popular player vigorously defended by the fans when he was subjected to racial epithets."

After that one brief stay with Toledo, Fleet spent the rest of his career in the minors. At that time, some of the more unsuccessful franchises were constantly being moved from one league to another, blurring the distinction between major and minor league.

In 1887, when Fleet was with Newark in the International League, Newark signed George Stovey, and together they formed organized baseball's first black battery. In that year the black presence was growing: seven blacks played for six teams in the prestigious league.

On July 14, before Newark's exhibition against Cap Anson's Chicago White Stockings (forerunners of the Cubs), Anson prohibited his team from taking the field. League directors immediately ruled black players would be forbidden in the future, citing opposition by white players.

This ruling was later modified and Walker played two more seasons in the IL, both with Syracuse. He was the only black in the league in 1889, when he helped lead Syracuse to the pennant. Two years later, he was charged with murdering a white man in a barroom brawl. When he was acquitted, the courtroom burst into applause.

Later he worked for the U.S. Postal Service and was indicted for mail theft. After serving one year in prison, he purchased an opera house in Cadiz, Ohio, which also showed motion pictures. Clark Gable, then in his youth and living nearby, saw his first movie in Walker's theater.

At about this same time, Walker was convinced the black man never would be treated fairly in America and in 1908 wrote a book, *Our Home Colony,* subtitled *A Treatise on the Past, Present and Future of the Negro Race in America.* He died in Cleveland in 1924 at 67.

This Was Brickhouse: He Knew Everybody and They Knew Him

FRIDAY, AUGUST 7, 1998

PHILIP K. WRIGLEY, THE LATE CUBS OWNER, called Jack Brickhouse into his office. It was May 1960, three weeks into the new season. The Cubs had already plunged into the National League cellar.

"Jack, I want to make a trade, and I want you to handle it for me."

"Who for who?"

"And Mr. Wrigley looked me in the eye," Brickhouse recalled, "and said, 'Lou Boudreau for Charlie Grimm.'"

And once again the Cubs made baseball history. Boudreau, who had been Brickhouse's sidekick on the club's telecasts, descended from the broadcasting booth and into the dugout to become the team's manager. In the exchange, Grimm replaced Boudreau.

So it was with Jack Beasley Brickhouse, the Hall-of-Fame broadcaster, who died Thursday at 82. He always seemed to be on the inside of the inside. More than likely, he was Wrigley's principal confidante for a quarter of a century.

"Jack, what about Leo Durocher?" Wrigley asked five years later. "I know he has a bad reputation."

Brickhouse acknowledged Durocher had stepped on a few toes but gave Wrigley a favorable report. Durocher was hired on the strength

201

of Brickhouse's recommendation. It may have been Brickhouse's only mistake.

Later, Brickhouse and Durocher had a big squabble. I don't remember what it was about, but I do remember Brickhouse's anger.

"I tried but I failed," he said. "I just can't get to like the guy."

Brickhouse wasn't alone. Many baseball people didn't speak kindly of the "Lip."

"Jack always had a happy face," recalled Jim Gallagher, who was the Cubs' general manager when Brickhouse climbed aboard in the late forties. Before that, in 1946, he was in New York, announcing Giants games with Steve Ellis ("It was the longest season of my life," Brickhouse said later).

"Even when he was a young announcer, he never missed a free meal," Gallagher added. "But he paid for his supper. Every time he went to a banquet, he always got up and made a speech. He sang for his supper."

I knew Brickhouse for more than 40 years. We were friendly but not close friends. When we were on the road and the Cubs had a free Saturday afternoon, he would invite me to go to the theater with him. And after the show, he would go backstage and speak to the players. He knew everybody and, of course, they knew him.

It was during these moments that I often thought he might be a frustrated actor, that he may have preferred a career on the stage.

Brickhouse was among the champions of the "gee whiz" school of broadcasting. The late Howard Cosell was at the other end, captain of the "aw nuts" brigade.

"I debated Howard about this," Brickhouse said in *A Voice for All Seasons,* his third and last biography. "I told him he's got his act and I've got mine. I don't want to be a stick-in-the-mud, but when you go overboard you don't hurt just the athlete. You hurt his wife going to the grocery store and his kid going to school. Why? What does that prove?"

Brickhouse did more than 5,000 baseball telecasts, probably a national record, and acknowledged there were times when he wasn't eager to get to the ballpark. He had his down days. But then he would open a letter from a shut-in or look down at the seats behind home plate and see the fans in wheelchairs and realize he was a lucky guy, getting paid for talking about a ballgame.

Brickhouse suffered with the ill-fated 1969 Cubs but didn't let it show. More than once, he would come into the press box and remind us we weren't covering the Nuremberg trials. Baseball was part of the entertainment business and nothing more.

Some of the cynics chided him for his Pollyannaish approach, saying that he always was trying to make the players and management look good. But it wasn't true. He was critical but never in a nasty manner. He never tried to point out his expertise by impaling someone else.

And he had a good sense of humor. Irv Kupcinet, his partner for 24 years of Bears broadcasts, recalled, "When the Bears were 1–13 [in 1969], Jack would say, 'The game we're broadcasting isn't necessarily the game being played on the field.'"

It's probably impossible for the current generation to realize how big Brickhouse was and to understand his contributions to broadcasting and specifically to WGN. He was its man for all seasons. He was at the mike at all the local sports events, big and small. He also covered politics and the theater and was among the first to do man-on-the-street interviews.

"He was a rare individual," Judge Abraham Lincoln Marovitz said Thursday. "He couldn't say no. He made more charity appearances, twice as many, as anyone I know, and he did it for the kids. He always had a wholesome message."

We were fortunate to have him in our midst.

A Great Companion

MAY 1972

MOE BERG IS DEAD and now I can tell the story. He would like that.

Many times, in recent years, I'd say to him, "Moe, you old son of a gun, when you die, I'm going to write your story, what you're really like."

Moe would laugh. He always was laughing, always enjoying himself. "Wonderful," he would shout, "marvelous." To him, so many things were wonderful and marvelous. They were his favorite words. Then he'd say, "Do it, do it, tell everything."

So I'll do it.

Moe was my roommate for the last 10 or 12 years. Whenever I'd come into New York, either with the Cubs or the White Sox, he would room with me. He knew the schedules and could estimate the arrival time. I would know, within minutes after checking in, if Moe was in town. He would call from the lobby and I'd say, "Moe, c'mon up," and we would spend the next three or four days together.

Life can be lonesome on the road and I always looked forward to seeing him. Sometimes he would join me in Baltimore, or in Boston, or in Philadelphia, or in Washington. The Eastern Seaboard was his province.

We spent little time together during the day. We would lie awake, after night games, talking about everything, including the game, and then he would ask, "What time do you want to get up?" He was an early riser, up and out by 7:00.

I never saw him when he awoke in the mornings, but I knew his routine. He would buy the newspapers, then go to a cafeteria for what he always called "a coffee." At 9:00 or 9:30, or whatever the specified time, he would call the room and announce: "Time to get up."

He would surface again at the dinner hour, when it was time to start for the ballpark. Usually we would take the subway, either to Yankee Stadium or to Shea Stadium. He always lightened my load and carried my briefcase. Most of the time, but not always, he would sit next to me during the game.

After the game, while I was writing my story, he would wait in the pressroom. Then we would return to Manhattan. Usually we would stop for something to eat, mostly at the Stage Delicatessen. If I ordered a salami omelette, Moe ordered a salami omelette. Food didn't interest him but, like a camel, he would stoke up.

Clothes didn't interest him, either. He always wore the same suit, a wash-and-wear charcoal gray, with a shirt and thin black tie. But he was meticulous about his person and each night would wash his clothes and hang them to dry. Many times, when he would see me packing, he would chide me and say, "What do you need all those clothes for?" One suit, he was convinced, was enough for any man.

Most former ballplayers won't walk across the street to see a ballgame. But not Moe. He loved baseball. He would attend as many as 50 to 60 games each season, maybe more. He often said the ballpark was his theater—and it was. He watched every pitch and every move of the catcher. He had been a catcher and he often criticized the catchers, not so much for what they did, but more for what they didn't do.

I can still recall the night last year when Baltimore beat Vida Blue in the first American League playoff game. Moe was impressed with Blue. The critical moment of the game came in the seventh inning when Blue was pitching to Paul Blair. Blue got two strikes on Blair and then fired four or five fastballs in succession, each pitch coming in with the same lightning speed.

With each succeeding pitch, Blair improved his timing, getting a little slice of the ball at first, then a bigger piece, then, his timing down perfect, Blair pulled a game-winning double to left field.

In the room that night, Moe repeatedly said, in anger, "Why didn't he give him the hook? Why didn't he throw the hook?" Moe knew that if Blue had changed speeds and thrown a curve, Blair, most likely, would have struck out, lunging. Typically, Moe didn't blame Blue. The Oakland catcher was at fault. It was the catcher's responsibility to call for the curve.

Moe didn't like to meet the modern players, but it wasn't because he thought the moderns weren't as good as the ancients. Not at all. He often said Johnny Bench of Cincinnati was the best catcher he ever saw. But many times, when we were together, there would be ballplayers nearby and I would ask Moe if he wanted to be introduced. He didn't. Later, I understood why.

He didn't want a player, or players, asking who he was, when he played, and who he played with, etc. He considered such identification demeaning.

"They think it all started with them," Moe would say. "Don't they know there were many of us here before they got here?" The modern players' lack of baseball history and their indifference to the past nettled Moe. So he did the gentlemanly thing. He avoided them.

Moe was the happiest, I think, at World Series time. He would see the games, return to the room for a nap, and take a long and leisurely bath. He was always taking baths. He would then set out for the press hospitality room where he would have dinner and remain until closing time. Wherever Moe sat became the head of the table.

In the main, his dinner companions usually were the genuine aristocrats of sportswriting, men such as the late Frank Graham, Red Smith, Arthur Daley, Leonard Koppett, and Jimmy Cannon of New York, Fred Russell of Nashville, Allen Lewis of Philadelphia, and Harold Kaese of Boston. Moe often said if he had to miss a game and was limited to only one account of the game, he would want Kaese's story. Kaese, he was confident, would come closest to telling him everything he wanted to know.

When Moe saw a good newspaper story, he would tear it out and show it around. He enjoyed Dick Young's stuff. More than 10 years ago, Young did a piece that had to do with the members of the proposed Continental League (which died before it got off the ground but forced expansion) meeting with the executives from the established major leagues. Young wrote that the Continentals likely would be advised to try another sport, "like flying a kite." Moe carried that story with him for months. "Isn't that a wonderful description?" he would say.

Generally, Moe was impressed with the current generation of baseball writers. He regarded the game stories of the 1971 World Series by Joe Durso of *The New York Times* as beautifully done. "Durso makes a narrative out of the game," Moe said.

But Moe had a vehement dislike of the so-called "chipmunks" and the new tendency to rush to the clubhouse and fill an entire story with locker-room quotes. "Just give me the facts; that's all I want," he would say.

He also said John McGraw couldn't manage today because of the demands of the press. He couldn't imagine McGraw defending or explaining his strategy to writers.

Moe had a working knowledge of about 10 languages and, of course, was highly educated. He had degrees from Princeton University and the University of Columbia Law School and he studied at the Sorbonne in Paris. Of his scholarly attainments, the only one I ever heard him express any pride about was that he was a founding member of America's most prestigious linguistic society!

Moe employed his knowledge of languages mostly when he was meeting people for the first time—and he was constantly making new acquaintances. If he met a waitress and her name was Standish or Stanislawski, he would spend 10 minutes dissecting her name, telling how and where the name originated, etc. Once I accused him of using his languages only to meet women. He laughed and indicated his father had told him the same thing.

Only once did I see him with a book. It was a dictionary of Sanskrit that needed bindery repair. It occurred to me at that time that Moe certainly wasn't intellectual in the usual sense. I never heard him engage in philosophical discussion or expound on great ideas or great books. He even refused to own Jim Bouton's *Ball Four*, which was warmly received by the intellectual establishment. Moe regarded it as gossip.

Moe didn't read magazines and had no interest in television, but he devoured newspapers. He repeatedly insisted that anybody could get a good education simply by reading *The New York Times* every day, which he did. He also bought the *Washington Post* and the *Boston Globe*.

My guess is that he turned to the sports sections first and I'm certain he would prefer to spend an afternoon with former teammates such as Heinie Manush and Joe Cronin, who, incidentally, was Moe's lifelong friend, than with a Shakespearean scholar or a scientist.

The New York baseball writers saw Moe several times a week, always at the ballparks or in the pressroom. Many times they referred to him as "Mysterious Moe." In reply, Moe invariably would put an index finger to his lips, confirming and sealing the mysteriousness of it all. It was a takeoff on the old World War II posters: "A slip of the lip can sink a ship."

Moe, of course, was pressed into service as a secret agent in World War II, working out of the Office of Strategic Services. He seldom spoke about his role as a spy.

I certainly don't want to diminish Moe's cloak-and-dagger contributions to the victory or to our acquisition of atomic secrets. I can only say that Moe was considerably more delighted to tell of the women he had known—a veritable chorus line of countesses and duchesses stretching from Italy and Denmark to the Baltic Sea. Though a bachelor, Moe had a fundamental appreciation of the feminine form.

But Moe did have a secret. He didn't have a regular job. He must have been rooming with me four or five years before this occurred to me. When I confronted him with my discovery, he would offer faint denials. Often he would mention he was involved in a shipment of aircraft to a foreign power or that he had a connection with the Arthur Little Company in Boston.

Above all, he was a free man, uncluttered and unencumbered. I can see him now striding down the avenue, newspapers folded under his arm, observing the world as it passed before him in review and saying, "Isn't that wonderful?" or "Marvelous, marvelous."

Baseball's Hitters
in Waiting

JULY 28, 1962

PINCH-HITTERS ARE FAST BECOMING PRIZED SPECIALISTS. But a good man who likes the work is still a rarity.

Either advanced beyond his time or terribly frustrated—and possibly both—Oliver "Patsy" Tebeau, manager of the Cleveland Spiders, tried a new experiment in the ninth inning of a National League game at Brooklyn in 1892. With his team trailing by two runs, he benched George Davies, his pitcher, and sent Jack Doyle, a reserve catcher, up to the plate to swing for him. Doyle responded with a single, advancing a runner to third. Thereby he became baseball's first pinch-hitter.

Although the Spiders lost the game, 2–1, Tebeau really started something. By the end of that pioneering 1892 season a total of seven pinch-hitters had been used in the major leagues. Last season the figure was 4,051, including 42 men who were pinch hitting for pinch-hitters, a phenomenon of modern tactics in which a pinch-hitter is sent up but immediately withdrawn for still another if the rival manager counters by changing pitchers.

Like relief pitchers, with whom they are often compared, pinch-hitters have gained in stature and are no longer merely extra men on the bench. Pinch-hitters were used in 97 percent of all major league games last year, and most clubs now have men who specialize in coming off the bench cold to hit in clutch situations. A team will pay as much as $20,000 a year, perhaps more, to the player who can deliver consistently under these circumstances. Not many can.

Soft Hours, Tough Job

Most major leaguers don't want to pinch hit anyway. They prefer to play every day as starters. About the only men receptive to becoming pinch specialists are veterans anxious to prolong their careers and extend their pension credits. The few who adapt successfully can add anywhere from two to five years to their big-league longevity.

Or take the case of 33-year-old Prentice "Pidge" Browne of the new Houston Colt .45's, who never had a look-in at the majors before. He spent a dozen seasons in the minors, including several stretches at Houston. After the city got its big-league franchise, he was signed on this year primarily as a left-handed pinch-hitter. As of late June he had come through with nine hits—several of them game-winners—in 25 official pinch at-bats. Manager Harry Craft was predicting that Pidge would break Sam Leslie's 30-year-old National League record of 22 pinch-hits in one season.

Pinch-hitting requires a rare combination of patience and fierce concentration. The pinch-hitter's workday is short, usually lasting for only a minute or two and sometimes for just one swing. Many big-name stars have not been able to distinguish themselves in pinch roles.

The late Ty Cobb, whose .367 batting percentage is the highest of all time, averaged .247 as a pinch-hitter. Babe Ruth's figure was a mere .200. Ted Williams, regarded as the best of the modern hitters, batted .316 in his final season of 1960 but had only a .053 pinch-hitting average, with a solitary single in 19 at-bats. His lifetime average in pinch appearances was .271.

Mickey Mantle, whose experience in the role has been very limited, says simply, "I don't like to pinch hit. I never did." Roger Maris, who did some of it at the start of his big-league career in Cleveland and Kansas City, is less emphatic. "I didn't mind—too much," he says, although he can't recall winning a game with a pinch-hit.

Jerry Lynch of the Cincinnati Reds is easily the best pinch-hitter in the majors today—he has been delivering at a .350 clip this season—but he yields to nobody in expressing distaste for the assignment.

Of the scores of past and present pinch-hitters who were interviewed for this article, one of the few who admitted to a liking for the job was big John Mize, a part-time first baseman and pinch-swinger when the New York Yankees were winning five successive pennants from 1949 through 1953. The Yankees gave $40,000 to get the aging slugger from the Giants and paid him a salary in excess of $25,000. He was more than worth it.

Mize considers pinch-hitting easier than batting regularly. His reasoning is that the man who comes up in a pinch situation generally gets better pitches to swing at than in normal circumstances. "The pitchers were in a jam by the time I got in there," Mize explains. "The pressure was on them, not me. They couldn't fool around. They had to throw strikes."

Cincinnati's Lynch vigorously states the other side of the case: "The pinch-hitter gets only one time at bat. He either does or he doesn't. The fellow playing regularly can strike out in the first inning, he can pop up in the fourth, but if he singles or doubles in a run or two in the sixth, he's had a good day. With us there's no second chance."

If Lynch doesn't enjoy being a spot hitter, opposing pitchers are even less happy to see him come up. Manager Fred Hutchinson last year sometimes would have Jerry climb out of the dugout as if preparing to bat even when there was no intention of using him.

Just the sight of Lynch coiled in the on-deck circle was frightening to many pitchers. Admitted Elvin Tappe, the Cubs' head coach for most of the 1961 season, "One look at him and our pitchers went to pieces. Even the guys in the bullpen began losing their stuff."

Psychological Warfare
The injection of psychological warfare into the use of pinch-hitters is nothing new. John McGraw of the Giants, one of the game's most original thinkers, was doing it back before World War I.

McGraw always made a real production out of sending up the fearsome Harry "Moose" McCormick. According to an account by Damon

Runyon, McCormick wouldn't step into the batter's box "until after a three-minute delay during which time the trainer would massage his legs with a bat to create the proper circulation and atmosphere for the Moose to stride majestically to the plate and look the quaking pitcher in the eye."

"This isn't quite true," McCormick said a while ago at his home in Lewisburg, Pennsylvania. "The trainer used cocoa butter."

McCormick is a legend among pinch-hitters, but neither he nor anybody else has had quite as devastating a single season as Jerry Lynch with Cincinnati last year. Lynch started off with three home runs in his first five tries and went on from there. All told, he made 59 appearances as a substitute hitter in 1961 and was safe more than half the time, drawing 12 walks and delivering 19 hits for a .404 pinch-batting average. More than half his hits were for extra bases.

Should Lynch Start?

Lynch's sustained success created one problem for manager Hutchinson. Should he continue to hold Jerry on the bench and use him only in the late innings, when a pinch-hit in the right spot could tie or win a game? Or should he start Lynch in left field, gambling that his productivity in the normal four times at bat would outweigh his defensive shortcomings?

Lynch started only 10 games during the first half of the season, but beginning in mid-August, he was in the regular lineup in 20 of 31 games. Had Hutch kept him in a reserve role all year long, Jerry undoubtedly would have broken most of the existing pinch-hitting records for one season.

After the Reds clinched the pennant on September 26, Hutchinson said he would use Lynch as a pinch-hitter in the Reds' remaining three games at Pittsburgh to give Jerry a shot at the record of six pinch homers in a season, set in 1932 by Johnny Frederick of the Brooklyn Dodgers.

Lynch had five pinch homers going into his final series, but was unable to add any more. Not only that, on the next-to-last day he took a called third strike for the first time in two seasons of heavy duty as a pinch-hitter.

He argued the call heatedly, claiming that the pitch—thrown by Clem Labine—had missed the outside corner and should have been ball three. "It was one of those borderline pitches," Lynch said months later, relaxing with his family at their home in Allison Park, Pennsylvania. "I'm sorry for some of the things I said. Landes [Stan Landes, the plate umpire] was right in throwing me out."

It was not surprising that Lynch got so worked up about the decision. Most professional pinch-hitters take the greatest pride not in how many hits they deliver but rather in how few times they strike out. Their object is at least to get a piece of the ball. Going down swinging is bad enough, but taking the third strike is unpardonable.

Bob Hale, an excellent pinch-batter, illustrates the point. In 1960, when he was with Cleveland, he had five pinch-hits in a row, tying an American League record set by John Mize. The record was tied again this year by Vic Wertz of Detroit. Hale finished 1960 with a total of 19, one short of Parke Coleman's league mark—since broken by Dave Philley. But that wasn't what gave Hale the greatest satisfaction. "I pinch hit in 70 ball games," he said recently, "and I took only one third strike."

Hale went on waivers last August to the Yankees and rode the bench with them to the pennant. It was, he concedes, an education just to sit in the Yankee dugout. Never had he been on a team with such depth. "Before, wherever I went I was the number one pinch-hitter. With the Yankees, I was number four." Johnny Blanchard, Bob Cerv, and Hector Lopez all rated ahead of him.

Aging Players Hang On

The Yankees, clearing some of the fringe players from their roster shortly after the 1961 season, sent Hale down to Richmond. "They were overly generous," Hale said in Chicago, where he was working in the off-season as a playground instructor. "I pinch hit seven times and they still voted me two-thirds of a Series share." Then Hale, who is 28, added, "I'll be back. I'll hit .300 at Richmond, and one of the big-league clubs will sign me. There is always a spot for a good pinch-hitter."

Elmer Valo, now a scout with the New York Mets, would be the first to agree. Last year, at 40, he was still in there swinging with the Phillies; it was his 20th season in the majors. He had played longer than anyone else then active except Stan Musial and Early Wynn.

During his last four years Valo survived almost exclusively as a pinch-hitter. As an American Leaguer in 1960 he got in 81 games as a substitute batsman, the first time a pinch-hitter had appeared in more than half a season's quota of games. He produced hits at a .261 pace.

Another veteran a few months older than Valo is eager to keep going. He is Dave Philley, a saddle-faced Texan now with the Boston Red Sox, who connected for a record 24 pinch-hits with the Baltimore Orioles last year. In 1958 with the Phillies he established still another mark with a string of eight consecutive pinch hits. He extended it to nine straight in his first appearance in 1959.

"It took me a couple of years to adjust to pinch-hitting," Philley says. "The toughest thing is learning to sit on the bench. Everyone wants to play. It's the natural thing. But I learned to sit. No one knows the pitchers like the pinch-hitters. We watch 'em like hawks."

Pinch-hitters fall into categories. Philley, for example, is a slap hitter who can be counted on to meet the ball. Men of this type are summoned for singles, and seldom for power. Others, such as Smoky Burgess of the Pirates, Charley Maxwell of the Tigers, Carl Sawatski of the Cardinals, and Chuck Essegian of the Indians, are called on when the situation demands a long ball.

Catcher Burgess, often tapped for pinch duty in games he doesn't start, has a career total of 11 home runs as a pinch-hitter—three short of George Crowe's major league record of 14. Outfielder Essegian—often a regular starter this season—is the only man to hit two pinch homers in a World Series. He did it in 1959 for the Los Angeles Dodgers against the Chicago White Sox.

Bob Cerv of the Yankees, who has hit 12 pinch homers, and Vic Wertz of the Tigers are noted for their ability to bring in runners with sacrifice flies. Julio Becquer, late of the Minnesota Twins, and Bob Boyd, recently of the Milwaukee Braves, were in the speed-merchant class—an important pinch-hitting asset when the manager is anxious to avoid the double play.

Earl Torgeson, who concluded his long playing career with the Yankees last year, exemplifies still another breed. Torgie was primarily a "pinch-looker"—almost always waiting out the pitcher and trying for a walk, which he often got. Such a man is ideal as a rally starter and is usually sent up to lead off an inning.

Most desirable of all is the versatile pinch-hitter like Jerry Lynch, who can be used under any circumstances—although preferably not with first base open, when the opposing manager can order an intentional base on balls, as happened in the third game of the 1961 World Series.

Lynch and Hale and most of the younger crop of pinch specialists prefer to swing at the first pitch—or the first "good" pitch, as they put it. "I'm swinging when I leave the bench," Hale has said, and Lynch declares, "I'm that way too. You've got to be aggressive."

Skip the First Pitch

Ron Northey, who developed into a remarkable pinch-hitter at the tag end of his playing career several years ago, was different. He decided early that he would never swing at the first pitch. Beginning with Johnny Mize's premise that the pressure was on the pitcher, Northey further reasoned that the first delivery would always be the pitch that was working best for the pitcher on that particular day.

Northey kept tabs. After two months he had established that eight times out of ten, the first pitch to him wasn't thrown for a strike anyway. More important, by standing and watching it go by, Northey could study the speed and break of the ball. He knew this same pitch would appear again, usually at the moment when the pressure was greatest. "That was the pitch I would hit," Northey says.

Northey, who is now a coach with the Pittsburgh Pirates, twice led the major leagues in pinch-hitting. His 1956 season with the White Sox was his best. In 39 official pinch at-bats he connected for 15 hits—13 of them with two strikes against him—and drove in the winning run in the late innings of eight different ball games. Mickey Mantle, who won the American League's triple crown that season, drove in the winning run in only nine Yankee games.

The Dodgers missed a chance to pick up Northey from the Charleston club in the American Association the year before because they decided he had grown too fat. With a Dodger scout in the stands, Northey put on a great hitting show, but nothing happened.

"They want you," Northey was told by Danny Menendez, the Charleston owner. "But they said you've got to lose 10 pounds."

Within four days Northey had pared off the weight, but the Dodger agent said he still was too heavy and didn't look good in a uniform. "What the hell do they want?" Northey asked Menendez. "A model or a ballplayer?"

Destruction by Dusty

Another memorable pinch-hitter was James "Dusty" Rhodes, now trying at 35 to work his way back from the minor leagues. In his day, which wasn't too long ago, Rhodes became famous as the only pinch-hitter ever to dominate an entire World Series as the New York Giants swept four straight from the Cleveland Indians in 1954. Rhodes won the first game with a three-run pinch-homer in the tenth inning. His one-run pinch-single helped to make the difference in a 3–1 game the next day. In the third game he contributed a two-run single to start the scoring. Dusty wasn't needed in the fourth game, which the Giants won going away.

"Rhodes thought he could hit anybody living," said Leo Durocher, who handled him. "And he did—that one year. I always tried to use him in the right spot, where they couldn't walk him. But I didn't put him in. He put himself in. When the number seven, eight, or nine men were due to hit he'd have his jacket off and be taking his practice swings. Then if we'd get a man on base, he'd come over, spitting tobacco juice and saying, 'Hey, Skip. Me? Now?'"

Durocher doesn't rate Rhodes as the best pinch-hitter he has seen, though. Leo picks two men who were active in his own playing days— Lew Riggs, of Cincinnati and Brooklyn, and Pat Crawford, who played for three National League clubs.

Everyone seems to have his own favorite. Dizzy Dean votes for Lefty O'Doul. The choice of Red Sox Manager Mike Higgins is Sheriff Dave Harris of the Senators. Charlie Grimm, who entered the majors prior to World War I, gives the nod to Moose McCormick. Clarence Rowland, a

Cub executive who goes back even farther than Grimm, recalls another McGraw pinch-hitter, Sammy Strang.

Pitchers Good in a Pinch

Some of the great pinch-hitters, surprisingly enough, have been pitchers, such as Red Lucas, Red Ruffing, and Jim Tobin of a generation ago, and Bob Lemon and Don Newcombe of more recent vintage. Red Lucas, now a tax collector in Nashville, Tennessee, had 114 pinch-hits in 16 years of National League service, the present career high.

The record is certain to tumble. As of a month ago, for example, Jerry Lynch had accumulated 69 pinch-hits since 1957. He has been at it on what could be considered a regular basis only since 1960. If Lynch doesn't remain a pinch specialist long enough to top Lucas, somebody else will, simply because there is so much more pinch-hitting nowadays.

Managers are completely sold on the practice. Some playing managers have been bold enough to pinch hit themselves. American League president Joe Cronin slammed five pinch home runs for the Boston Red Sox in 1943. Lou Boudreau won two key games down the stretch with pinch-hits while piloting Cleveland to the 1948 pennant.

Frank Frisch's last major league hit came in a pinch role. His Cardinals, trailing the Braves by one run in the ninth, had the bases loaded with two out. Frisch was looking down the bench trying to decide whom to send up to the plate when a spectator yelled, "Hey, grandma, why don't *you* hit?" Frisch did, singling to win the game.

As a rule, however, the manager turns to a specialist to do the big job in the clutch. Perhaps the ultimate in rendering aid to a manager was achieved by Singing Sam Leslie, after establishing his National League record of 22 pinch-hits for the Giants in 1932.

Following the season Leslie had Bill Terry, his boss, as a houseguest in Pascagoula, Mississippi. One morning they were out fishing in a boat and Terry, who couldn't swim, fell overboard. As he had so many times before, Leslie came through for his manager. He jumped in and brought Terry safely ashore.

Introduction to
My Greatest Day in Baseball

ORIGINALLY PUBLISHED IN 1945, REPRINTED IN 1996

WE SHOULD BE GRATEFUL TO JOHN PETER CARMICHAEL for this collection of 47 as-told-to stories by some of baseball's best-known luminaries who sat for interviews and recalled their greatest moments in baseball. They are individual recollections but when stitched together become an excellent framework of diamond history, in effect, an antecedent to Larry Ritter's classic *Glory of Their Times*.

I was among the fortunate who not only knew Mr. Carmichael but also worked alongside him. When I was a young sportswriter breaking in on the Chicago baseball beat, he was a veteran and much-decorated sports columnist for the *Chicago Daily News*. I don't know if the "greatest day" series was his idea, or if it flowed from his good friend, Lloyd Lewis, at that time the *Daily News* sports editor. What I do know is, Carmichael always understood the beauty of turning his column over to his subjects.

On many occasions it was their column, not his. The best example of his approach—and for me, it has been unforgettable—occurred almost 40 years ago when we were in Tampa, Florida, covering the White Sox during spring training. It was the custom for the writers to meet at the headquarter hotel for 5:00 cocktails; for the next hour or so the happenings of the day were reviewed. Carmichael wasn't anchored to the White Sox and traveled to other camps, usually in the company of fellow columnists. He had been to Bradenton and had interviewed Charlie Dressen, the manager of the Milwaukee Braves.

"Charlie Dressen gave me a terrific column," Carmichael announced, obviously pleased with his day's production.

And, immediately, it occurred to me that most sportswriters, perhaps all, would have said, "I wrote a terrific column on Charlie Dressen today," giving themselves, not Dressen, the credit.

That would have been the natural reaction. But Carmichael knew that Dressen, a good talker, had supplied the column. Carmichael was the host; Dressen was the attraction. I am not suggesting that Carmichael was just a typist. He was among the very best sportswriters of his time, in my view among the best of all time. But like a good baseball manager, he knew when there was no need to interfere.

My Greatest Day in Baseball is the epitome of this sensible and honest approach. Except when moralizing, which is usually a mistake—pontificating is a better word—the best sports columns are entertaining and informative, ideally a combination of both. Essentially an anecdotist, Carmichael added a third dimension, what can be described as "a gentle ramble."

Readers of the sports pages are knowledgeable. They know what's going on, especially since the advent of television, and, I am convinced, are weary of the shrill daily assaults on players, owners, managers—the so-called "aw nuts" school of sportswriting. "Aw nuts" can be a proper approach if offered sparingly, but many of the practitioners can't play in any other key. They're constantly beating a dead horse. Carmichael was of the "gee whiz" genre. He seldom wrote a harsh sentence. If he didn't like somebody— and he certainly had his dislikes—he withdrew and didn't offer access; he ignored them.

Once I asked him why his column was always cheerful, why he was such a nice-guy writer. His reply:

> The only time I meant to be vicious was against Bill Cox. He owned the Phillies. Judge Landis threw him out for betting on

baseball. Cox was an arrogant son-of-a-bitch. When he fired Bucky Harris, his manager, I really blasted him. It was the only time I was mad enough at anyone to do it. I never believed in castigating a lot of people, I don't know why. Maybe it was because I always had a feeling that if you turn out to be wrong, you've done irreparable damage.

Carmichael also abhorred peephole journalism. I recall a story by one of the *Daily News* staffers who was assigned to an owners' meeting at the Edgewater Beach Hotel in Chicago. After listening through an air vent, the reporter presented a running account of some of the dialogue. Carmichael expressed disdain. He insisted it wasn't ethical, that baseball owners were entitled to privacy, same as a meeting of the directors of a corporation.

This book is about events on the field, not behind closed doors. Many historic moments are covered. And all the players aren't portrayed as saints. But the criticism, where it appears, is justified. For example, here is Mordecai "Three Finger" Brown of the Cubs recalling how Christy Mathewson of the Giants, the Great Matty, took the field for the replay of the controversial "Merkle boner" game, which forced a playoff for the 1908 National League pennant:

> I can still see Christy Mathewson making his lordly entrance. He'd always wait until about 10 minutes before game time, then he'd come from the clubhouse across the field in a long linen duster like auto drivers wore in those days, and at every step the crowd would yell louder and louder. This day they split the air. I watched him enter as I went out to the bullpen, where I was to keep ready. [Frank] Chance still insisted on starting [Jack] Pfeister.

Certainly, a revealing glimpse of the aristocratic Mathewson—who at the time of his retirement held the National League record for the most victories. A companion reminiscence of the Merkle game is offered by Johnny Evers, the Chicago second baseman. It was the most controversial game of the 20th century. Evers reveals the crucial event, in Pittsburgh 19 days earlier, that prompted the ninth-inning, force-play call by umpire

Hank O'Day that denied the Giants of what appeared to be a routine victory.

Carmichael was the coauthor of 15 of these 47 chapters. In the original presentation they were in a beautifully illustrated *Chicago Daily News* series. The stories ran in the winter, during the baseball off-season, usually two a week, when the sports pages were empty. In those days, baseball was *the* major sport. Football and basketball were covered but were secondary.

A significant number of contributions were written by "outsiders": Chet Smith of Pittsburgh, for example, was teamed with Honus Wagner, the Pirates' star shortstop. Ernie Mehl of Kansas City was assigned to Satchel Paige, the great black star who for many years made his home in that city. Shirley Povich of Washington interviewed Clark Griffith, the so-called Old Fox who owned and operated the Washington Senators and before that was a big-league pitcher. Similarly, Bill Leiser of San Francisco drew Lefty O'Doul, and New York's Ken Smith did Frankie Frisch.

Carmichael's pieces are among the best. Born in Madison, Wisconsin, on October 16, 1902, the son of the general manager of a dental supply company, he attended Campion Academy in Prairie du Chien, Wisconsin, and Marquette University in Milwaukee. He dropped out of Marquette during his junior year. He did not intend to be a journalist but was supposed to major in accounting and commerce. When I interviewed him in 1972 he explained what had happened:

> I was walking with another fellow, this was when I was at Marquette, going up the hill to Barnett Hall, and I said, "Gee, I hate this 8:00 class. Why don't they have classes at a civilized hour?"
>
> He said, "You should have gone into journalism. They don't have any classes until 9:00 or 10:00 in the morning."
>
> The Journalism Building was right across the way. So I left him and enrolled in journalism.

His first newspaper job was covering the morgue as a night-shift cityside reporter for the *Milwaukee Journal*. He switched to the now defunct

Milwaukee Leader where he remained for two years as a drama critic and reporter. He came to Chicago on a vacation in 1927 and ended up on the sports desk of the old *Herald & Examiner.* He joined the *Daily News* in 1932 and two years later was rewarded with a column.

"Howard Mann was the sports editor and he asked me to think up a name for it," Carmichael recalled. "I said, 'The Barber Shop.'

"He asked me why and I told him, 'There is no damn use in putting a column on the sports page with a heading "Inside Sports" or something like that. What the hell, they know it's on sports.' I told him I grew up in small towns and the barbershop was the place where everybody settled everything."

"The Barber Shop" had a long run: 38 years. Carmichael estimated he had written 11,000 columns. The sports editors of all four Chicago dailies—*Tribune, News, Sun-Times,* and *Chicago Today*—served as cochairmen of a giant City of Hope testimonial banquet on his retirement in 1972. He died in 1986 at the age of 83.

From the beginning his column was well received; it wasn't long before he had a national reputation. He was among the country's most prolific and well-traveled sportswriters and was welcome at every stop. Connie Mack and Ted Williams, among others, repeatedly said he was their favorite sportswriter.

In addition to his column, he wrote hundreds of sidebars and feature stories, along with dozens of lengthy profiles on theatrical personalities, all of which were bannered and took an entire page. The theatre fascinated him. After interviewing Tallulah Bankhead in New York, where she was playing in *The Little Foxes,* she insisted he appear with her and stationed him at a table on the rear of the stage. He was also in constant demand as a speaker.

Except for writing down dates, Mr. Carmichael never took notes. Early on, he discovered the pad and pencil not only slowed the process but were discomfiting and inhibiting to his subjects. This was long before the invasion of electronic journalism. There were no portable tape recorders. To put his subjects at ease, Carmichael worked at developing his memory.

When he sat down at the typewriter he was able to reconstruct the dialogue with remarkable accuracy.

Some of the pieces written by others, in spots, are stiff. We can easily detect when the writer is using his words in transmitting the recollections. This is never true with Carmichael. Like Ring Lardner, who was among his Chicago predecessors, Carmichael had a great ear. His piece on Dizzy Dean is a genuine classic, perhaps the best sports story I have read. I still marvel, a half century later, how he did it without taking notes.

After Dean beat Detroit 11–0 in the final game of the 1934 World Series, he recalls a clubhouse conversation with Frankie Frisch, his manager:

> Frisch came by and do you know what he said? "Anybody with your stuff should have won 40 games instead of a measly 30. You loaf. That's the trouble. Thirty games! You ought to be 'shamed of yourself."
>
> Imagine that, and me just winning the Series for him: ol' Diz out there pitchin' outta turn too, don't forget that. He wanted me to pitch although he'd said Bill Hallahan was gonna work the last game. But he came to me the night before and he asked: "Diz, you wanna be the greatest man in baseball?" I told him I already was, but he didn't even hear me 'cause he went on: "You pitch that game tomorrow and you'll be tops." I just told him, "Gimme that ball tomorrow and your troubles are over." He wanted me to pitch. I knew that. Hell, I was afraid he would let Hallahan start.

INDEX

A Memoir of a Modest Man (Angle), 160
Aaron, Hank, 54, 144
ABC television, 80
Abernathy, Ted, 50
Adams, Bobby and Dick, 31
Adams, Franklin P., 137, 139
Adcock, Joe, 190
Agee, Tommie, 52
Ainge, Danny, 170
Alexander, Gary, 42
Alexander, Hugh, 75–77
Alexander, Pete, 41
All-American Conference, 123
Allen, Ethan, 118
Allen, Maury, 155
Allen, Richie, 142
All-Star Game
  creation of the, 120–23
  Cubs in 1969, 51
Allyn, John, 129
Alomar, Roberto and Sandy, Jr. (sons), 32
Alomar, Sandy, Sr. (father), 31
Alou, Felipe (father), 9, 25, 32, 33, 189
Alou, Moises (son), 32
amateur free agents, major league draft of, 81–86
American Association, 9, 199
American Civil Liberties Union (ACLU), 145
American League (AL)
  and creation of the All-Star Game, 120–23
  first black players for, 129
  Manager of the Year award, 24
  Most Valuable Player award, 68, 167
  Rookie of the Year award, 82
  scoreless innings records, 110
  Twins 1965 pennant win, 3
American Negro League, 76
amyotrophic lateral sclerosis (Lou Gehrig's disease), 173
Angle, Paul M., 160
Anson, Adrian "Cap," 157, 158, 199–200
Aparicio, Luis, 44–46, 105, 151
Applachian League, 19
Appling, Luke, 45, 101, 105, 155
Arch—A Promoter Not a Poet (Littlewood), 120
Arizona Rookie League, 29
Atlanta Braves, 43, 144
Attell, Abe, 113, 114, 115

Babe Ruth (Meany), 91–92, 95
Bahnsen, Stan, 40, 42
Baines, Harold, 83
Baird, Tom, 76
Baker, Dusty, 24, 26, 189, 190, 191
Baker, Gene, 180
Ball Four (Bouton), 208
Baltimore Orioles, 9, 32, 99, 172, 215
  no-hitters, 38, 42, 43
Bankhead, Tallulah, 223
Banks, Ernie, 50, 51, 52, 76, 101, 104, 106, 107, 138, 142, 178–80, 183, 190
Baseball America, 82, 86
Baseball Digest, 90, 152
Baseball Hall of Fame
  baseball writers in, vi–vii, 34, 136
  broadcasters in, 118, 196, 201
  eligibility for, 105–7
  exclusion of Shoeless Joe Jackson from, 111
  Hall of Famers on Old Timers' All-Star team, 101–4
  and how it began, 133–36
  shortstops in, 44–46, 105
  20-game loser pitchers in, 5
Baseball Hall of Fame inductees
  Aparicio, Luis, 44–46
  Brock, Lou, 163, 165
  Chance, Frank, 139
  Evers, Johnny, 139
  Galvin, Pud, 4
  Greenberg, Hank, 69
  Tinker, Joe, 139
  Veeck, Bill, 127, 129, 192
Baseball Magazine, 121
Baseball: The President's Game (Mead and Dickson), 155–56
Baseball Writers Association of America (BBWAA), 44, 45, 106, 107, 118
basketball and baseball careers, 169–71
Beckert, Glenn, 51, 52, 138
Becquer, Julio, 215
Bell, David (grandson), Buddy (son), and Gus (grandfather), 32
Bell, George, 177
Bench, Johnny, 106, 206
Berg, Moe, 204–9
Berra, Dale (son), 32, 33
Berra, Yogi (father), 32, 33, 60

Berres, Ray, 46
Bescher, Bob, 41
Bevens, Bill, 38, 39, 42
black ballplayers, 78–80, 146, 147, 186–88, 222
  first, 198–200
  See also individual players
Black Sox scandal, 111–16
Blair, Paul, 205–6
Blanchard, Johnny, 214
Blue, Vida, 205–6
Boeckel, Tony, 12
Bohne, Sam, 41
Boland, Bernie, 41
Bonds, Barry (son) and Bobby (father), 31, 176
Boone, Aaron (son), 32
Boone, Bob (father), 32
Boone, Bret (son), 7, 32
Boone, Ray "Ike" (grandfather), 32
Boston Beaneaters, 41
Boston Braves, 11–14, 122, 186, 193
Boston Globe, 119, 208
Boston Pilgrims, 9
Boston Red Sox, 24, 80, 167
  ambidextrous pitchers, 8, 9
  Buckner, Bill, with, 124, 125–26
  early black ballplayers and, 186–87
  no-hitters, 41, 42, 43
  pinch-hitters, 215, 218
Boudreau, Lou, 101, 170, 201, 218
Bouton, Jim, 208
Boyd, Bob, 215
Boyer, Ken, 106
Braves Field, Boston, 12
Breadon, Sam, 121
Brett, Ken, 40, 42
Brick Alley Press, Stillwater, MN, 2
Brickhouse, Jack Beasley, 130, 201–3
Bridges, Tommy, 41, 173
broadcasters
  Brickhouse, Jack, 201–3
  Buck, Jack, 118
  Caray, Harry, 195–97
  Totten, Hal, 95–96
Brock, Lou, 152, 163–65, 170
Broeg, Bob, 34–35, 106
Broglio, Ernie, 163–65
Brooklyn Dodgers, 9, 79, 102, 213

225

marathon game between
    Boston Braves and, 11–14
  in 1947 World Series, 38, 39
  no-hitters, 41, 42
  replacement players, 167, 168
  Robinson, Jackie, and,
    187–88
Brooklyn Robins, 41
Brooklyn Superbas, 41
Brosnan, Jim, 63–66, 108,
    109, 184
Brown, Bobby, 8–9
Brown, John, 17
Brown, Mordecai "Three
    Finger," 221
Brown, Prentice "Pidge," 211
Brown, Tommy, 168
Brown, Warren, 95
Buck, Jack, 118
Buckner, Bill, 80, 124–26
Bunning, Jim, 156
Bureau scouts, 85
Burgess, Smoky, 215
Burns, Bill, 41, 113
Burns, Edward, 95
Burroughs, Jeff, 151
Busch Stadium, St. Louis, MO,
    53
Bush, Donie, 46
Bush, George, 117–18, 156
Bush, Guy, 93
Butler, Art, 41
Butler, Brett, 148–49

Cadore, Leon, 11–14
Cain, Bob, 34
California Angels, 5, 40, 42,
    84, 98, 125, 170
Campanella, Roy, 180, 188
Campanis, Al (father), 33,
    78–80, 146
Campanis, Jim (son), 33
Campbell, Nolan, 29
Campusano, Sil, 43
Cannon, Jimmy, vii, 206
Canseco, Jose, 82
Caray, Harry, 179, 195–97
Carlton, Steve, 5, 65
Carmichael, John Peter, 219–24
Carolina League, 21
Cash, Norm, 109
Castillo, Frank, 40, 43
Cermak, Anton, 93
Cerv, Bob, 214, 215
Chamberlain, Elton "Ice Box,"
    9
Chance, Frank, 137–39
Chandler, Happy, 168
Chattanooga Lookouts, 3
Chicago American, 188
Chicago Bears, 203
Chicago Cubs, 5, 28, 32, 147
  as Anson's Colts, 157

Banks, Ernie, Mr. Cub,
    178–80
Boudreau-for-Grimm trade,
    201
Brickhouse, Jack, as
    announcer for, 201–3
Broglio-for-Brock trade,
    163–65
  Brosnan, Jim, with, 63, 64
  Bush, George, and, 117–19
  Dawson, Andre, with,
    181–83
  double-play legend, 137–39
  last pennant won by, 168
  and lights in Wrigley Field,
    47, 49
  in 1932 World Series, 92–96
  1969 season, 50–52
  no-hitters, 40, 42, 43
  owner Philip K. Wrigley,
    160–62, 201
  player in 30/30 club, 176
  replacement players, 166
  Rose, Pete, and, 56, 57
  Santo, Ron, and Hall of
    Fame eligibility, 106–7
  scouts for, 76, 77, 84
  Sosa, Sammy, with, 175–77
  Sunday, Billy, with, 157–59
  Veeck, William L., Sr., and,
    193–94
Chicago Daily News, 161, 164,
    219, 221, 222, 223
Chicago Evening American,
    192
Chicago Herald & Examiner,
    223
Chicago Historical Society, 112
Chicago Inter Ocean, 192
Chicago News, 223
Chicago Player of the Year
    Award, 124
Chicago Sun-Times, vii, 188, 223
Chicago Today, 223
Chicago Tribune, v, vii, 120,
    121, 122, 123, 223
Chicago White Sox, 5, 9, 16,
    23, 32, 46, 61, 83, 167
  Aparicio, Luis, with, 44
  Brosnan, Jim, with, 63, 65
  Caray, Harry, as announcer
    for, 196–97
  Jackson, Shoeless Joe, and,
    111–16
  Jordan, Michael, with, 169,
    171
  in 1959 World Series, 189,
    215
  no-hitters, 39, 40, 41, 42
  scout with, 76, 77
  Veeck, Bill, ownership of,
    127, 128, 129, 161–62

White House reception for,
    154–55
Chicago White Stockings,
    199–200
Chicago World's Fair, 120
Chilcott, Steve, 86
Church, Marguerite Stitt, 154
Cincinnati Reds, 7, 20, 32, 98,
    164, 168
  Brosnan, Jim, with, 63
  Durocher, Leo, and, 101, 103
  no-hitters, 41, 42, 43
  pinch-hitters, 212, 213
  Rose, Pete, with, 54, 56–57
  and Schott, Marge, contro-
    versy, 144
  sign stealing, 189, 191
Clarkson, John, 41
Class A baseball
  Class A Midwest League, 27
  umpire salaries in, 28–29
Class B Carolina League, 21
Class C Mid-Atlantic League, 77
Class D Appalachian League, 19
Class D Northern League, 77
Cleveland Buckeyes, 186
Cleveland Indians, 69, 99, 167
  first black player, 129
  in 1954 World Series, 102
  no-hitters, 38, 39, 41, 42, 43
  pinch-hitters, 214, 217, 218
Cleveland Naps, 41
Cleveland Spiders, 41, 210
Clymer, Otis, 41
coaches, pitching, 98
Cobb, Ty, 46, 54–55, 56, 57,
    58, 111, 211
Cobbledick, Gordon, 95
Coleman, Parke, 214
Colorado Rockies, 43
Colt Stadium, Houston, 98
Comiskey, Charles A., 115
Comiskey Park, Chicago, 39,
    40, 44, 48, 76, 95, 124,
    154
Conley, Gene, 170
Conlon, Jocko, 101, 102, 141
Continental League, 207
Corcoran, Larry, 9
Corcoran, Tommy, 189–90
Cortesio, Ria, 27, 28, 29, 30
Corum, Bill, 91, 95
Cosell, Howard, 202
Cox, Bill, 69, 220–21
Cox, Theresa, 29–30
Craft, Harry, 211
Cramer, Doc, 39, 42
Cravath, Gavvy, 41
Crawford, Pat, 217
Crawford, Shag, 142
Cronin, Joe, 45, 208, 218
Crowe, George, 215

Index

Cuccinello, Tony, 167–68, 189
Cy Young award, 87, 98

Dahlgren, Babe, 174
Daily Times, 95
Dale, Jerry, 30
Daley, Arthur, 206
Daniel, Dan, 95
Dark, Alvin, 102, 179
Davies, George, 210
Davis, Eric, 82, 149
Davis, Jody, 89
Dawidoff, Nicholas, 111
Dawley, Bill, 182
Dawson, Andre, 181–83
Dayton Daily News, 147
Dean, Dizzy, 16, 217, 224
DeBakey, Michael, 102, 103
DeBusschere, Dave, 170
Delahanty, Ed, 41
DeLeon, Jose, 5
Delsing, Jim, 34
depreciation of ballplayers, 128
designated hitter, 178
Detroit Tigers, 16, 17, 47, 167
  Greenberg, Hank, with, 68,
    69
  Manuel, Jerry, with, 25, 26
  midget pinch-hitter in game
    against, 34
  in 1934 World Series, 224
  no-hitters, 39, 40, 41, 42, 43
Devine, Bing, 86, 169–70
Dickey, Bill, 73
Dickson, Paul, 156
DiMaggio, Joe, 130–32, 155,
  166
Doby, Larry, 129, 188, 198
Dodger Stadium, Los Angeles,
  148, 149
Donatelli, Augie, 142
double plays, 137–39
Doubleday Field,
  Cooperstown, NY, 149
Doubleday, Nelson, vi
Downing, Brian, 82
Doyle, Jack, 210
Drabek, Doug, 43
Drabowsky, Moe, 179
draft, baseball, 81–86
Drebinger, John, 62, 94, 95
Dressen, Charlie, 189, 190, 220
Drysdale, Don, 140, 149–50,
  179
Duffy, Hugh, 41
Dunlop, Harry, 20–21
Dunston, Shawon, 57, 84, 85,
  88, 138, 183
Duquette, Dan, 8, 85
Durham, Leon, 56
Durocher, Leo, 50, 101–4,
  163, 201–2, 217

Durso, Joe, 207
Dybzinski, Jerry, 24–25, 40

Einhorn, Eddie, 146
Eisenhower, Dwight D., 156
Eisenreich, Jim, 2
Eisenstat, Harry, 69–70
Elias Sports Bureau, 166
Elliott, Harold, 12
Ellis, Steve, 202
Elson, Bob, 154, 196
Engel, Bob, 58
Epstein, Mike, 73
Erickson, Scott, 5
Ernie Banks International, 180
Esasky, Nick, 125
Essegian, Chuck, 215
Everett, Carl, 38, 43
Evers, Johnny, 138–39, 221–22

Face, Elroy, 22
Farrell, Turk, 98
fastballs
  of ambidextrous pitchers, 8
  Feller, Bob, 15, 17–18, 98
  Maddux, Greg, 88
  Ryan, Nolan, 97–98
father-son duos, 31–33
Feller, Bob "Rapid Robert,"
  15–18, 69–70, 98
Fenway Park, Boston, 72, 126,
  132
Ferdenzi, Til, 59–60
Ferris, Dave "Boo," 9
Filiatrault, Phil, 19, 20
Fisk, Carlton, 32
Fitz Gerald, Ed, 39, 42, 154
Flanagan, Mike, 42
Flood, Curt, 184–85
Florida Marlins, 25, 181
Fonseca, Lew, 17–18, 46
Foote, Barry, 126
Fox, Nellie, 39, 74, 105
Foxx, Jimmie, 61, 73, 167
Franco, Julio, 38, 43
Francona, Tito (father) and
  Terry (son), 32
Frederick, Johnny, 213
free agency, 184–85
free-agent scouts, 81–86
freedom of speech
  and Marge Schott contro-
    versy, 144–47
Fregosi, Jim, 109
Frick, Ford, 61, 133–36, 155
Friend, Bob, 22, 156, 179
Frisch, Frank, 218, 222, 224
Frontier League, 19

Gable, Clark, 200
Gaedel, Edward Carl, 34–37
Galarraga, Andres, 43
Galehouse, Denny, 69, 168

Gallagher, James Timothy,
  47–49, 168, 202
Gallico, Paul, 95
Galvin, Pud, 4
game losses, historic
  20-game losers, 4–6
Gandil, Chick, 112, 113, 114,
  115, 116
Garagiola, Joe, 34
Garrelts, Scott, 43
Garrett, Wayne, 52
Gedman, Rich, 82
Gehrig, Lou, 68, 93, 119,
  172–74
general manager, baseball
  owner as, 1
Gera, Bernice, 29
Giamatti, Bart, 30
Gibson, Bob, 65
Gilkey, Bernard, 43
Gillespie, Gordon, 71–72, 74
Glory of Their Times (Ritter),
  219
gloves, baseball
  reversible six-finger glove, 7
  Gold Glove awards, 152
Goldsberry, Gordon, 84–85
Goler, Robert A., 112
Gomez, Lefty, 18, 132
Gooden, Dwight, 66, 84, 85
Gordon, Joe, 39, 42
Gorman, Lou, 125
Gossage, Goose, 98
Gowdy, Hank, 12, 13
Grace, Mark, 138
Grady, Sandy, 180
Graham, Frank, 206
Grant, Jimmy, 39
Gray, Brett, 19
Gray, Pete, 166–67
Green, Dallas, 77
Greenberg, Hank, 61, 67–70,
  128
Greenberg, Steve, 144, 145,
  146
Griffey, Ken, Sr. (father) and
  Ken, Jr. (son), 31, 33
Griffith, Calvin, 1–3
Griffith, Clark, 3, 222
Griffith Stadium, Washington,
  DC, 39
Grimes, Burleigh, 93
Grimm, Charlie, 92, 162, 201,
  217
Griner, Dan, 41
Groat, Dick, 22, 170
Grove, Orval, 39, 42
Guest, Edgar A., 67–68
Guidry, Ron, 5
Gullic, Ted, 41
Guzman, Jose, 40, 43

Hairston, Jerry (son), 32, 40, 42
Hairston, Jerry, Jr. (grandson), 32–33
Hairston, John (son), 32
Hairston, Sam (grandfather), 32
Hale, Bob, 214, 216
Hall of Fame. *See* Baseball Hall of Fame
Halladay, Roy, 43
Hands, Bill, 50
Harding, Warren G., 156
Harrelson, Ken, 99
Harridge, Will, 37, 121, 122
Harris, Bucky, 221
Harris, Dave, 41, 217
Harris, Greg, 7–8, 9
Hart, Eugene, 13
Harvey, Doug, 140–42
Head, Ed, 9
Hearst Corporation, 45
Helms, Tommy, 56, 103
Hemond, Roland, 127
Henderson, Rickey, 165
Hendrick, George, 42
Henrich, Tommy, 166
Herman, Billy, 101
Hernandez, Keith, 82
Hershiser, Orel, 110
Herzog, Whitey, 86
Heydler, John, 122
Hickman, Jim, 52
Higgins, Mike, 217
Higginson, Bobby, 43
Himes, Larry, 177
Hirdt, Steve, 166
history, baseball
  first black ballplayers, 198–200
  longest game, 11–14
  replacement players during WWII, 166–68
  20-game losers (pitchers), 4–6
  youngest and oldest players, 168
hitting, art of, 71–74
Hoffman, John C., 161
Holke, Walter, 12–13
Holland, John, 162
Holman, Brian, 43
Holtzman, Jerome, v–vii, 133–36, 220
Holtzman, Ken, 42, 50, 51, 52
home runs, 61–62, 63, 68, 69–70
  Banks, Ernie, 179
  Maris, Roger, and Ruth, Babe, records, 59, 61
  Ruth, Babe, called-shot home run, 90–96
Hooper, Harry, 41
Hoover, Herbert, 93, 156
Horlen, Joel, 169

Horner, Bob, 149
Hornsby, Rogers, 92, 111, 193
Houk, Ralph, 25, 61
Houston Astros, 3, 43, 51
Houston Colt .45s, 98, 211
Houtteman, Art, 42
Howard, Elston, 42
Hriniak, Walt, 74
Huggins, Miller, 172
Hundley, Randy (father), 32, 51, 52, 147
Hundley, Todd (son), 32
Hurley, Ed, 35
Hurst, Bruce, 125
Hutchinson, Fred, 212, 213

injuries
  playing in pain, 182, 183
Institute to Study Athletic Motivation (ISAM), 85–86
intercollegiate baseball, 199
interleague games, 192, 194
International League, 199
Irvin, Monte, 188
Isaminger, Jimmy, 95
Ivor-Campbell, Fred, 158

Jack Brickhouse: A Voice for All Seasons (Petterchak), 202
Jackson, Jesse, 145
Jackson, Reggie, 86, 155, 178
Jackson, Shoeless Joe, 111–16
Jacobs, Leonard J., 198
Jenkins, Ferguson, 50, 51, 52, 106, 147
Jennings, Hugh, 41
Jethroe, Sam, 186
Jewish ballplayers, 67–70
Jim Evans Umpire Academy, 27
Johnson, Davey, 24, 42
Johnson, Howard, 176
Johnson, Randy, 15
Johnson, Wallace, 43
Johnson, Walter, 5, 65, 98, 110
Jordan, Michael, 169, 170–71
Joyner, Wally, 42
Jurges, Bill, 92, 94

Kaese, Harold, 206, 207
Kaline, Al, 109
Kamzic, Nick, 84, 85
Kansas City Athletics, 86
Kansas City Monarchs, 76, 186
Kansas City Royals, 33, 125
Keane, Johnny, 164, 165
Keeler, Wee Willie, 132
Keller, Charley, 166
Kelly, Edward J., 120
Kelly, Joe, 41
Kendall, Fred and Jason, 32

Kennedy, Bob (father), 32, 33, 80
Kennedy, John F., 129
Kennedy, Terry (son), 32, 33
Kerr, Dick, 113
Kessinger, Don, 51, 52, 138
Kieran, John, 174
Kiner, Ralph, 53, 54, 55
King, Clyde, 83
Kingman, Brian, 4–6
Kinney, Robert, 147
Kladis, Nick, 127
Klippstein, Johnny, 109
Kluczynski, John, 154
knuckleballs, 5, 167
Koenig, Mark, 92
Konetchy, Ed, 13
Koney, Chuck, 84
Koosman, Jerry, 52
Koppel, Ted, 78, 79, 80
Koppett, Leonard, 206
Koufax, Sandy, 65, 66, 99, 142
Krehbiel, Fred, 129
Kroc, Ray, 2
Krueger, Ernie, 12
Krukow, Mike, 171
Kubek, Tony, 60
Kuenn, Harvey, 156
Kuenster, Jack, 161
Kuhn, Bowie, 146, 155
Kuntz, Rusty, 182
Kupcinet, Irv, 203
Kurowski, Whitey, 167

Labine, Clem, 213
Lachemann, Marcel, 170
Lamont, Gene, 24
Landes, Stan, 214
Landis, Kenesaw Mountain, 49, 111, 121, 123, 168
Lane, F. C., 121
Lane, Frank, 76
Lang, Jack, 44, 45
Lardner, John, 128
Lardner, Ring, 193, 224
Lasorda, Tom, 110, 148, 150, 175
Lau, Charlie, 74
Lavagetto, Cookie, 39, 42
Law, Vance (son), 32
Law, Vernon (father), 22, 32
League Park, Cleveland, 69
Leary, Tim, 5
Lee, Manny, 38
Lee, Thornton (father) and Don (son), 32
Leiser, Bill, 222
Lemon, Bob, 218
Leonard, Jeff, 82
Leonard, Will, 90
Leslie, Sam, 211, 218
Lewis, Allen, 206

Lewis, Bob, 48
Lewis, Duffy, 187
Lewis, Lloyd, 219
Leyland, Jim, 25
Lieb, Fred, 189–90
Life magazine, 17
lights
    in Wrigley Field, 47–49
Lisenbee, Hod, 168
Littlewood, Tom, 120
London Werewolves (CT), 19
Long Season, The (Brosnan), 64
longest game, baseball's, 11–14
Lopes, Davey, 57
Lopez, Al, 46
Lopez, Hector, 214
Los Angeles Dodgers, 33, 51,
    99, 162, 175
    and dismissal of Al Campanis,
    78–80, 146
    in 1959 World Series, 189,
    215
    Piazza, Michael, with, 148,
    149–50
    scout with, 77
Lotshaw, Andy, 93
Lou Gehrig's disease, 173
Louisville Colonels, 9, 41
Louisville Courier Journal, 192
low-ball hitters, 74
Lucas, Red, 218
Lynch, Jerry, 212, 213–14,
    216, 218
Lyons, Ted, 41

MacCarl, Neil, 38
MacGregor Coaches Clinic, 71
Mack, Connie, 92, 122
Maddux, Greg, 87–89, 103
Magerkurth, George, 95
Mahler, Rick, 82
major league draft
    of amateur free agents,
    81–86
major league records
    Aparicio, Luis, 46
    DiMaggio, Joe, 56-game hit-
    ting streak, 131
    Gehrig, Lou, 2,130-game
    streak, 172–74
    Ryan, Nolan, lifetime walks
    and strikeouts, 98–99
    scoreless innings records, 110
    stolen-bases record, 137, 165
Major League Scouting Bureau,
    85
Malloy, Jerry, 199
Malone, Pat, 93
Maloney, Jim, 98
Manager of the Year award, 24,
    26
managers, baseball

black, 78–80, 146
    managing sons, 33
    Manuel, Jerry, 23–26
    pinch-hitting, 218
Mann, Arthur, 61
Mann, Howard, 223
Mantle, Mickey, 59, 61, 75, 76,
    181–82, 211, 216
Manuel, Jerry, 23–26
Manush, Heinie, 208
Maranville, Walter "Rabbit,"
    44, 45
Maris, Roger, 59–62, 63, 155,
    211
Marovitz, Abraham Lincoln, 203
Marshall, Mike, 109
Martin, Hersh, 166
Martinez, Carmelo, 28
Martinez, Pedro, 15
Mathewson, Christy, 65, 221
Mattingly, Don, 82, 179
Maxwell, Charley, 215
Mays, Willie, 61, 142
Mazeroski, Bill, 22
McCarthy, Joe, 92, 95, 173
McCaskill, Kirk, 5
McClellan, Scott, 29
McCormick, Barry, 13
McCormick, Bertie, 120, 121
McCormick, Harry "Moose,"
    212–13, 217
McCosky, Barney, 17
McCoy, Hal, 147
McDonough, John, 163
McDonough, Joseph, 29
McDowell, Roger, 84
McGraw, John, 122, 207, 212
McGraw, Tug, 9
McJames, Doc, 41
McKenna, Andrew, 129
McKeon, Jack, 24
McLain, Denny, 5
McLish, Cal, 9
McRae, Hal (father) and Brian
    (son), 32, 33
Mead, William, 155–56
Meany, Tom, 91–92, 95
Mehl, Ernie, 222
Melton, Bill, 40
Menendez, Danny, 217
Merchant, Larry, 59
"Merkle boner" game, 221–22
Metheny, Bud, 166
Mid-Atlantic League, 77
midget pinch-hitter, 34–37
Midwest League, 27, 30
military service
    ballplayers in the armed
    forces, 15, 16–17, 68
Miller, Jay, 145–46
Miller, Marvin, 156, 185

Milnar, Al, 39, 42
Milner, Eddie, 42
Milwaukee Braves, 54, 190, 215
Milwaukee Brewers, 85
Milwaukee Journal, 222
Milwaukee Leader, 223
Minnesota Twins, 1, 3, 215
Mitchell, Kevin, 82
Mize, John, 212, 214, 216
Montreal Expos, 7, 9, 25, 43,
    182, 189
Montreal Royals, 79, 187
Moore, Mike, 5
Moreland, Keith, 56
Morgan, Joe, vi, 125, 126
Morgan, Tom, 99
Morris, Hal, 7
Most Valuable Player (MVP)
    award, 68, 82, 167, 179,
    182
Muchnick, Isadore, 186
Mullane, Tony, 9, 199
Municipal Stadium, Cleveland,
    69
Murff, Red, 98
Murphy, Dale, 149
Murphy, Johnny, 173
Muser, Tony, 176
Musial, Stan the "Man,"
    53–55, 73, 140, 214
Mussina, Mike, 38, 40, 43
My Greatest Day in Baseball
    (Carmichael and
    J. Holtzman), 220

National Italian-American
    Sports Hall of Fame, 130
National League (NL)
    and creation of the All-Star
    Game, 120–23
    double plays in, 138
    Manager of the Year award,
    24
    Most Valuable Player award,
    82, 179, 182
    Old Timers' All-Star team,
    101–4
    Reds 1961 pennant win, 63
National Livestock and Meat
    Board, 97
Necciai, Ron, 19–22
Negro Leagues, 76, 187, 188
Newcombe, Don, 79–80,
    179–80, 218
Newhouser, Hal, 167
Newsweek, 128
New York Daily News, 118
New York Giants, 41, 54, 102,
    122, 137, 188, 202, 217,
    218
New York Globe, 137
New York Herald-Tribune, 94

New York Journal-American, 59
New York Mets, 9, 98, 165
  drafts of amateur free agents,
    82, 84, 86
  Gooden, Dwight, with, 66,
    84
  Kiner, Ralph, as announcer
    for, 54
  1969 season, 51, 52
  in 1986 World Series, 125
  no-hitters, 40, 42
  scouts for, 98, 214
New York Post, 155
New York/Penn League, 29
New York Times, 11–12, 13,
  62, 94, 95, 207, 208
New York World-Telegram, 91
New York Yankees, 5, 8, 17,
  18, 33, 61
  drafts of amateur free agents,
    81, 82
  and Gehrig, Lou, 2,130-
    game streak, 172–74
  in 1932 World Series, 92–96
  in 1947 World Series, 38, 39
  no-hitters, 42, 43
  pinch-hitters, 212, 214,
    215–16
  replacement players, 166, 167
Niekro, Joe, 50
Niekro, Phil, 5
Nixon, Otis, 43
Nixon, Richard M., 3, 154–56
No Cheering in the Press Box
  (J. Holtzman), vii, 133–36
no-hitters lost with two outs in
  ninth, 38–43
Northern League, 77
Northey, Ron, 216–17
Northrup, Jim, 109
Northwest League, 199
Nuxhall, Joe, 168
Nye, Rich, 50

Oakland Athletics, 4, 5, 42, 43,
  155
Oakland Tribune, 6
Oberkfell, Ken, 43, 82
O'Day, Hank, 222
Odom, Blue Moon, 42
O'Doul, Lefty, 217, 222
Oeschger, Joe, 11–14
Ojeda, Bob, 82
Old Timers' games, 45, 101–4,
  163
Olson, Ivy, 12
O'Malley, Peter, 146
O'Malley, Walter, 162
one-armed outfielder, 166–67
O'Neill, Paul, 43
one-legged pitcher, 167
Orta, Jorge, 40
Osborn, Don, 64

Our Home Colony (M. Walker),
  200
outfielders
  one-armed outfielder,
    166–67
  Sunday, Billy, 157–59
owners, baseball club
  Griffith, Calvin, 1–3
  Steinbrenner, George, 81, 82
  Veeck, Bill, 127–29, 192
  Wrigley, Philip K., 160–62,
    201

Pacific Coast League, 155
Paige, Satchel, 222
Palmer, Jim, vi
Parker, Dave, 56, 82
Parrish, Larry, 82
Paschal, Ben, 41
Paul, Gabe, 162
Pegler, Westbrook, 95
Pennock, Herb, 41
Peoria Chiefs, 196
Pepe, Phil, 118
Perez, Tony, 147
Perry, Gaylord, 106
Phelps, Ken, 43
Philadelphia Athletics, 41, 92,
  122
Philadelphia Daily News, 59
Philadelphia Phillies, 50, 57,
  220
  no-hitters, 41, 43
  pinch-hitters, 215
  replacement players, 167
  scouts for, 77, 170
Philadelphia Stars, 186
Philley, Dave, 214, 215
Phillips, Wally, 97
Piazza, Michael Joseph, 148–50
Piazza, Vincent, 150
Pick, Charley, 12
Pierce, Billy, 39, 42, 105, 154
pinch-hitters, 210–18
  aging players, 214–16
  Lynch, Jerry, 212, 213–14,
    216, 218
  midget pinch-hitter, 34–37
  Rhodes, James "Dusty,"
    217–18
Piniella, Lou, 147
Pipp, Wally, 172
pitchers
  ambidextrous, 7–10
  and the art of hitting, 71–74
  Brosnan, Jim, 63–66, 108,
    184
  Cadore, Leon, 11–14
  Feller, Bob, 15–18, 69–70, 98
  Kingman, Brian, 4–6
  Koufax, Sandy, 65, 66, 99
  Maddux, Greg, 87–89

Necciai, Ron, 27 strikeouts,
  19–22
one-legged pitcher, 167
pitcher as youngest player in
  big-league history, 168
relief pitchers, 210
Ryan, Nolan, 97–100
20-game losers, 4–6
Pittsburgh Courier, 186, 187
Pittsburgh Pirates, 5, 64, 69, 92
  Necciai, Ron, with, 21–22
  no-hitters, 41, 43
  pinch-hitters, 216
Pizarro, Juan, 61
Players' Association, 156
Pole, Dick, 170–71
Polo Grounds, New York, 54,
  165
Postema, Pam, 27–28, 30
Povich, Shirley, 222
presidents, U.S., and baseball,
  49, 93, 117–19, 154–56
Pud Galvin Memorial Trophy, 4
Purkey, Bob, 179

Qualls, Jimmy, 40, 51
Quick, Jim, 56
Quinn, Bob, 147
Quisenberry, Dan, 83
*Quotations from Chairman
  Calvin* (pamphlet), 2

Radbourne, Charlie "Old
  Hoss," 12
Rainey, Chuck, 42
Reagan, Ronald, 156, 197
Reardon, Jeff, 83
Rebechini, Ferdinand, 130
records. *See* home-runs; major
  league records; scoreless
  innings records; stolen-
  bases records
Reed, Ron, 170
Regan, Phil, 50
Reinsdorf, Jerry, 146
relief pitchers, 210
Remy, Jerry, 40, 42
replacement players, 166–68
Replogle, Hartley L., 112–16
reserve clause, baseball's
  Curt Flood's challenge to,
    185
Reusse, Pat, 3
Rhoads, Bob, 41
Rhodes, James "Dusty,"
  217–18
Richard, Bee Bee, 98
Richards, Paul, 9–10, 75
Richardson, Bobby, 60
Rickey, Branch, 65, 79, 187,
  188
Rickey Ratings system, 65–66

Index

Riggleman, Jim, 181
Riggs, Lew, 217
Rigney, John, 167
Ripken, Cal, Jr., 172, 173
Ripley's Believe It Or Not!, 9
Ritter, Larry, 219
Riverfront Stadium, Cincinnati, 101
Roberts, Robin, 156
Robertson, Jax, 81
Robinson, Brooks, 45, 106, 107
Robinson, Jackie, 73, 78, 79, 80, 146, 186, 187, 198
Robinson, Ray, 173
Robinson, Ron, 43
Robinson, Wilbert, 13
Rockwell International, 98
Rohr, Billy, 42
Roosevelt, Franklin D., 49, 93
Root, Charlie, 64
Rose, Pete, 54, 56–58, 103, 119, 131
Rose, Pete, Jr., 57
Rosen, Al, 83
Ross, Gary, 50
Rowland, Clarence "Pants," 162, 217–18
Rucker, Nap, 41
Ruffing, Red, 218
Ruhl, Bill, 7
Runyon, Damon, 95, 212–13
Russell, Fred, 206
Ruth, Babe, 59, 61, 62, 68, 69, 70, 119, 122, 155, 168, 211
  called-shot home run, 90–96
Ryan, Nolan, 15, 97–100

Saberhagen, Bret, 82, 87
St. Louis Browns, 16, 34–35, 41, 69, 128, 131, 167, 168
St. Louis Cardinals, 33, 52, 86, 122
  Broglio-for-Brock trade, 163–65
  Musial, Stan, with, 53, 54
  no-hitters, 41, 42, 43
  pinch-hitters, 218
  replacement players, 167, 168
  Smith, Ozzie, with, 151, 152
St. Louis Post-Dispatch, 35
Saltzgaver, Jack, 173
San Diego Padres, 51, 88, 152
San Francisco Giants, 24, 43, 51, 150, 169, 183, 189
Sandberg, Ryne, 56, 82, 89, 137, 138, 183
Sanders, Reggie, 7
Sanford, Jack, 179
Santiago, Benito, 88
Santo, Ron, 51, 52, 63, 106–7

Saucier, Frank, 34
Sawatski, Carl, 215
Schaefer, Germany, 41
Scheffing, Bob, 162
Scherger, George, 57
Schiff, Sidney, 128
Schoendienst, Red, 51, 54
Schott, Marge, 144–47
Schueler, Ron, 177
Schultz, Howie, 167, 170
Schwartz, Jeff, 9
Science of Hitting, The (T. Williams), 73
scoreless innings records, 110
Scott, George, 42
Scott, Mike, 43
scouts, baseball, 98, 148, 152, 187, 214
  Alexander, Hugh, 75–77
  free-agent scouts, 81–86
Seattle Mariners, 5, 32, 33, 43
Seattle Pilots, 129
Seaver, Tom, 40, 42, 51, 65
Segar, Charles, 138
Selig, Bud, 190
Selkirk, George, 132
Selma, Dick, 50, 51
Shafer, Sid, 127
Sharman, Bill, 170
Shaughnessy, Dan, 119
Shea Stadium, New York, vi
Shepard, Bert, 167
shortstops
  Aparicio, Luis, 44–46, 105
  Dunston, Shawon, 57, 84, 88, 183
  with former basketball careers, 170
  Koenig, Mark, 92
  Robinson, Jackie, 187
  Smith, Ozzie, 151–53
sign stealing, 189–91
Simmons, Ted, 63
Simons, Herbert F., 90–91, 95
Simpson, Allan, 82, 86
Simpson, Harry, 42
Sisler, Dick and David, 32
Sisler, George, 32, 132
Skinner, Bob (father) and Joel (son), 32
Slapnicka, Cy, 16
Smith, Chet, 222
Smith, Curt, 117
Smith, General "Howlin' Mad," 17
Smith, Ken, 222
Smith, Lee, 57
Smith, Ozzie, 151–53
Smith, Red, 206
Smith, Wendell, 186–88
Smith, Willie, 50
Sorensen, Lary, 57

Sosa, Sammy, 175–77
Soto, Mario, 42
Southern Association, 3
Spelius, George, 27
Sports Illustrated, 81, 82, 111, 160
sportswriters, v–vii, 59, 61–62, 180, 197, 208
  Baseball Writers Association of America (BBWAA), 44, 45, 106, 107, 118
  Broeg, Bob, 34–35
  Brosnan, Jim, 63–66
  Carmichael, John Peter, 219–24
  Frick, Ford, 61, 133–36
    on Ruth, Babe, called-shot home run, 90–92, 94–95
  Smith, Wendell, 186–88
  Veeck, Bill, 128–29
  Veeck, William L., Sr., 122, 192–93
    at White House baseball conference, 117, 118, 119
spring training, 108–10
Stahl, Chick, 41
Stainback, Tuck, 166
Staley, Gerry, 154
Stanka, Joe, 154–55
Stanky, Eddie, 39
Stargell, Willie, 64, 149
Starrette, Herm, 87
stealing signs, 189–91
Steinbrenner, George, 2, 81, 82, 146
Stengel, Casey, 23
Stieb, Dave, 38, 43
Stirnweiss, George "Snuffy," 167
stolen-bases records, 137, 165
Stone, Steve, 197
Stoneham, Horace, 122
Stottlemyre, Todd, 31
Stovey, George, 199
Strang, Sammy, 218
Strawberry, Darryl, 149
strikeouts
  father-son strikeout against Ted Williams, 32
  Koufax, Sandy, 99
  Necciai, Ron, 27 strikeouts, 19–22
  Ryan, Nolan, as strikeout king, 97, 99
Sukeforth, Clyde, 187
Sunday, Reverend W. A. "Billy," 157–59
Sutcliffe, Rick, 89
Swift, Bob, 35
switch-hitting, 152

Tamman, Larry, 31
Tanner, Chuck (father) and Bruce (son), 32

Tappe, Elvin, 212
Tartabull, Jose (father) and
  Danny (son), 32
Taubensee, Ed, 7
Taylor, Zack, 34, 35
Tebeau, Oliver "Patsy," 210
Terrell, Walt, 42
Terry, Bill, 218
Tesreau, Jeff, 41
Texas Rangers, 8, 176–77
third basemen
  Ron Santo, 106–7
30-game winner (pitcher), 5
30/30 seasons
  players with, 176
Thoreau, Henry David, 129
Thornton, Andre, 82
three-generation families in
  baseball, 32
three-hit games, 124–26
Time magazine, 64
Tinker, Joe, 137–39
Tinker-to-Evers-to-Chance
  double plays, 137–39
Tobin, Jim, 218
Torgeson, Earl, 215–16
Toronto Blue Jays, 38, 43
Torre, Joe, 152
Totten, Hal, 95–96
Touching Second (Evers), 139
Traber, Jim, 38, 43
Trachsel, Steve, 5
trades, baseball
  Boudreau-for-Grimm trade,
    201
  Broglio-for-Brock trade,
    163–65, 170
  free agency and Curt Flood
    trial, 184–85
  player trades and sign
    stealing, 191
Tribune magazine, 90, 95
Triple A baseball, 25, 27
Trout, Paul "Dizzy" (father)
  and Steve (son), 31
Turner, Ted, 2
20-game losers (pitchers), 4–6

Ueberroth, Peter, 79
umpires
  Harvey, Doug, 140–43
  lady, 27–30
USA Today, 6
USS *Alabama*, 15, 16–17

Valentine, Bobby, 8
Valo, Elmer, 214–15
Van Dyck, Dave, 5
Vance, Dazzy, 41
Vaughan, Irving "Pop," 95
Veach, Bobby, 41
Vecsey, George, 119

Veeck as in Wreck (Veeck),
  35–37, 193
Veeck, Bill (son), 1, 34, 35–37,
  83, 122, 127–29, 161–62,
  188, 192, 193, 194
Veeck, Mary Frances (wife of
  Bill), 34, 128, 129, 193
Veeck, Mike (grandson), 129
Veeck, William L., Sr. (father),
  122, 162, 192–94
Veryzer, Tom, 42
Vidmer, Richards, 94, 95
Vonachen, Pete, 196
Vukovich, John, 56–57, 88

Wade, Ben, 148
Wagner, Honus, 46, 222
Wagner, Paul, 43
Walker, Chico, 143
Walker, Moses "Fleetwood"
  and Welday, 198–200
Wallis, "Tarzan" Joe, 40, 42
Wanninger, Pee Wee, 172
Ward, Archibald Burdette
  (father), 120, 121, 122,
  123
Ward, Gary, 82
Ward, Thomas (son), 121, 123
Washington Post, 208
Washington Senators, 3, 69,
  132, 222
  no-hitters, 41, 42
  owner Calvin Griffith, 1, 3
  pinch-hitters, 217
  replacement players, 167, 168
Weir, Tom, 6
Wertz, Vic, 214, 215
Westcott, Cliff, 48
Western Association, 10
WGN television, 203
Wheat, Zack, 12
White, Bill, 164
White, Frank, 82
White House conference on
  baseball, 117–19
Wilcox, Milt, 40, 42
Williams, Billy, 51, 52, 101,
  102, 105, 107, 142, 143,
  175, 190
Williams, Claude, 113, 114
Williams, Dick, 25
Williams, Joe, 95
Williams, Lefty, 112
Williams, Marvin, 186
Williams, Ted, 32, 45, 71–74,
  132, 211
Williams, Walter, 40, 42
Willis, Vic, 5
Wills, Maury (father) and
  Bump (son), 32
Wilson, Charlie, 10
Wilson, Hack, 61, 105

Winslow, William, 86
Wise, Rick, 42
Wojciechowski, Gene, 27–28
women umpires, 27–30
Wood, Wilbur, 5
Worcester Ruby Legs, 41
World Series
  1919, White Sox in, 111–16
  1932, Yankees vs. Cubs,
    92–96
  1934, Dizzy Dean in, 224
  1947, Yankees vs. Brooklyn
    Dodgers, 38, 39
  1954, New York Giants vs.
    Indians, 217
  1959, Los Angeles Dodgers
    vs. White Sox, 189, 215
  1961, Jerry Lynch in, 216
  1971, game stories of the, 207
  1986, Red Sox vs. Mets, 125
  and Ruth, Babe, called-shot
    home run, 91–92
World War II, 48–49, 128
  ballplayers in the armed
    forces during, 15, 16–17,
    68
  use of replacement players
    during, 166–68
Wren, Christine, 29
Wright, Clyde and Jaret, 31
Wrigley Field, Chicago, 56, 76,
  87, 148, 149, 175
  Bush, George, on, 117, 118
  lights in, 47–49
  1932 World Series at, 93–96
Wrigley, Philip K., 122,
  160–62, 179, 201
Wrigley, William (father), 193
writers, baseball. *See* sportswriters
Wyatt, Whit, 41
Wynn, Early, 214

Yale University, 117, 118–19
Yankee Stadium, New York, 131
  Lou Gehrig Appreciation
    Day at, 174
Yastrzemski, Carl, 106, 167
Youmans, Floyd, 84
Young, Cy, 5, 41
Young, Dick, 207
Young, Don, 51
Young, Matt, 5
Youngblood, Joel, 191
*You've Got to Have B*lls to
  Make It in This League*
  (Postema), 27–28

Zeller, Jack, 47, 49
Zimmer, Don, 118, 182